STUDIES IN COMPARATIVE EDUCATION

TEACHER TRAINING
AND MULTICULTURALISM:
NATIONAL STUDIES

Edited by Raúl Gagliardi

This book presents a selection of studies from the IBE's project 'Basic Education for Participation and Democracy: Key Issues in Human Resources Development (Teachers and Multicultural/Intercultural Education)'. Many of the texts reproduced here are shortened versions of the original research reports submitted by the authors. The complete versions of these texts are available from: Dr Raúl Gagliardi, International Bureau of Education, P.O. Box 199, 1211 Geneva 20, Switzerland.

The ideas and opinions expressed in this work are those of the authors and do not necessarily represent the views of UNESCO:IBE. The designations employed and the presentation of the material throughout the publication do not imply the expression of any opinion whatsoever on the part of UNESCO:IBE concerning the legal status of any country, territory, city or area, or of its authorities, or concerning the delimitations of its frontiers or boundaries.

Published by UNESCO: International Bureau of Education,
7, place de Fontenoy, 75700 Paris, France.

ISBN: 92-9145-002-2

Printed in Switzerland by Presses Centrales Lausanne, S.A.

Preface

Since its creation, some fifty years ago, UNESCO has considered the dialogue between cultures as a basic element in its strategies to consolidate peace. The ways in which this dialogue is conducted, however, must be continuously renewed in order to confront situations and requirements which are changing with considerable rapidity. Current trends, such as the world-wide economy, the information technology revolution, the crisis in traditional ideological paradigms, massive migrations, the growing concern with global problems such as the environment, drugs and AIDS, have modified not only traditional social relationships but also culture's role in the development process. Two apparently contradictory trends dominate modern society: the standardization of cultural patterns; and the search for basic reference points for cultural identity. The tensions, the imbalances and – in many cases – open conflicts have worsened to such a point that some analysts estimate that future conflicts will take on a cultural character. Even if these forecasts could be contested, there is no doubt that the dialogue between cultures is more vital today than ever before and that the modalities of this dialogue will have to be reviewed.

Education, both formal and non-formal, is at the centre of this renewal of methods for cultural dialogue. At present, all societies are becoming multicultural societies and it was not by accident that the last two International Conferences on Education, convened by UNESCO, were intended to discuss problems concerning the relationship between education and culture in general, and the culture of peace and democracy in particular. What came out of both conferences was that nobody can remain indifferent for long faced with the upsurge of xenophobia and violence witnessed by a number of political, ethnic, cultural or religious claims. Nevertheless, discussions and adopted agreements demonstrate one fundamental fact: *it is not sufficient to condemn, one must rather prevent and anticipate.* Educational action strategies should, therefore, dissuade by preventing the appearance of such phenomena of historical regression and, in this way, to furnish those responsible for political decisions with a greater capacity to anticipate.

What are the main elements in an education strategy intended to promote dialogue between cultures and to obstruct the appearance of the phenomena of cultural intolerance? On this subject, a common element in the answers that have been proposed to this question is the critical importance of teachers. They are, together with the mass communication media and the family, the most important agents in the socialization process for future generations. It follows that knowing about and intervening in the attitudes of future teachers who will be faced with cultural diversity represents one of the most important lines of preventive action that can be identified at the national and international levels.

In this context and with the generous contribution of the Italian Co-operation, UNESCO:IBE has launched a project intended to study and improve the training of teachers for multi- and intercultural education. The activities of this project began in 1993 as a follow-up to the Recommendation adopted by the forty-third session of the International Conference on Education. The project's basic activities are:

1. To analyse the worldwide bibliography and organize a databank on innovations in multicultural/intercultural teacher training and education.
2. To organize and carry out comparative evaluation of selected innovations in multicultural/intercultural teacher training and education, and to formulate general policies for teacher training in this field.
3. To organize comparative research on the conceptions and attitudes of future teachers as they relate to other cultures, racism, etc., and on their conceptions of multicultural/intercultural education, using a research model developed in Geneva by experts in psycho-sociology. The main instrument is a multiple-choice questionnaire. This has been translated into local languages and adapted to both local environments and to the indigenous characteristics of students through the assistance of national institutions collaborating with the project. In each country, a sample of 300 students intending to become teachers will answer the questionnaire. So far, the questionnaire has been applied in Bolivia, the Czech Republic, Lebanon, Mauritius, Mexico, Pakistan, Poland, Senegal and Spain.

4. To organize and implement local research activities in teacher training for multicultural/intercultural education in the following countries: Bolivia, the Czech Republic, Jordan, Lebanon, Mauritius, Mexico, Pakistan, Poland, Senegal and Tunisia. The basic activities being developed at country level are:
   - Analysis of the curriculum of primary school-teachers' training, in order to identify the components related to multicultural/intercultural education.
   - Analysis of the methods used in the training of future teachers to develop their capacity for multicultural/intercultural education.
   - Analysis of the bibliography relating to teacher training for multicultural/ intercultural education (see 1. above).
   - Identification and analysis of positive experiences in teacher training for multicultural/intercultural education (see 2. above).
   - Analysis of future teachers' conceptions of other cultures, racism, etc., and their conceptions of multicultural/intercultural education, using a basic instrument that will be used in different countries for comparative studies (see 3. above).

This book presents the outcomes concerning the initial training systems of teachers in eight countries at different levels of development in different regions of the world but who are faced with a common challenge to educate for cultural diversity.

Both the conclusions of each particular study and the general outcomes demonstrate the complexity of the problems and the benefits of comparative analysis. Overcoming prejudices and stereotypes is not an easy task nor likely to be achieved in the short term. Mentalities change far more slowly than knowledge and, because of this, educational strategies need to be applied in the long term. This study also shows that it is necessary to improve the exchange of experiences as well as contacts between people and institutions who are confronted with the same problems in different contexts. The publication of the initial outcomes of this project is intended to enrich the quality of discussions between specialists and institutions who, in different parts of the world, are concerned by multicultural education as an instrument to promote understanding, respect and dialogue between cultures.

JUAN CARLOS TEDESCO,
Director

Contents

CHAPTER I

An integrated model for teacher training in a multicultural context

Raúl Gagliardi

BACKGROUND

The multicultural approach to education is relatively new to most countries. As a first priority, teacher training needs to be reorganized in order to improve the capacity of teachers to teach in a multicultural context. The sharing of positive experiences can help countries to improve teacher training in this field.

PRELIMINARY RESULTS

The main issues in teacher training for multicultural/intercultural education

A project's contribution to improving national capacity for teacher training in multicultural/intercultural education should be to determine the main issues involved. The activities of the IBE's project 'Basic Education for Participation and Democracy: Key Issues in Human Resources Development (Teachers and Multicultural/Intercultural Education)' have enabled experiences from very different situations to be considered. Analysis suggests that the main issues in teacher training for multicultural/intercultural education are as follows:

– *The solving of educational problems in the multicultural context cannot be achieved by isolated measures.* It is necessary to reshape policies on

1

teacher training and education in order to adapt them to individual communities' educational needs.

– *The curricula for basic education are frequently mono-cultural.* They dwell on the history and beliefs of the dominant groups. This situation may reinforce feelings of discrimination among pupils from minorities, which may in turn cause pupils to lose their cultural identity and self-esteem. It is also a cause of low school achievement among pupils from discriminated minorities and thus a big disadvantage for them both in obtaining good jobs and in their integration into society. Appropriate curricula for multicultural/intercultural education should integrate some of the history and characteristics of all communities. A territorial approach (see chapter II, 'Teacher training for multicultural education in favour of democracy and sustainable development: the territorial approach') can be very useful in achieving this goal. Teacher training should incorporate strategies and methods that will improve school achievement among pupils from discriminated minorities.

– Multicultural/intercultural education is a way of reinforcing the cultural identity of pupils from all communities, including those discriminated against. Such education stimulates pupils' self-esteem by developing their knowledge of the characteristics and achievements of their own communities. By the same token, it also enables negative attitudes towards other communities to be overcome.

– *Decision-makers and those responsible for education frequently lack awareness of the problems caused by cultural and linguistic differences in the classroom, or pay little attention to these problems.* Any improvement of education in the multicultural context starts with awareness of pupils' difficulties among those responsible for education.

– *Cultural and linguistic diversity is frequently considered to be a negative element in education.* However, such diversity can be a resource in classroom activities if teachers are capable of accepting pupils' conceptions and knowledge and stimulating pupils to share them. Pupils' family life, cultural background and experiences can all be important resources for teachers. Viewing them in this light stimulates pupils' self-esteem and can help to surmount shyness and discriminatory feelings by developing mutual understanding and solidarity between pupils from different communities.

– *Mono-cultural education sets homogeneous educational objectives for the entire population.* However, different communities may have different educational objectives. To accept these differences and adapt to them is an important issue for schools. This can be difficult when communities have very different objectives. In this case a 'bicultural school' seems a possible solution. Teacher training should include information about the educational objectives of different communities and on how to integrate them in curricula.

- *It is necessary to help teachers surmount ethnocentrism and negative attitudes towards minorities.* Such attitudes are obstacles to understanding pupils' cultures and accepting particularities. Analysis of teachers' conceptions and attitudes relating to pupils' communities is an important factor in organizing teacher training in multicultural/intercultural education.

- *Learning is not simply the acquisition of new information.* Rather, it is a complex process of transforming conceptual frameworks. The learning processes depend on a web of ideas, beliefs, logical abilities, language, knowledge and skills that individuals develop and use for integrating new information and building new knowledge and skills. This web is organized in a system called a 'cognitive system'. It may facilitate the learning of some knowledge and the development of some skills, while hindering the learning of others. By identifying obstacles to students' learning, teachers can design training programmes that help the student overcome them. Learning obstacles can be affective, religious, cultural, logical or conceptual.

- *The meaning given to information depends on conceptions, beliefs and attitudes.* If pupils have conceptions, beliefs and attitudes that are different from those of their teachers, they may ascribe different meanings to the information they receive. Teacher training should provide teachers with elements for understanding and overcoming this problem.

- *Multicultural/intercultural education requires the capacity in an educator to adapt teaching to pupils in a learner-centred approach.* Some teachers' conceptions and attitudes relating to teaching and learning can obstruct the development of this capacity. For example, teachers frequently think that 'to teach' is identical to 'to transmit information' and that 'to learn' is equivalent to 'to listen and to remember'. Such teachers are not much concerned by individual pupils' characteristics and do not adapt teaching to pupils' learning difficulties. Teacher training should help teachers to modify their conceptions so that they may develop the capacity to take into account pupils' characteristics and learning difficulties in a learner-centred approach. Analysis of teachers' conceptions and attitudes about teaching and learning is, therefore, an important element in teacher training.

- *One important element to take into account in teaching is the 'temporal structure' of pupils* (monochrone or polychrone). Differences in temporal structures can be a source of misunderstanding between teachers and pupils. Teacher training should inform teachers about pupils' temporal organizations and develop their capacity to adapt teaching to them.

– *Understanding pupils' learning difficulties is a fundamental element in any educational activity, particularly when the teacher comes from a community other than that of the pupils.* Analysis of pupils' conceptions and attitudes is an important component in a learner-centred approach. Teacher training for multicultural/intercultural education should include methods for analysing pupils' conceptions, attitudes, and learning obstacles, and should develop strategies and methods for helping them to overcome the latter.

– *Frequently, teachers have problems in communicating with pupils from different cultures.* If teachers do not know the precepts of communication used by pupils, they may have difficulty establishing good relations with them. A related problem arises from pupils' taboos. If teachers do not take into account pupils' taboos, they can harm sensibilities and provoke feelings of rejection. Teachers should learn to use the communication precepts of the pupils' communities and should be aware of taboos, adapting their activities accordingly.

– *Some research suggests a positive correlation between pupils' culture and some learning difficulties.* For example, pupils from cultures without mathematical concepts evidently have numerous problems with mathematics. They may, however, have other capacities that can be harnessed by the teacher. Experience suggests that integrating, for example, the capacity to understand very complex systems of kin relationships, the capacity to undertake traditional activities, or knowledge about the territory, can help pupils to surmount learning difficulties. In the multicultural context, analysis of culture and learning difficulties and the strategies and methods for helping pupils overcome the latter are therefore important elements in teacher training.

– *Different cultures have different 'learning styles'.* To adapt teaching to pupils' learning styles can facilitate learning and solve some of the pupils' difficulties.

– *Pupils are ethnocentric and frequently have negative attitudes and conceptions about other cultural and ethnic groups.* Helping pupils to understand other communities and to develop solidarity with them is fundamental to the promotion of peace and democracy. Teacher training should include the study of methods of analysing pupils' attitudes, and strategies and methods that will help develop understanding and solidarity between different communities.

– *In the multicultural context, pupils' language development is a fundamental educational issue.* Children who have limited capacity in the

4

teaching language have many difficulties achieving proficiency. This situation increases the probability of poor school achievement. Of particular concern is the situation of children coming from families with impoverished language skills or migrant children who lack the opportunity to speak either their mother language or the dominant language fluently. The outcome of some research suggests that bilingual children who do not speak either language well have special learning difficulties. Effective multilingual education requires the participation of all teachers, and not only language teachers. Teachers should be trained in methods of analysing pupils' language development as well as in methods of helping pupils develop their mother language.

− *A characteristic of racism and xenophobia is the proclivity to accept simplistic answers to complex problems.* To avoid the trap of simplistic answers, the capacity to understand complex systems and networks of causality processes, such as social systems and environmental systems, is required. Some research shows that pupils frequently fail to develop this capacity. Teachers must be trained to help pupils develop the capacity to understand complex systems and avoid simplistic thinking. This would be an example of integrating teacher training for multicultural/intercultural education with teacher training for education towards sustainable development.

− *Pupils from minorities frequently have serious health, social and economic problems.* Education for sustainable development, adapted to improve the quality of life in different communities, can help solve these problems. One important objective is to improve the capacity to negotiate and the capacity for organizing collective activities. This is another example of the possible integration of education towards sustainable development with multicultural/intercultural education.

− *Multicultural education needs a community-centred approach.* Therefore, teacher training needs to include the imparting of basic information about ethnic and cultural groups, such as traditional knowledge, religion, taboos, language, social organization, communication precepts, temporal organization, etc. However, it is important to avoid stereotypes about communities frequently transmitted by teachers; these are an obstacle to an understanding of pupils' problems. Teacher training should develop the capacity for using the basic information about pupils' communities while developing teachers' capacity for adapting teaching to real, unstereotyped pupils.

− *Each community has its own empirical knowledge, which is transmitted to new generations through tales, stories, songs, proverbs, etc.* It is important to encourage the integration of traditional knowledge in teaching (in particular in science teaching) as it facilitates learning, allows pupils to learn about their own community, develops cultural identity and self-esteem and permits the conservation of empirical knowledge that would otherwise be lost. This integration is the basis for developing the national capacity for sustainable development founded in the use of all resources and knowledge and the participation of all communities. Teachers should be trained in the use of traditional knowledge in science teaching and in other subjects.

– *The participation of pupils' families in school activities is an important element in pupils' achievement.* Teacher training should develop a teacher's capacity for establishing good communications with the families of pupils from different communities, and for stimulating them to participate more actively in school activities.

– *Training materials are frequently mono-cultural, presenting only a 'dominant ethnic and cultural model'.* Such material may harm the feelings of pupils from minorities and can reinforce discriminatory conceptions and attitudes. Multicultural education needs training material presenting all cultures and the history of all communities. Teachers should be trained in the production of multicultural training materials.

– *Teachers should be trained in education for conflict management.* This training can provide teachers with concepts and methods for developing pupils' capacity for managing conflicts and for stimulating active participation by pupils in solving peacefully any conflicts between communities.

The necessity of educational research at the local level

Multicultural/intercultural education needs precise information about pupils' communities. This information should be kept updated in order to trace the cultural, social and economic changes in different communities. Research on how to obtain and update this information should be carried out at local level. The information, once obtained, should be incorporated in teacher training courses and transmitted to teachers. Therefore, a well-organized system of research and transmission of information is an important element in multicultural/intercultural education.

From the multicultural viewpoint, other necessary information is required on pupils' main learning obstacles. This information will allow teaching to be adapted to pupils' difficulties. Comparative educational research should be organized so that this information can be obtained.

The 'ideal profile' of a teacher in a multicultural context: a researcher

The problems mentioned in the earlier section, 'The main issues in teacher training for multicultural/intercultural education', are difficult to solve. Information about pupils and about their communities is required. However, communities and pupils change, and new information is therefore always necessary. This potentially problematic situation can be resolved once teachers gain the capacity to analyse their pupils as an ongoing activity, and can adapt their teaching to change. In other words, teachers should be 'researchers in the classroom', analysing pupils' learning obstacles and using strategies and materials adapted to them. In the multicultural context, therefore, teachers should be capable not only of establishing good communications with their pupils, but should also have an 'open mind' and a 'scientific approach to teaching'. Our experience shows that teachers are not only capable of developing these attitudes and capacities, but can also gain from analysing pupils' conceptions and learning obstacles, by developing the capacity to integrate this analysis into their daily activities.

The integrated model of teacher training for multicultural/intercultural education

The project is preparing an *'integrated model of teacher training for multicultural/intercultural education'*, which will include research methods for analysing: future teachers' conceptions and attitudes concerning pupils' communities; pupils' conceptions and attitudes and learning obstacles; information about pupils' communities; information about education towards sustainable development and the territorial approach; and a synthesis of positive experiences in teacher training for multicultural/intercultural education. The integrated model should be developed autonomously in each country because it incorporates information at the local level. The integrated model will permit:
- Teachers to overcome ethnocentrism and negative conceptions and attitudes about pupils' communities.
- Development of teachers' capacity to help pupils overcome negative conceptions about other communities.
- The education of teachers about the history and characteristics of different communities (cultures, social organizations, religions, kinship organizations, taboos, communication precepts, temporal organizations, relationships with environmental systems, relationships with other communities, main economic activities, etc.) and development of their capacity to exploit this information in teaching.

7

- Informing of teachers about traditional knowledge circulating within communities and the development of their capacity to exploit this information in teaching.
- The training of teachers in methods of analysing pupils' conceptions and learning obstacles and of adapting their teaching in accordance with this information.
- The enhancement of teachers' capacity for surmounting learning obstacles caused by pupils' lack of language development, in particular in the case of bilingual children who may have limited skills in both languages.
- Making teachers aware that some cultures and languages lack mathematical and scientific elements, and enhancing their capacity to exploit traditional elements in teaching such as kinship relationships.
- Making teachers aware of the main obstacles to participation of pupils' families in school activities, and enhancing their capacity to establish good relationships with the pupils' families and communities.
- Making teachers aware of the main quality-of-life problems in pupils' communities (housing, environmental degradation, employment, health, etc.) and development of their capacity to become 'agents for sustainable development' in these communities.
- The development of teachers' capacity for integrating different disciplines into a global approach focused on analysis of the characteristics and resources of a territory, its use by different communities, and the environmental impact of human activities upon it.
- The increasing of national capacities for preparing teaching material adapted to individual communities.

Activities for preparing an integrated model of teacher training in multicultural/intercultural education

The model will be developed at national level by experts who will:
- Organize comparative research about future teachers' ethnocentrism and their conceptions and attitudes relating to pupils' communities.
- Design, select and evaluate methods of overcoming future teachers' ethnocentrism and negative attitudes towards pupils' communities.
- Analyse the main learning difficulties of pupils from different communities (difficulties in developing the capacity for abstraction among some bilingual pupils, language difficulties, taboos, lack of basic scientific and technical concepts, difficulties originating in different communication precepts, difficulties originating in different temporal organizations, ethnocentrism, negative attitudes towards other communities, etc.).

- Select, evaluate and adapt appropriate training methods in order to help pupils overcome their main learning difficulties.
- Collect folk tales, proverbs, etc., and analyse traditional knowledge from different communities.
- Design strategies in order to incorporate traditional knowledge and folk tales in multicultural education.
- Analyse the main economic and social problems and other problems related to the quality of life in different communities (health, housing, employment, discrimination, etc.).
- Analyse the use of environmental resources in different communities and the negative environmental impact thereof.
- Select, evaluate and adapt educational methods for sustainable development appropriate to different communities.

The results obtained will be used to:
- Prepare an integrated curricula of teacher training for multicultural/ intercultural education based on the integrated model developed by the project.
- Put forward proposals for educational policies applicable to teacher training for multicultural/intercultural education.
- Propose teacher training strategies and methods for multicultural/intercultural education.
- Prepare and distribute documents on teacher training for multicultural/ intercultural education.
- Organize seminars on teacher training for multicultural/intercultural education addressed to decision-makers and those responsible for teacher training institutions.

CONCLUSION

The preliminary results of activities carried out in the first year of the project suggest that developing teachers' capacity for multicultural/intercultural education means providing them with information about pupils' communities and training them in how to use this information in teaching. Multicultural/intercultural teacher training also needs to develop the teachers' capacity for communicating with pupils from different cultures. Teachers should also be trained in methods for analysing pupils' conceptions and learning obstacles. They should know how to teach about sustainable development and how to train pupils to improve the quality of life. Therefore, teacher training for multicultural education should be a blend of information and pedagogical methods. It must not be reduced to a few lessons about pupils' culture or to an isolated discipline. Instead, it should permeate all the disciplines of education. Training teachers in multicultural/intercultural education is not sufficient if teachers are ethnocentric and if they have negative conceptions and attitudes concerning pupils' communities. Therefore, teacher training should include activities which analyse teachers' conceptions and attitudes. It should also include activities which help teachers to change negative attitudes towards pupils' communities and to surmount ethnocentrism.

All these elements are contained in an integrated model for teacher training which is being developed by the project. Each country should develop this model at the national level, and should integrate strategies and methods for analysing pupils' conceptions and attitudes with information about pupils' communities. All this should be assembled in a package which is designed to assist teachers in helping pupils to understand and master issues related to sustainable development.

BIBLIOGRAPHY

Amadio, M. Two decades of bilingual education. *Prospects* (UNESCO, Paris), vol. XX, no. 3, 1990, p. 343-47.

Barton, B. He Maturanga Tau Ahua Reorua: He Kitenga O tetahi Kalako [Bilingual mathematics education: a practitioner's point of view]. *Science and mathematics education papers – 1990*. Hamilton, New Zealand, Centre for Science and Mathematics Education Research, University of Waitako, 1990, p. 159-76. (SAME papers – 1990.)

Begg, A. Communication and assessment in mathematics education. In: Stephens, M., et al., eds. Communicating mathematics: perspectives from classroom practice and current research. Victoria, Australia, The Australian Council for Educational Research Ltd., 1993, p. 288-90.

Calvo Buezas, T. Attitudes and prejudices of teachers and pupils regarding other peoples and cultures. *European teachers' seminar: towards intercultural education: training for teachers of Gypsy pupils*. Council for Cultural Co-operation, Council of Europe, Strasbourg, France, 1990, p. 44-47.

Clarkson, P.; Thomas, J. Communicating mathematics bilingually. In: Stephens, M., et al., eds., op. cit., p. 263-73.

Cruz, B.C. How to improve home-school relations in minority communities. *N.A.S.S.P. Tips for principals* (National Association of Secondary School Principals, VA), 1993. 2 p.

Cushner, K.; McClelland, A; Safford, P., eds. *Human diversity in education: an integrative approach*. New York, McGraw-Hill, 1992. 371 p. (Quoted in Cruz, op. cit.)

Food and Agriculture Organization of the United Nations. *A summary of the process and evaluation of the strategic campaign extension on rat control in Malaysia*. Rome.

Ferguson, T. Communicating in the multilingual classroom. In: MacGregor, M.; Moore, R., eds. *Teaching mathematics in the multicultural classroom: a resource for teachers and teachers educators*. Melbourne, Australia, School of Science and Mathematics Education, Institute of Education, The University of Melbourne, 1991, p. 33-47.

Gagliardi, R. Les concepts structurants de la biologie [The structurant concepts of biology]. *Actes des Vèmes Journèes internationales sur l'éducation scientifique* (Chamonix, France), no. 5, 1983, p. 545-52

—. Concepts structurants en éducation à la santé [Structurant concepts in health education]. *Actes des IXèmes Journées internationales sur l'éducation scientifique* (Chamonix, France), no. 9, 1987, p. 543-50.

—. *Model training kit for extensionists on fish technology and quality control at artisanal level. Analysis of the required characteristics of a model training kit. Project report.* Rome, Food and Agriculture Organization of the United Nations, 1991. 52 p.

Gagliardi, R.; Alfthan, T., eds. *Environmental training: policy and practice for sustainable development.* Geneva, International Labour Office, 1994. 140 p.

—. eds. La formation pour le développement durable [Training for sustainable development]. *Actes des XVes Journées internationales sur la communication, l'éducation et la culture scientifiques et techniques* (Chamonix, France), No. 15, 1993, p. 549-55.

Gagliardi, R.; Bernardini Mosconi, P., eds. Education à l'environnement: utilisation des représentations des élèves pour la preparation d'un curriculum sur l'écologie [Environmental education: use of pupils' representations in preparing a curriculum on ecology]. *Actes des Xèmes Journées Internationales sur l'Education Scientifique* (Chamonix, France), No. 10, 1988, p. 521-26.

Gagliardi, R.; Bernardini Mosconi, P.; Bocchiola, M.T., eds. *Il bambino, il maestro e le scienze (Testo di formazione per insegnanti di scuola elementare* [The child, the teacher and science (Training test for primary schoolteachers)]. Pavia, Italy, Edizioni Antares, 1993. 166 p.

Gilbert, J.; McComish, J. *Science learning, language and feminist pedagogy. Science and mathematics education papers – 1990* (Centre for Science and Mathematics Education Research, University of Waitako, Hamilton, New Zealand), 1990, p. 32-59. *(SAME papers – 1990)*

Giordan, A; De Vecchi, G. *Les origines du savoir* [The origins of knowledge]. Neuchâtel; Paris, Delachaux et Niestlé, 1987. 214 p.

Hafner, A.L.; Spencer Green, J. Multicultural education and diversity: providing information to teachers. *Annual meeting of the American Association of Colleges of Teacher Education* (San Antonio, TX), 1992. 30 p.

Hall, E.T. Making sense without words. In: Fersh, S., ed. *Learning about peoples and cultures.* Evanston, McDougal, Litell, 1974.

—. *Au-delà de la culture* [Beyond culture]. Paris, Editions de Seuil, 1987. 234 p.

Hall, E.T.; Reed-Hall, M. *Hidden differences – doing business with the Japanese.* New York, Anchor Press/Doubleday, 1987. 192 p.

Hanlon, C.; Stewart, T. Aboriginal girls and education. *Feminity and reality: factors that affect girls learning.* Canberra, Australia Department of Employment Education and Training, 1992, p. 10-14.

Harris, S. *Two-way Aboriginal schooling – education and survival.* Canberra, Aboriginal Studies Press, 1990. 176 p.

Kepert, B. Aboriginal students communicating mathematics. In: Stephens, M., et al., eds., op. cit., p. 274-82.

MacGregor, M. Language, culture and mathematics learning. In: MacGregor, M; Moore, R., eds., op. cit., p. 6-20.

—. Interaction of language competence and mathematics learning. In: Stephens, M., et al., eds., op. cit., p. 51-59.

Marthaler, F. Le four solaire est pour aujourd'hui [The solar oven is with us]. *Actes des XIIIèmes Journées internationales sur la communication, l'éducation et la culture scientifiques et techniques*. Chamonix, 1991, p. 352-57.

McDiarmid, G.W. What's the matter? Preparing teachers for culturally diverse classrooms. Reno, NV, Far West Region Holmes Group, 1989. (Quoted in McDiarmid, 1992.)

——. What to do about differences? A study of multicultural education for teacher trainees in the Los Angeles Unified School District. *Journal of teacher education* (Washington, DC), vol. 43, no. 2, March–April 1992, p. 83-93.

McDiarmid, G.W.; Price, J. *Prospective teachers' views of diverse learners: a study of the participants in the ABCD Project*. East Lansing, MI, Michigan State University, National Center for Research on Teacher Education, 1990. (Reseach Report 90-6.) (Quoted in McDiarmid, 1992.)

McPherson Waiti, P. A Maori person's viewpoint on the education of Maori children and, in particular, science. *Education.Science and mathematics education papers-1990*. Hamilton, New Zealand, Centre for Science and Mathematics Education Research, University of Waitako, 1990, p. 177-201. (SAME papers-1990.)

Morton, K.A.; Hull, K. Parents and the mainstream. In: Jones, R.L., ed. *Mainstreaming and the minority child*. Reston, VA, Council for Exceptional Children, 1976. (Quoted in Cruz, 1993.)

Moore, R. Teaching mathematical language in the classroom. In: MacGregor, M.; Moore, R., eds., op. cit., p. 61-83.

Obel, E. Women and afforestation in Kenya. *Voices from Africa*. Geneva, Non-Governmental Liaison Service – UN (NGLS), 1989.

Ohia, M. The unresolved conflict and debate: an overview of bilingual education in New Zealand secondary schools. *Science and mathematics education papers-1990*. Centre for Science and Mathematics Education Research, University of Waitako, Hamilton, New Zealand, p. 111-32. (SAME papers-1990.)

Ohia, M.; Moloney, M.; Knight G. A survey of mathematics teaching in New Zealand secondary school bilingual units. *Science and mathematics education papers-1990*. Centre for Science and Mathematics Education Research, University of Waitako, Hamilton, New Zealand, p. 133-58. (SAME papers-1990.)

Orr, E.W. (1987) Twice as less. *Mathematical behaviour* (New York, Norton), no. 11, p. 261. (Quoted in MacGregor, 1993.)

Paccaud, M . Personal communication to the author.

Perez de Eulate, L.; Gagliardi, R. Les représentations des élèves dans la formation des instituteurs en biologie [Pupils' representations in the training of biology teachers]. *Actes des Xèmes Journées internationales sur l'éducation scientifique*. Chamonix, France, 1988, p. 551-54.

Plotkin, M.J. *Tales of a Shaman's apprentice*. Harmondsworth, United Kingdom, Ed. Viking Penguin, 1993. 318 p.

Raichvarg, D. Vers la compréhension des êtres infiniment petits [Towards the understanding of very tiny beings]. In: Giordan, A., ed. *Histoire de la biologie*. Vol. 1. Paris, Ed. Technique et Documentation – Lavoisier, 1987, p. 91-198. (Petite Collection d'Histoire des Sciences.)

Skutnabb-Kangas, T.; Toukomaa, P. *Teaching migrant children's mother tongue and learning the language of the host country in the context of the socio-cultural situation of the migrant family*. Helsinki, The Finnish National Commission for UNESCO, 1976. (Quoted in Clarkson & Thomas, 1993.)

Tedesco, J.C. *Equidad y conocimiento: eje de la transformación productiva con equidad*. Santiago, ECLAC/UNESCO, 1992. 8 p.

Werner, D.; Bower, B. *Helping health workers learn.* Palo Alto, CA, Hesperian Foundation, 1982. (Quoted in Gagliardi, 1991.)
World Health Organization. *The community health worker.* Geneva, 1987. 461 p.
Zeichner, K. *Educating teachers for cultural diversity.* East Lansing, MI, Michigan State University, National Center for Research on Teacher Education, 1992. (Quoted in McDiarmid, 1992.)

CHAPTER II

Teacher training for multicultural education in favour of democracy and sustainable development: the territorial approach

Raúl Gagliardi and Paula Bernadini Mosconi

BACKGROUND

Intolerance, racism and xenophobia manifest themselves in similar characteristics: the tendency to find simplistic answers to complex problems, and the adoption of an ethnocentric attitude. To develop the capacity to understand complex systems and to help pupils surmount ethnocentrism are important educational objectives for a democratic society.

Democracy and sustainable development cannot be achieved without the participation of the whole population. Therefore, democracy and sustainable development need special educational activities in order to develop the necessary change in attitudes and the development of new capacities and knowledge in the population.

For sustainable development, it is necessary to disseminate information about existing resources and their possible sustainable uses. However, this information is not very useful if people do not have the capacity to understand the complex network of relationships between human activities and environmental systems. It is also important to know the histories of different communities and about their economic, cultural, religious and social activities, as well as the impact the latter have on environmental systems.

Thus, three elements are important for education towards sustainable development:
- Knowledge about existing resources and the way they may be exploited.

- The capacity to understand the complex network of relationships between human activities and environmental systems.
- Knowledge about the history of different communities, plus their economic, social, cultural and religious activities, and their impact on environmental systems.

These elements are also important for education in favour of democracy. They are the basis for:
- Developing the capacity for decision-making and negotiation, taking into account the needs of all communities and members of society.
- Raising the levels of mutual understanding and solidarity between different communities.

Further, multicultural education needs to develop this knowledge and these capacities in order to increase the ability to understand the needs and potentials of each community, as well as the relationship of each community with environmental systems, and their achievements and history.

To achieve democracy, it is necessary to encourage mutual understanding and respect between members of different communities and to promote the active defence of human rights for all members of society.

Democracy and sustainable development imply both the capacity to make decisions which take into account the needs of different social and cultural groups, and increasing the capacity for negotiation between different communities, or cultural and social groups.

One of the main obstacles to mutual understanding and tolerance is ethnocentrism. People who think that the only 'normal' way of thinking is their own are unable to accept other cultures.

The inability to understand complex systems also has a negative effect because it can lead to the acceptance of simplistic answers to complex problems, and the approval of racist and xenophobic propositions.

Ignorance of the characteristics of other cultures, and of their histories and achievements, is another element obstructing mutual understanding and tolerance.

Therefore, helping pupils overcome ethnocentrism and developing their capacity to understand the relationships between different communities and environmental systems are basic educational objectives.

UNDERSTANDING COMPLEX SYSTEMS

Sustainable development implies the better use of environmental resources and the maintenance of human activities within certain limits imposed by

15

the environment. The sustainable use of environmental resources and the prevention of environmental degradation therefore implies knowledge about environmental systems and their relationships with human activities.

The capacity to exploit environmental resources is very ancient. For example, farmers had already acquired practical knowledge about agriculture thousands of years ago. They selected domestic plants and animals without knowing the theory of genetics. They produced a favourable environment in which to cultivate plants without having a theoretical ecological basis. The accumulation of empirical information over long periods was sufficient for the development of agriculture. However, ecology has only been developed as a science over the last century, and most of the world's population is not yet familiar with it. Empirical observations were enough to create new methods of production, but were not sufficient to build a scientific theory of the environment.

Environmental degradation provoked by human activities is not a new problem. Desertification, deforestation, climatic change, the disappearance of species and other environmental problems have been provoked by the unsustainable use of environmental resources over hundreds of years. Empirical knowledge about environmental resources has not been sufficient to avoid environmental degradation.

The basic scientific concepts required to understand environmental systems, such as the transfer of matter and energy, the molecular structure of matter, chemical reactions, synergy, levels of organization, multiple constraints, thresholds, equilibrium, the structure and dynamics of populations, self-building systems, micro-organisms, etc., are not well-known to most people. Frequently, vague ideas substitute for scientific knowledge about environmental systems, for example considering the environment as God, or as an organism capable of taking action for its own survival.

Environmental systems are difficult to understand, and the results of their interaction with human activities are difficult to foresee because environmental transformations are not linearly related to their causes. If the impact of human activity goes beyond a certain threshold, a 'cascade' of processes begins, and leads to environmental degradation. A difficulty arises from the fact that negative effects may appear at a great distance from their sources. It is important also to understand the possible synergy between different environmental processes. For these reasons, an understanding of the relationships between human activities and environmental systems requires the capacity to understand complex systems that do not display linear behaviour, that is, systems made up of a huge quantity of components organized in a web of causality processes. Ecosystems, social systems and living organisms are examples of complex systems. Information about environmental systems and their relationship with human activities is therefore not very useful if students do not have the capacity to understand complex systems.

An understanding of environmental systems and their relationships with human activities cannot be achieved by a summary of scientific information. It also requires the development of a student's capacity to organize in the mind many simultaneous and interrelated causal processes. Therefore, in order to go beyond vague notions about environmental protection and to be capable of assembling organized scientific knowledge about environmental systems, it is necessary to develop the capacity to understand complex systems.

Similar problems to those described above are faced in trying to understand other complex systems – the cell, the living organism, physiological systems or social systems – these cannot be understood without the capacity to build 'networks in the mind'. Sciences, such as cybernetics, which have provoked enormous changes in all scientific disciplines, cannot be developed without this capacity.

The capacity to deal with complex systems will allow the quality of life to be improved and more resources to become available, by the undertaking of new, environmentally sound economic activities, as well as by the solving of existing environmental problems.

The acquisition of this capacity is not a spontaneous development. Educational research carried out in different countries (Argentina, France, Italy, Spain, Switzerland and Venezuela) suggests that school-leavers often do not understand complex systems and think linearly, although environmental phenomena occur in a non-linear manner, in a complex web of causality. This is true despite the fact that their study programmes include disciplines related to complex systems, such as ecology, biology and physiology. These results suggest the necessity for designing new strategies and methods to improve the students' ability to understand complex systems.

Any strategy or teaching method for developing student capacity is not, however, useful if the teachers themselves do not have this capacity in the first place. Experience from teacher training suggests that many teachers have not developed the ability to understand complex systems and therefore cannot teach them. It is therefore necessary to analyse the importance of this phenomena and to determine the best solutions.

RESEARCH METHODOLOGY

The basic assumption of the research methodology is that the learning processes depend on a web of ideas, beliefs, logical abilities, language, knowledge and skills, that individuals develop and use for integrating new information and building new knowledge and skills. This web is organized into a 'cognitive system'. It may facilitate the learning of some knowledge and the development of some skills, while hindering the learning of others. By identifying the obstacles to students' learning, teachers can design training programmes that help the students to overcome them.

Acquiring basic scientific knowledge is not easy. Listening to a teacher imparting scientific information is often inadequate for the acquisition of new knowledge. Researchers of the teaching sciences analyse the learning of scientific concepts and suggest methods for helping the learner. A basic assumption is that learning is not the simple acquisition of new information. Rather it is a complex process of transforming conceptual frameworks. Obstacles to learning can be affective, religious, cultural, logical or conceptual.

To identify obstacles to learning, it is possible to apply a research methodology developed by social psychology and adapted and used for science teaching over the last fifteen years by the Laboratory of Didactics and Epistemology of Sciences at the University of Geneva, the Centre for Studies on Didactics of the Faculty of Sciences of the University of Pavia, and the University of Paris VII and other research and training institutions working on teaching methodology in science and in teacher training.

The research methodology consists essentially of an analysis of students' conceptions (ideas, beliefs, opinions, knowledge), capacities and attitudes using open-ended questionnaires complemented by individual interviews and group discussions. The questions are oriented to analyse the students' conceptions about a subject and their ability to master it, and not to analyse the information they have about the subject. The questions should be open and should not provide any indication of the 'correct' answer. Designs and schemes can complement the questions. The validity of the answers is confirmed by using complementary questions about the same subject. The 'secret' is to ask questions that cannot be answered by using memorized information. This research methodology requires special training, in particular to analyse the conceptions and abilities that lie 'behind' the answers. Interviews and group discussions allow more details to be obtained about students' capacities, conceptions and learning obstacles and to confirm the results obtained from the questionnaires.

This research methodology is currently used for the analysis of students' conceptions and learning obstacles in different scientific domains at primary, secondary and university levels. Sciences, such as biology, ecology, physiology, chemistry and physics, and areas such as environmental education and health education, are taught using it. The methodology is also used for the training of nurses and it has been proposed for training in environmental protection, teaching traditional communities how to conserve food, and for other training activities. It has also been proposed for the analysis of students' conceptions and learning obstacles in any field.

The research methodology has also been applied when training teachers for science teaching and it has been proposed as a basic element in the training of teachers in any field. Its use in teaching activities permits a continuous analysis of the students' learning obstacles. This information is useful for organizing tailor-made courses in which activities can be adapted to deal with learning obstacles. It is also a good instrument for evaluating strategies, curricula and teaching methods. If the students do not transform their conceptions and overcome the learning obstacles facing them, they cannot acquire the offered knowledge.

ANALYSIS OF LEARNING OBSTACLES
IN ENVIRONMENTAL EDUCATION

Since 1986, the methodology described above has been in use in Lombardy, Italy, where it has been used to analyse students' conceptions and learning obstacles with regard to environmental systems. Activities combine educational research and teacher training and have been organized by the Regional Institute for Research, Experimentation and Teacher Training of Lombardy (Istituto Regionale de Ricerca, Sperimentazione e Aggiornamento Educativi), an institution responsible for the in-service training of teachers. One research activity lasted two years, with the participation of forty teachers from secondary and high schools throughout the region. The participants prepared and evaluated questionnaires and used them to analyse their own students' conceptions, abilities and learning obstacles. The questions called for the solution of problems that can only be solved by establishing networks of relationships between causality processes. The answers were analysed by each teacher individually and also in teacher teams. The teacher teams identified the structural concepts necessary for overcoming learning obstacles and for building up scientific knowledge about environmental systems. They also proposed strategies, methods and contents for the teaching. This activity allowed the participating teachers to improve their awareness of students' capacities and stimulated the introduction of teaching innovations. It also encouraged an improvement in the teachers' scientific knowledge about environmental systems, in particular aiding them to identify structural concepts.

Similar research developed in other regions of Italy and in other countries produced comparable results: most students have neither the basic scientific background to understand environmental systems, nor the capacity to understand the complex network of processes that are typical of them.

These results were confirmed by other research on environmental education, including a research project on students' conceptions of the main problems encountered during various historical periods. The answers suggested a tendency to consider the environment as a unity, without structure, and not as a complex web of processes.

Another research project was developed in Italy as part of the 'Project for environmental education in secondary and high schools in Lombardy'.

The students' answers suggested three main attitudes towards the environment:

- *Pantheism*: 'nature' has the capacity to protect animals and plants. It is not the same thing as living organisms.
- *Anthropocentrism*: the environment exists for human exploitation.
- *Pessimism*: the relationship between man and the environment is always deleterious for the latter. There is no way of avoiding this situation.

The students were also asked about the main problems of given historical periods. Students saw the main problems in prehistoric periods as food, wild animals and defense. In ancient Greece and Rome the only problem was warfare. During feudalism the problems were health, war and hygiene, and today the most important problem is pollution. The main problems in developing countries are food, agriculture and health. They do not mention pollution or unemployment as problems in developing countries. Concerning Italy, the students indicated that the main problems were pollution, social and political problems, the Mafia, unemployment, health, drugs and bad governments!

These answers show that students have a very simplistic idea of day-to-day problems in different periods and in different countries. They probably use stereotypes transmitted by the mass media (prehistoric men fighting with wild animals, war in feudal castles, etc.). Another important problem is the incapacity to situate the problems of other people or other communities.

Research about pupils' conceptions confirms these results. In particular, a research project on pupils' conceptions of environmental problems and resources in different periods shows that understanding of the relationship between man and the environment is limited. Environmental elements (rivers, forests, fields, etc.) are understood as a resource or as a problem. Pupils have difficulty in understanding that a river, for example, can be a resource *and* a problem, depending on the situation and the characteristics of the community.

The results are consistent: pupils are ethnocentric, have limited understanding of environmental systems and are unaware of the basic problems of other communities or countries.

INTEGRATION OF CONCEPTS TAUGHT IN DIFFERENT DISCIPLINES

A student who wants to understand social and environmental systems should learn disparate disciplines to an advanced level and then attempt to integrate them. But there is always a risk that such training will merely convey to the student a large quantity of disorganized information.

Education for sustainable development should be a well-organized set of learning activities that help students develop their capacity to understand and manage complex social and environmental systems. Chemistry, physics, thermodynamics, mathematics, statistics, economy, geography, biology and ecology should be integrated in a student's mind and used to understand environmental processes.

Concepts such as energy, entropy, the molecule, chemical reactions, respiration and photosynthesis should be integrated with concepts such as the cell, the organism, self-building systems, the micro-organism, species, population, the ecosystem, economic activity and territory.

Teachers assume that a concept learned in one discipline can be applied elsewhere. Teachers in biology, for example, assume that pupils know and bring with them the concepts taught in physics and chemistry. Frequently this hypothesis is wrong. Many students do not transfer the concepts taught in different disciplines. Educational research shows that secondary school students do not spontaneously integrate concepts that are taught in different courses. In a student's mind, the energy learned about in physics is not the same as the energy learned about in biology or geography. Students do not use the concepts of the molecule and chemical reaction learned in chemistry to explain biological or environmental processes. Yet the integration of concepts is as important as the learning of them. In fact, without the integration of concepts the information is soon forgotten. This accounts for the rapid loss of scientific information learned by rote in schools.

A possible cause of this phenomenon is the curriculum: history, geography, ecology and economy are separate disciplines. Each teacher has a main

21

objective – to convey the programme of his/her course – and gives no importance to the use of concepts taught in other disciplines.

THE TERRITORIAL APPROACH

A training technique called 'the territorial approach' was set up with the objective of stimulating the integration of concepts taught in different disciplines, in order to develop the capacity for understanding complex systems, so as to surmount ethnocentrism and enable pupils to learn about different communities, their history and their relationships with environmental systems.

The territorial approach is based on the study of the territory where students live, analysing the specific environmental, economic and social systems and their evolution. The relationships between all these systems are also analyzed. The consequences of human activity on environmental systems are studied. The histories of different communities are integrated with their relationships to other communities and to environmental systems.

The main learning difficulties encountered by students – dealing with dimensions, changes of scale in processes, relationships between macro and micro levels, etc. – can be discussed in relation to each discipline. Each teacher should present each concept imported from other disciplines showing the particular meaning given to it by the discipline he/she is teaching. Different disciplines can be integrated around a particular theme, such as the local territory or area. Studying the area where they live can motivate students and enable them to establish relationships between the human sciences (history, politics, human geography) and other sciences (ecology, geology, chemistry, physics, biology, etc.). Each of these disciplines can focus on a particular aspect of the local area while simultaneously incorporating the other disciplines. For example, a teacher of history can teach about the main historical processes and, at the same time, discuss associated environmental transformations, geographical aspects, economic evolution, etc. A teacher of ecology can start with a description of the main ecosystems in the area but can also analyse the impact of economic activities and the relationship of these to historical processes. Students must be stimulated to establish relationships between the different disciplines.

One advantage of this methodology is that it eliminates the isolated themes that so lack relevance for students. It shows how all areas of knowledge can be integrated and used to build new knowledge.

This approach was tested with science teachers in the 'Park of Ticino'. The 'Park of Ticino' covers 22,000 square kilometres on the east bank of the Ticino river, in Northern Italy, including the town of Pavia, forty villages and a nature reserve park. What was, many hundred of years ago, a marshy swamp has today become an agricultural plain through canalization of the river.

Teacher training took place in the form of an initial meeting, a guided tour and a week-long seminar. During the seminar, teachers followed courses on didacticism in the sciences (in particular analysis of students' conceptions, determination of learning obstacles and structural concepts). Other courses discussed the history, economy, geography and ecology of the park. The participants, organized in multidisciplinary teams, analyzed old maps and documents looking for the former river bed, the location of houses, churches, castles and roads, and their relationship to economic and social activities. They analyzed the evolution of technology and the impact of human activity on environmental systems. Analysis of transformations in economic, social and religious activities was integrated with analysis of the transformation of environmental systems, and with study of the evolution of technology.

During a second phase of the seminar, the teams analyzed the existing resources in each historical period, their use by different communities, the transformations that were necessary for human use, and the effect on the environment. With all these elements teachers determined a series of concepts (structural concepts) and proposed strategies and methods to teach them, integrating different disciplines around the same conceptual network. Questionnaires for the analysis of students' conceptions were also pre-pared.

The seminar's participants were stimulated by the territorial approach. Teachers from different disciplines started to focus teaching on two main objectives: developing students capacities for understanding complex systems and integrating the different disciplines in order to obtain a basic conceptual network covering history, geography, ecology, economy, religion and technology.

FUTURE DEVELOPMENT

The territorial approach should be developed in each country because it is centred in the characteristics and potential for sustainable use of national or local territories. It can be proposed for teaching sustainable development and for multicultural/intercultural education. It is integrated in the 'Guides for training teachers for multicultural/intercultural education' and other materials produced as part of the IBE's project 'Basic education for participation and democracy: key issues in human resources development (Teachers and multicultural/intercultural education)'.

The territorial model is also the basis for the preparation of projects for teacher training for basic education addressing the poorest countries, and for the preparation of projects on education for sustainable development.

The territorial approach needs a particular teacher training strategy in order to stimulate the organization of teams incorporating teachers from different disciplines focused on the study of the local territory.

BIBLIOGRAPHY

Gagliardi, R. Les concepts structurants de la biologie [The structural concepts of biology]. *Actes des V^es Journées internationales sur l'éducation scientifique* (Chamonix, France), no. 5, 1983, p. 545-52.

—. Model training kit for extensionists on fish technology and quality control at artisanal level: analysis of the required characteristics of a model training kit. *Project report.* Rome, Food and Agriculture Organization of the United Nations, 1991. 52 p.

Gagliardi, R.; Alfthan, T., eds. *Environmental training: policy and practice for sustainable development.* Geneva, International Labour Office, 1994. 140 p.

—. La formation pour le développement durable [Training for sustainable development]. *Actes des XVes Journées internationales sur la communication, l'éducation et la culture scientifiques et techniques* (Chamonix, France), no. 15, 1993, p. 549-55.

Gagliardi, R.; Bernardini Mosconi, P., eds. Education à l'environnement: utilisation des représentations des élèves pour la preparation d'un curriculum sur l'écologie [Enviromental education: the use of pupil's conceptions in the preparation of an ecology curriculum]. *Actes des X^es Journées internationales sur l'éducation scientifique* (Chamonix, France), no. 10, 1988, p. 521-26.

Gagliardi, R.; Bernardini Mosconi, P.; Bocchiola, M.T., eds. *Il bambino, il maestro e le scienze (testo di formazione per insegnanti di scuola elementare)* [The child, the teacher and science (training test for primary school researchers)]. Pavia, Italy, Edizioni Antares, 1993. 166 p.

CHAPTER III

Intercultural bilingual education and the training of human resources: lessons for Bolivia from the Latin American experience[1]

Luis Enrique López

INTRODUCTION

Historically, the training of professionals to meet the needs of bilingual education in Latin America has nearly always been a secondary concern in terms of the provision of resources. Nonetheless, concern with this issue has considerably increased in recent years, possibly as a consequence of the greater attention being given to bilingual education generally. It has to be admitted, however, that the provision of education and training in disciplines related to the introduction of bilingual programmes is still inadequate to meet the needs of any country in the region.

Until recently, the emphasis in bilingual education was placed almost exclusively on developing educational methodologies and materials, principally for the teaching of indigenous[2] languages as mother tongues, and Spanish as a second language. Training in the new methods and materials was given to teachers in various projects, in their role as mediators between those who designed the innovations and the students. But, as we shall see later, training was always thought of as a functional activity tied to the development of each individual project, rather than as action to provide the teachers with basic training or more thorough professional grounding of longer-term value.

Lately, initiatives which go beyond the mere provision of basic skills have been launched, leaning towards true professional training in bilingual education. In this paper, we shall take stock of the main examples of these in the region, as the basis for an analysis of the needs of professionals for effective and high-quality bilingual education. This overview will then enable us to relate needs to provision, in order to draw conclusions which may aid the formulation of new initiatives, at a time when Bolivia is beginning a process of educational reform which stresses the need for a new system to meet the demands of its multiethnic, multicultural and multilingual population.

THE NEEDS OF HUMAN RESOURCES

In order to analyse training needs for bilingual education, we must start from the consideration that this approach, as it is conceived in most countries in the region, means something more than developing a specific project designed to satisfy a particular want, as might be the case in a project on the methodology of reading, writing or arithmetic, for example. An intercultural bilingual education programme means, in fact, a far-reaching transformation which calls all educational elements into question – from the principles of educational provision to the plans, programmes and educational materials needed for the new proposal. In other words, to conduct intercultural bilingual education means to transform the current education system so as to meet the basic learning needs of indigenous learners, and not merely the introduction of an innovation into one specific aspect of the system. Intercultural bilingual education is much more than languages education, or education in first and second languages, as it was thought to be when it began.[3]

The complexity of intercultural bilingual education thus presents us with a wide range of staff requirements. In order to ensure successful application it is necessary to take training action in fields such as research, planning, curriculum development, educational administration, educational supervision and, of course, teaching and classroom activities.

In the field of research, professionals have to be able to conduct basic investigations such as:
- Sociolinguistic diagnoses of, for example, the expectations and attitudes of various parties (parents, teachers, learners, etc.) towards the use of indigenous languages in education.
- Descriptive studies of aspects of the languages and cultures concerned.
- Research designed to describe and analyse teaching practice in the classroom.

Such research will establish the training needs of the teachers who will be responsible for implementing the intended innovations. To this type of research should be added evaluation, either conducted while the innovation is being carried out or once it is completed. The interdisciplinary nature of intercultural bilingual education also means that research must cover a number of disciplines such as education, descriptive linguistics, psycholinguistics, sociolinguistics, social psychology applied to the field of linguistics, cognitive psychology, cultural anthropology, cognitive anthropology, applied or educational linguistics, and bilingual teaching practice, the latter a new and rapidly emerging field.

With regard to planning, there is a need for professionals who can make use of the results of research in order to plan action, especially in two fields: language planning and educational planning. Their decisions will relate to tasks of major sociopolitical importance such as the normalization of vernacular languages,[4] including codification and the development of grammars, and to questions such as the basic needs of learners, the orientation of the programmes, the design of curricula, the development of educational materials, etc.

There is also a need for professionals trained to intervene in various aspects of curriculum development, from identification of the skills which learners need to develop, to the preparation of textbooks and guides for teachers and pupils in each area. Professionals who can address educational administration and supervision are also required.

Finally, educators trained to teach bilingually are needed, and this in turn leads to an urgent need for full professional training programmes. This need is not just for training in basic skills to overcome situations caused by inadequate – because it was thought universal and homogenous – teacher training received in the past. There is a basic requirement for teachers with the ability to guide the learning of mother tongues and a second language, exploiting both the languages and the subordinate and dominant cultures as teaching resources.

In view of the undeniable importance of having teachers so trained, it is also important that there should be trainers of trainers: those who will take responsibility for teacher training, so that the innovation takes root at classroom level and teachers' practices are changed. At the present time, this is the most urgent need of intercultural bilingual education in all the countries in the region.

One need which we wish to stress is for a new concept of training, which will play a major role in the implementation of innovations at classroom level. In order for bilingual education to succeed, traditional training has to be substantially transformed, because, in many cases, the radical ideas of bilingual education do not outweigh tradition. This brings us to a primary requirement: for the observation and description of current teaching practices, so that we can infer the view of learning and of bilingualism in schools and society. Training based on exhaustive knowledge of teachers' real practices can thus be provided to modify their performance in the classroom.

THE PROVISION OF TRAINING

Training

In the running of bilingual education programmes, the participation of teachers – indigenous and others – in tasks which are seen as priorities, such as developing new textbooks and guides for children and teachers, has been in response to various requirements. These include the desire to have a native, bilingual speaker able to use both the indigenous language and Spanish fluently, to the wish to employ someone who would implement the innovations in the classroom, or someone who could give professional teaching advice from his or her experience and knowledge. As a result, throughout the history of intercultural bilingual education in Latin America, indigenous teachers have played a variety of roles: as 'informants'[5] of linguists and anthropologists involved in grass roots research; as recorders in writing of the traditions, oral history, and skills and knowledge of the peoples to which they belong; as co-authors of the new educational materials written in the relevant indigenous language and/or in Spanish; as introducers of radically different methodologies in the classroom; as collectors of teaching information for researchers; and as trainers of teachers.

In order to be effective, programmes have generally included in their design a training element to fill gaps in the areas of linguistics, anthropology and teaching, and in matters of ideology and politics. The earliest antecedents of this type date from more than forty years ago, when courses were organized in Mexico to train indigenous young people to write in their own languages with the aims of enabling them to start translating the Bible and to use primers devised by the missionary linguists of the Summer Institute of Linguistics. This strategy was later emulated in most countries in the region. Thus, for example, in Peru, the first course of this type was launched in summer 1953, with the participation of eleven young people from six Amazonian ethnic language groups who started teaching reading and writing to 270 learners in indigenous Amazonian languages, within their own communities of origin. Here in Bolivia, a similar strategy was put into effect between 1952 and 1985 among various indigenous peoples in the provinces of Oriente, Chaco and Amazonia.

Since the 1960s, training courses have expanded and become diversified with the growth in intercultural bilingual education courses, and they are presently provided in all the countries where there are projects, from Mexico to Argentina and Chile. In Nicáragua, for example, forty-five training courses were held between 1984 and 1987 for 1,026 teachers. For more than twenty years, projects run in Ecuador, Guatemala, Mexico and Peru have regarded the training of teachers as a priority area. In Bolivia, the Intercultural Bilingual Education Project (Ministry of Education and Culture–UNICEF) has, since it began in 1990, trained some 400 teachers in annual courses lasting from two to four weeks before the beginning of the school year, complemented by week-long workshops during the school holidays in the middle of the year. These measures were in addition to those previously serving the same teachers and carried out under two bilingual education projects involving international co-operation: the Rural Education Project I (Bolivia–USAID) and the Altiplano Integrated Education Project (Bolivia–World Bank). In the first, between 1978 and 1986, 506 classroom teachers, forty-five section heads and six supervisors were trained.

One problem to be faced is the design of the training courses, seminars and workshops, which must take into account their short duration and the quantity of material which has to be covered, given the general absence of experience and information about the field among teachers. This is compounded by the variety of basic teacher training which teachers bring with them, and by the fact that those with a teacher's certificate are the products of the very system which the bilingual and intercultural standpoint intends to change.

This situation gives rise to serious difficulties when innovations are put into practice, with respect to both teaching and political ideology. Problems are related to the fact that teachers have been prepared to serve learners whose characteristics differ significantly from those of indigenous, vernacular-speaking children; and the problems of political ideology are that the teachers have often adopted the dominant system's homogenizing ideology and are reluctant to consider the possibility of using and taking advantage of indigenous languages in school. Thus, for example, in Bolivia there are still frequent cases of teachers insisting that their indigenous students, both male and female, cut their hair, discard traditional clothing and even cease using their mother tongue in school.[6] The situation can be yet more complicated in the case of skills, knowledge, values, attitudes and beliefs which learners have acquired in their peasant or indigenous home. A teacher, having learnt to give greater value to the hegemonic culture with its 'civilizing' zeal, is required to 'convert' the indigenous learners.

This brings us to the conclusion that, in the case of intercultural bilingual education, training is not only a question of teaching practice but also of teachers' vision and individual behaviour in the face of diversity. The scale of efforts at homogenization has been such that it has affected not only Spanish-speaking teachers, white and *mestizo*, but also teachers of peasant origin who speak an indigenous language. This means that the teacher factor has become one of the main problems of intercultural bilingual education programmes and that training alone is no panacea, since change has also to take place in the affective domain and in teachers' perceptions of themselves and of the world around them. Teachers must be convinced of their pupils' real potential for learning and intellectual development, and of the potential of the given indigenous people, of their skills, knowledge, languages, values, beliefs – in sum, of their culture.

Problems of this nature have been mentioned in every exchange of experience and in almost all reports on intercultural bilingual education projects. The majority of programmes have reached the conclusion that training courses are insufficient to meet the needs, expectations and requirements of the programmes, and of the beneficiaries and their parents.

This has caused some programmes to plan longer periods of training before introducing innovations, i.e. pre-service training. This occurred in the intercultural bilingual education project in Ecuador in 1985. Since, given the lack of vernacular-speaking teachers, it was necessary to work with a number of 'improvised' teachers, the possibility was considered of arranging courses lasting four months before teachers joined the project. Although this was feasible in the first year, in later years and as grade coverage was extended, training time was reduced considerably, finishing up as the two or three weeks that most projects allow for that purpose. This situation became even more difficult when it was a matter of training several different groups of teachers at once. There was no other solution but to adopt the pattern which is characteristic of every intercultural bilingual education programme today, if several activities are to be carried out simultaneously – research, curriculum development, textbook production, distribution, community work, and so on – i.e. by substantially reducing the time devoted to training.

Programmes still face growing problems, given that every training activity has to start by training the intercultural bilingual education teachers in writing the indigenous language – which they usually speak but cannot write – so as to reawaken their linguistic awareness and interest them in studying the language that they will use as the medium of education.

Training needs are greater still if indigenous young people with limited schooling are selected as teachers; this is frequently the case among small indigenous ethnic groups in the region. In such cases, the responsibility goes beyond training itself and has to take into account complementary schooling courses so that the young people at least complete secondary education. This is a situation that affects the implementation of intercultural bilingual education programmes among most indigenous peoples, with the possible exception of the major ethnic groups such as the Quechua and Aymara, where there is a greater availability of qualified persons, or at least of graduates of secondary education.

It should of course be stated in this context that in many cases, and especially when intercultural bilingual education forms part of a wider framework of linguistic and cultural revival, the young people who take on the role of teachers in intercultural bilingual education programmes perform their work effectively, despite their limited schooling, motivated perhaps by teaching children of their own ethnic group. Here in Bolivia, this can be seen, for example, among Guaraní-speaking young people who have been mandated by their organization, the Assembly of the Guaraní People (APG) to act as temporary teachers of Guaraní children attending primary school, using a bilingual intercultural approach.

In view of the limited time available, it could be useful to introduce training where face-to-face course time was complemented by ongoing monitoring of teaching: i.e. a teacher with experience of intercultural bilingual education, together with one or more leaders of the innovation, would be responsible for overseeing the teacher training, and their main function would be to accompany and assess the teachers in the transformation of their practice.

However, in order for this to take place, the assessment would have to be long enough and frequent enough to guarantee a minimum of continuity and feedback. Given the coverage and range of activities of intercultural bilingual education projects, no one can really guarantee a minimum of a weekly visit to each teacher undergoing training and, if several different grades were to be monitored at once in the same school, the scheme would be impracticable and could not be replicated or generalized on the scale presently needed, given the conditions prevailing in the Ministries of Education in the region. Whole regiments of advisers would be needed, and would have to be constantly in the field: regiments that would, indeed, themselves have to be trained.

Moreover, if priority attention is given to teachers, this often means the neglect of other equally important factors such as the development of educational materials. This has happened to a number of projects, such as that of the Ayacucho in Peru. After more than a decade of activity, there were still only textbooks for the first two or three grades of primary school.

With the challenge of wider coverage, and the growth of intercultural bilingual education out of projects considered experimental, for example in Guatemala, Ecuador and Peru, teacher training needs now tend to exceed all possible capacity to respond. The challenge for Bolivia is all the greater since Education Reform Law No. 1565 defines intercultural bilingual education as the means by which *all* vernacular-speaking learners shall be served. This refers to approximately seventy per cent of learners of school age, and to a larger percentage of those entering primary school in rural and marginal urban areas.

In order to escape from this impasse, substantial changes need to be made in current teacher training programmes. A new concept of training is required which links immediate skills training to a more thorough professional grounding.

Similarly, it is imperative for every intercultural bilingual education programme to have a more direct influence on teacher training, and it might even be preferable to initiate every intercultural bilingual education programme from a teacher training centre. In that way, the innovation might be more sure of continuity since, by becoming involved in the development of an experimental programme, the teacher training college or institute of education would face the challenge of constantly modifying its practice and the training which it provides for future teachers.

Certification programmes for serving teachers

In the face of situations such as those described, special programmes have been devised for serving teachers who entered the service without passing through a teacher training centre or having completed school education. These certification or professionalization programmes for teachers,[7] as they are commonly called, are also for teachers working in indigenous areas and conducting intercultural bilingual education programmes. This is the case, for example, in Colombia, Ecuador, Peru and Mexico.

Since the mid-1980s, the Ethnic Education Division of the Ministry of National Education in Colombia, in association with the teacher training colleges within its jurisdiction, has organized training programmes which progress through ten stages, coinciding with school holidays. A teacher can attend up to three stages per year, so that he or she can complete the training in a total of three and a half years. The Colombian programmes combine face-to-face tuition with distance methods and also accept indigenous teachers who have completed primary-level education.

Something similar takes place in Ecuador, under a project developed in the Quechua-speaking area of Cotopaxi. For ten years, the Cotopaxi Indigenous Education Service (SEIC) has been opening new schools, using indigenous young people of varied educational backgrounds, many of whom have only completed primary education. The only way of bringing schooling to these rural areas is to turn anyone who knows a little more than his or her future pupils into a teacher, and training such people in action partly by face-to-face methods which, as is conventional, include tasks to be undertaken by the teachers on their own.

In Peru, the situation is a little different in that certification programmes serve teachers who have completed at least secondary education. There are various programmes, but only three of them were designed with the specific needs of teachers working in intercultural bilingual education programmes in mind. These are those of Puno, Pucallpa and Condorcanqui, Bagua. The last two serve Amazonian teachers, and the first Quechua and Aymara-speaking teachers. We should also mention that the Condorcanqui programme arose from a demand by an indigenous organization: the Interethnic Association of the Peruvian Selva (AIDESEP). Training is the responsibility of the respective higher institutes of education and takes the same period of time as that devoted to the training of school teachers (five years); however, instead of proceeding over ten academic semesters in accordance with the usual calendar, it takes only five summer periods (of three months each) and is complemented by distance learning activities. These are, however, organized in a spontaneous manner, with inadequate design and insufficient supervision.

Since nearly all certification programmes for serving teachers contain elements of distance learning, we think it right to digress a moment from this review and make one or two remarks about this method as it relates to an indigenous context. Besides the limitations referred to in the last paragraph, programmes which are only partly face-to-face have an almost insoluble difficulty in serving indigenous teachers: that of their mastery of Spanish and their difficulties of reading comprehension.

This is one of the question marks hanging over the Bolivian efforts since the early 1990s, when a distance-based education model of certification for serving teachers was introduced. As will readily be understood, many such teachers work in rural areas and speak an indigenous language. The Bolivian Distance Education System (SEBAD) has provided nearly 6,000 unqualified teachers throughout the country with written educational materials (modules) and is now awaiting an external evaluation which will determine its degree of success, part of which will relate to the level of internalization of the contents of the modules and the reading comprehension of the teachers served.

In order to overcome this potential deficiency, SEIC, without much success, initially included materials recorded on cassette in its distance component, which students were supposed to listen to and process, in recognition of the oral nature of the entire indigenous context and with a view to mitigating somewhat the indigenous young people's reading problems. Although the intention was good, the reaction of the serving teachers was not positive: they pointed to difficulties associated with the speed with which the information flow was presented, the inability to ask questions about something they had not understood, and the excessive individual attention required by interaction with the cassette. The teachers showed clearly that they preferred the face-to-face method in which they could not only listen but could also be listened to, and could work co-operatively with their fellows.[8]

The results of a similar method were better for the Quechua-speaking young teachers of Urubamba, Cuzco, served by the certification programme run by the Pontifical Catholic University of Peru, McGill University of Canada and the Higher Technological and Educational Institute of Urubamba. This programme also combined face-to-face and distance education using cassettes and listening guides, the last of which may have led to the method's being well received by users. The cassettes provide the information, and the listening guides give the teachers instructions on how to work with the cassette and where to stop, besides offering simple reading passages to complement the information needed by the teacher to reach a particular objective. It would be interesting to compare experiences and to determine why the method was accepted in Urubamba and rejected in Cotopaxi, and to know whether the use of recorded material and of oral and visual media in distance education would be culturally relevant and educationally adequate for other teachers needing a gradual initiation into the world of the written word.

Difficulties such as those indicated have led to careful analyses of the certification and professionalization programmes for serving teachers. In Peru, for example, AIDESEP has evaluated the results of its teacher certification programme in Condorcanqui in order to design a whole training strategy for unqualified teachers which makes use of and is related to the experience of the teacher training run by that organization in Iquitos (see next section).

In Mexico, it is a national university that has committed itself to the difficult task of 'raising the level of more than 13,000 teachers from an indigenous environment, who have completed the *bachillerato* secondary education examination or basic teacher training'.[9] The goal of the National Pedagogical University (UPN), in close association with the Directorate General of Indigenous Education, is to raise indigenous teachers to the status of university graduates. The curriculum of this programme, which takes eight academic semesters of training, is based on teaching practice. 'The aim of the programme is to meet the requirements of innovative educational practice which, taking actual conditions as its starting point, can help to solve the complexity and diversity of indigenous education today' (National Pedagogical University, 1990, p. 5). Moreover, by enabling serving teachers to gain a university degree, it opens up to them the possibility of pursuing postgraduate studies if they so desire. It should be remembered that in Mexico, as is the case in nearly all countries in the region, teaching is a terminal career, so that a qualification as primary or high-school teacher from an institute of education or a teacher training college does not entitle the holder to pursue university studies.

On the same lines, plans are going ahead for UPN to launch a two-year Master's programme in indigenous education for vernacular-speaking professionals wishing to deepen their analysis of their teaching practice. Perhaps such programmes will begin to turn out the professionals specializing in intercultural and bilingual education to whom we referred earlier.

The Mexican case, although different from the others on which we have commented, merits analysis because it goes a stage further, beyond the mere certification of teachers who are working without the pieces of paper which make them qualified, and aims at professionalization, introducing them to university life and the practice of research and constant reflection. As is pointed out in the documents produced by UPN, the intention is to 'contribute to the professionalization of pre-school and primary teachers working in the indigenous environment' (National Pedagogical University, 1990, p. 19), to which end it develops a partly face-to-face method that accustoms serving teachers to meeting their colleagues in workshops for discussion and study of the materials of the programme. The aim of these workshops is to 'consider a given problem from the various angles provided by a teacher education approach' (ibid, p. 20).

Fortunately, as has been seen, different responses have been coming to the fore in recent years in various countries in the region, with the aim of giving increased attention to serving teachers, using methods which overcome the limitations of training programmes. In all the cases reviewed, the results of certification programmes are better than those of training programmes. For one thing, serving staff are catered for over longer periods than those used in training, and for another, greater continuity is ensured by the use of an ad hoc curriculum in which aspects dealt with in training courses in a few hours comprise one or more major subjects.

Other advantages relate to the number of teachers who can be covered, regardless of whether they are teaching an intercultural bilingual education programme or not. For example, in the training courses for unqualified teachers provided by the Higher Institute of Education of Puno, Peru between 1984 and 1988, 456 primary school teachers obtained qualifications, among whom twenty-three were teaching an intercultural bilingual education programme in their respective schools. All of them received training in various aspects linked to intercultural bilingual education: the writing and grammar of indigenous languages, curriculum design, mother tongue teaching, second language teaching, and social and natural sciences, besides other more general training subjects.

An additional benefit in Bolivia and Peru is related to the mobility which is characteristic of the rural teaching force. In an effort to move gradually closer to the city, many rural teachers change school every two or three years, even every year, and this creates further difficulties for any intercultural bilingual education programme: the effects of any short training course are diminished by the constant turnover of teachers, and in any course it is necessary to revise basic concepts and strategies – such as reading and writing in indigenous languages – in order to ensure that there is a minimum common language and practice among all teachers, before matters of methodology can be addressed. As may be imagined, this does not happen in professionalization and certification programmes: by catering to serving teachers, regardless of the schools where they work, the continuity of the training is ensured.

Despite these advantages, such training programmes are neither perfect nor free of difficulties. One of these arises from the lack of technical staff able to take on the organization and teaching of specialized courses on intercultural bilingual education. In a situation in which there are few professional programmes in linguistics or anthropology, the administrators of the training programmes have serious difficulty in providing, for example, courses on the descriptive disciplines of linguistics, with reference to indigenous languages. The problem is not unique to language-based subjects: it is equally difficult to find trainers to teach more applied subjects such as the teaching of the indigenous language as a mother tongue, the teaching of Spanish as a second language, etc. The central difficulty lies in the lack of any intermediate level of training for the training of intercultural bilingual education trainers.

Moreover, reference should be made to the usual structure of the curriculum of these courses, which is one of their major drawbacks. A review of some of the study plans of the programmes provided in Colombia and Peru, for example, leads us to the conclusion that these are only 'halfway' solutions, as the emphasis is placed only on adapting the content of the national curricula in order to respond to some of the sociocultural peculiarities and training needs of indigenous teachers, but not on designing an ad hoc curriculum structure. In the Bicultural Curriculum for the Professionalization of Sikuani Teachers, for example, we see that of the fifteen training areas, only one is devoted to the reading and writing of the indigenous language and to developing the indigenous teachers' knowledge of their language; and we observe that out of a total of 2,400 hours of training, only 640 relate to the specific preparation required by native teachers (Colombian Ministry of National Education, 1988).

Professional training in and for bilingual education

It was not until the mid-1970s that a new phase began, in which mid-term and long-term alternatives with a more thorough approach to training began to appear, although there had already been significant training in descriptive linguistics applied to indigenous languages in certain countries in the region since the beginning of the previous decade. The first professional programmes of descriptive linguistics in indigenous languages on which we have information were those provided in Peru, under the Language Promotion Project of the Greater National University of San Marcos (UNMSM) in Lima which, from 1960, began training linguists specializing in the study of Quechua.

However, the first human resources development programme specifically for bilingual education was held in Mexico, between 1979 and 1982, with the aim of stimulating the linguistic and ethnic development of indigenous Mexican peoples through the training of professionals specializing 'in various fields, including a sector ... able to plan, implement and evaluate the various ethnic and linguistic development plans' (Centre for Research and Advanced Studies in Social Anthropology (CIESAS), 1983). The programme arose out of lengthy educational experience in indigenous communities, through the observation that none of the established professional careers met the requirements of putting into practice indigenous education and programmes to revive ethnic and cultural identity. The programme was held in Pátzcuaro, Michoacán, over eight academic semesters, to train ethnolinguists from the various Mexican ethnic groups, and served a total of sixty-seven students from seventeen indigenous peoples. This first course was followed by a further session starting in 1983. At the end of these two courses, the programme was regrettably discontinued, although, as we shall see below, the institutions which sponsored it, CIESAS and the Indigenous National Institute (INI) used it as the basis for creating a Master's programme in Indoamerican linguistics in 1990.

The Mexican programme, in contrast with that of UNMSM, was principally aimed at indigenous young people who had already trained as teachers and therefore had some direct experience of indigenous education, either as pupils or as teachers; it was also of a more practical nature, having been designed for the purposes of bilingual or cultural revival programmes. The programme aimed at training individuals in 'theoretical knowledge and practical skills for the study of the problems associated with ethnic and linguistic development and for the design and implementation of action plans as the basis for continuing ideological and theoretical reflection leading to a change in attitude, a process of intellectual and . . . emotional decolonization' (CIESAS, 1983).

In recent years, the attention given to this type of programme has grown, although many appear to suffer the same fate as bilingual education and intercultural bilingual education programmes and are not always sure of continuation. Such programmes can be grouped into:

- those training teachers to use bilingual methods;
- those providing training in linguistics applied to intercultural bilingual education;
- those placing greater emphasis on more theoretical, academic training in a linguistic discipline with reference to one or more indigenous languages.[10]

Teacher training programmes: Examples of this type of programme are the Mexican scheme for an indigenous secondary school leaving certificate (*bachillerato*), the programme of the Shuar Bicultural Bilingual Institute (INBISH) in Ecuador, and the programmes run by three Higher Institutes of Education in Peru: in Pucallpa, Iquitos and Puno.

An essential feature of all these programmes, with the exception of that of Iquitos, Peru, is that they are the result of negotiations with the official system which authorized them only to *adapt* the national teacher training curricula. Thus, for example, INBISH is authorized to include only thirty per cent of specific cultural content, that devoted to the study of Shuar language and culture. The same happened in the case of the Higher Institutes of Education in Puno and Pucallpa, tertiary institutions which began their activities in the field in 1985 by creating a special department to train teachers in bilingual education over ten academic semesters.

The Mexican scheme for an indigenous *bachillerato* is of equally recent date and has similar characteristics. A draft curriculum was worked out in 1987 for an indigenous teaching *bachillerato* lasting six academic semesters, with the aim of modifying the curricula of certain teacher training colleges and raising the quality of indigenous education. The syllabus is based on a common core (similar to the other *bachilleratos*, which exist in the country) providing bilingual, bicultural educational training.

Something similar occurred with the Shuar people's INBISH, in which teachers are trained over eight semesters, four of which form part of secondary-level studies, to meet the needs of the bilingual education by radio directed by the Shuar people.

The experiences to which we have referred are all recent and are attempts to find possible solutions to the training of intercultural bilingual education teachers. Despite the various schemes' limitations and their continuing concessions to the official teacher training programmes, we consider that they can provide a basis for more far-reaching changes to the systems of teacher training.

Something of this nature appears to have happened in Peru when a programme to train native intercultural bilingual education teachers was approved in 1988 at the Loreto Higher Institute of Education in Iquitos, using an *ad hoc* curriculum. This was the first attempt in that country, and perhaps in the region, to devise a truly differentiated training for the preparation of indigenous teachers.

The new programme comprises six years of training, divided into a number of college-based and non-college-based stages. In the first of these, lasting three months each, students from different indigenous peoples work in seven areas of training (anthropology, history, linguistics, ecology, mathematics, art, physical education and education); and in the non-college-based stages, lasting from six to eight months, they return to their communities of origin accompanied by one of their tutors, to carry out specific research tasks which feed into the college training received or prepare the ground and provide material for the next college-based stage. Although the arrangement of such a scheme is not devoid of problems and conflicts arise within the group of professionals directing it, the intention is worthy of praise for the importance which it gives to anthropological and linguistic content.[11]

This was the first time that the Peruvian State authorized a curriculum plan and a regime of study significantly different from the 'official'; this may be due to the fact that an indigenous organization is taking part in the management of a programme of this type, perhaps for the first time: the Interethnic Association of the Peruvian Selva (AIDESEP). Innovative programmes such as this, with considerable human and financial resources, should also translate into the production of materials for teacher training and cultural and linguistic reflection, supplementing other experiences under way and encouraging wider discussion of the training of indigenous teachers required by intercultural bilingual education.

One outcome of trials lasting a number of years in this field is the 'Curriculum model for teacher training and professionalization in bilingual intercultural education', approved and published by the Peruvian Ministry of Education at the end of 1993. The document is the product of three collective drafting workshops in which indigenous leaders, teacher training experts and specialists in the relevant disciplines took part. The scheme reduces face-to-face training time from ten to six academic semesters, devoting the last four to practical teaching combined with research, preparation of a dissertation and the development of a number of courses during the holidays. The scheme 'permits diversification of curricula in response to the needs of each Higher Institute of Education or University in accordance with the populations served, by being a general, open-ended and non-fragmented programme' (Peruvian Ministry of Education, 1993).[12]

Among the objectives of this scheme are 'combining the indigenous forms of knowledge transmission with the support of the various pedagogical themes that enable the teacher to devise and manage a methodology and techniques appropriate to the educational reality in which he or she will work', 'promoting the participation of the community in the educational process', and 'integrating the world view of the cultures on the relationship between man and nature into the curriculum' (ibid). The model, which was supposed to be implemented in ten higher institutes of education in the Andean and Amazonian regions of Peru, includes:

– Curricula organization in areas (ecosystem, society and culture, language, mathematics, education, religious education) and functions (research, community work, and teaching and learning) which future teachers will have to handle.
– Presentation of the way in which research, community work and professional practice are interrelated during the ten semesters of training.
– Range, objectives and content and the way in which these are integrated.
– The methodological recommendations for their implementation.

It appears, however, that the scheme did not succeed in all these fields, for want of the necessary human resources.

In Bolivia, in the context of education reform, the possibility of changing the strategy and models of teacher training is being created under Law No. 1565 of 7 July 1994, which provides for the institutional and curricular transformation of teacher training colleges. Besides giving importance to intercultural bilingual education, the reform allows the organization of teacher training centres explicitly devoted to the training of indigenous and Spanish-speaking teachers for bilingual education. At the present time, in fact, teachers are not being trained for intercultural bilingual education in any teacher training college. The only thing which has been included in syllabuses in recent years is one intercultural bilingual education subject, which means in practice nothing more than a good intention arising from greater awareness of its diversity in the country. Not surprisingly, given the lack of a specific programme of study, of the relevant educational materials and trained teachers to implement it, this subject has been taught in a different way and to a varying standard in each of the teacher training colleges in which it has been introduced. In many colleges, this has even led to the absurd situation of regarding the learning of an indigenous language, or of reading and writing in Quechua or Aymara using literacy materials developed for teaching illiterate adults, as the content of that subject.

Programmes of linguistics applied to intercultural bilingual education: One of the problems facing programmes such as those sketched out in the previous section relates to the lack of human resources available to manage or apply them. Such requirements refer specifically to professionals with a sufficient theoretical grounding in linguistics, anthropology and education and an interest in the practical problems arising from the application of intercultural bilingual education. There are few specialists in applied linguistics in the region, and in order to be trained they have generally had to study in foreign universities, particularly in North America or Europe.

Because of such considerations, the National University of the Altiplano in Peru (UNA-P) and the Experimental Bilingual Education Project in Puno (PEEB-P) organized a postgraduate programme in Andean linguistics and education. The Puno programme started in 1985, providing training at two levels: as a first degree specialization, for qualified teachers; and at Master's level for professionals of various social disciplines, including linguistics and education, who were all Quechua or Aymara-speaking. The Puno programme provides its students with an interdisciplinary training drawn from several branches of linguistics, anthropology and education, although the greatest emphasis is on the application of linguistic knowledge and findings to the resolution of the educational problems of the vernacular-speaking population.

An internal evaluation report of UNA-P states that 'It is commonly agreed . . . that this postgraduate programme has amply met what was expected of it and that it should continue to provide its services for the sake of revalidating, encouraging and studying Andean languages. Graduates have become key players in the conduct of bilingual education programmes, not only in Puno but also in neighbouring regions. Thus, for example, through membership of the APLYCA (Association of Professionals in Andean Language and Culture), graduates of the programme organized and conducted training courses for rural teachers in summer 1991, both in Puno and in Cuzco, in association with the relevant official branches of the Ministry of Education' (UNA-P, 1993). Ten former students of the programme are presently working as university teachers in various faculties of the same university, five are responsible for courses in Quechuan or Aymaran language and intercultural bilingual education at the Higher Institute of Education in Puno, and two likewise at the Higher Institute of Education in Huancavelica; two are teaching subjects related to intercultural bilingual education at the San Agustín National University in Arequipa, three are involved in intercultural bilingual education in other departments in the country, and thirty-five are supporting the efforts of the Bolivian education system to promote the development of intercultural bilingual education.

Six years later, also arising out of a bilingual education project, the Intercultural Bilingual Education Project of Ecuador (PEBI) led to the creation of a special first degree in intercultural bilingual education at the University of Cuenca. This course, initially lasting one year and now one and a half years, was established to serve indigenous young professionals who had finished studying for a degree but had not completed their dissertation.

At present, the Puno and Cuenca programmes are the only ones in the region offering a specialization in linguistics applied to intercultural bilingual education. Their attraction lies in the combination of theory and practice, and naturally in the growing demand for this type of professional. Between 1985 and 1993, three groups graduated from Puno with a Master's degree, and four with a minor specialization, totalling eighty-seven professionals, among whom thirty are Bolivian teachers and eighteen Master's students. Twenty-eight minor specialization students are currently pursuing courses there, among whom twenty-three are Bolivian.[13] Between 1991 and 1994, some forty-five persons graduated with a first degree from Cuenca in two groups, and the third intake began work at the beginning of the second semester of 1994. The University of Cuenca, like that of Puno, has also contributed to the development of Bolivian intercultural bilingual education in that it trained two Quechua-speaking Bolivian graduates in its second group.

To a certain extent, this is also the direction taken by the Native Languages degree specialization (Quechua and Aymara) offered by the Greater University of San Andrés in La Paz (UMSA), although it has not achieved all the success hoped for, partly because of the extremely limited number of graduates (three) which it has trained during the thirteen years in which it has been operating. The programme is also marred by the shortage of specialist professionals which the University has to teach the course, and by the composition of its current syllabus.

The UMSA specialization was designed using North American modern languages programmes (from departments of modern languages) which provide a general education, and emphasize the learning of one language in particular in combination with translation, literature, linguistic description, sociolinguistics and languages teaching. During the ten semesters of the course, students do not really succeed in specializing in any of the disciplines mentioned. What is missing in Bolivia, in our view, is a programme of indigenous linguistics applied to intercultural bilingual education and to the teaching of indigenous languages, whether as mother tongues or as second languages.

Similar efforts have been made in other universities in the country. At the University of San Francisco Xavier in Chuquisaca, teachers of Quechua are trained in ten semesters, in a Quechua-English specialization, and at the Twentieth Century University in Potosí, the La Paz course has been replicated with the help of UMSA.

It is encouraging that a new project is being launched by the Education Department at UMSA to train first degree graduates in intercultural bilingual education, on the basis of a syllabus specifically designed to prepare trainers of teachers serving Quechua and Aymara-speaking pupils. The new project, designed initially as a special degree offering five or six semesters of complementary studies to qualified staff of teacher training colleges who have wide teaching experience, will also contribute indirectly to the substantial modification of teacher training programmes for primary schools. The proposed syllabus links teacher training with research and gives particular attention to applied aspects relating especially to curriculum design for intercultural bilingual education and to mother tongue and second language teaching.

Programmes such as those of Puno and Cuenca, and soon that of La Paz, contribute to the development of intercultural bilingual education in their own region through the training of a vernacular-speaking intelligentsia capable of giving a lead to the evolution and adaptation of intercultural bilingual education in contexts beyond that of the initial experiment. Moreover, the practical orientation of such training appears to coincide with the regional need for specialists able to design and plan intercultural bilingual education programmes. Its graduates are currently fulfilling needs such as this at various levels, both in the State and the private sector, in the field of rural education, and specifically of Andean bilingual education.

On the basis of such achievements, we regard it as unfortunate that the Mexican programme of ethnolinguistics was suspended, and we note with satisfaction the launch of new initiatives such as: that of the National University of Amazonia in Peru, which has organized a degree programme in intercultural bilingual education; the first degree in bilingual intercultural education for young Aymara-speakers in northern Chile launched by the 'Arturo Pratt' University of Iquique; and the courses provided by the Catholic University of Chile in Temuco, in education in Mapuche and Spanish.

At the postgraduate level, there is the possibility of an Andean subregional programme involving professionals and higher education centres in five countries: Colombia, Ecuador, Peru, Bolivia and Chile. This new programme, which will receive technical and financial support from the German Government, will link the universities in these countries which have shown interest in the question of education for their indigenous population in a network, and will comprise three lines of action: research, training and documentation, both the copying of materials and the publication of the outcomes of research and proposals of relevance to intercultural bilingual education. The emphasis of the new programme will be on the development of an intercultural and bilingual teaching system, and on the training of professionals who will subsequently be able to strengthen the action of their universities to promote the development of intercultural bilingual education projects and programmes.

The training of professionals in indigenous linguistics: Unusual interest has recently been shown in various countries in the region in developing professional studies and programmes in linguistics relating to the description of indigenous languages and to the application of linguistics to intercultural bilingual education activities. This is happening in Mexico, Guatemala, Colombia, Peru and Brazil.

In Guatemala, there are postgraduate programmes in sociolinguistics (University of El Valle) and intercultural bilingual education administration (Rafael Landivar University). These programmes offer Master's degrees and professional qualifications respectively, and they are open to professionals, indigenous and others, with a first degree in education or social science. The Rafael Landivar University also offers a programme in ethnolinguistics for indigenous professionals so that they can describe and analyse their own languages.

Of the various Master's programmes in linguistics being run in Colombia, two are most closely related to intercultural bilingual education: those of the University of the Andes and the National University. Both are supported by the increased awareness of the indigenous communities of their languages and cultures, which leads to requests for assessment when writing systems are being established, to the collection of ancestral traditions and knowledge, and to the design of alternative education systems.

The programme of the National University is presently faced with a difficult situation because of a lack of students, perhaps due to a failure to determine exactly the needs in this area and the interests of the students served. Twenty students have graduated from the programme.

That of the University of the Andes, possibly because of the academic and financial support continuously received from the CNRS and the French Government since 1985, is now catering to a third group of students, following a break of two years when its project staff returned to Paris.[14] These Master's courses in ethnolinguistics are attended by indigenous and non-indigenous Colombian professionals interested in describing Amerindian languages.

The Master's programme in ethnolinguistics has succeeded in training thirty-one researchers, of whom eight are indigenous. The first graduates are preparing their doctoral theses in Paris.

The work of this programme has been strengthened by the creation of a studies and documentation centre which brings together the graduates and teachers of the course and promotes research and practical activities, including publication of students' dissertations and of records and outcomes of the activities promoted. Some of the activities of the centre are conducted under contract for the Ethnic Education Division of the Colombian Ministry of National Education.

The programmes of both the University of the Andes and the National University were designed as academic programmes for training Colombian linguists to meet the country's current needs in the area of description of indigenous languages, to fill gaps in such material and to supplement the partial work of uneven quality undertaken in that field by the Summer Institute of Linguistics.

The emphasis of a programme such as that of the University of the Andes is therefore placed on a solid grounding in ethnolinguistics, combining periods of desk work with time devoted to research in areas where the language in which the student is specializing is spoken. It is interesting that despite the rather academic nature of the programme, its relationship with indigenous organizations and their demands has led it to seek links with intercultural bilingual education and 'ethnoeducation', as the method of serving the indigenous population in Colombia is known. The programme thus includes a seminar in its last semester on a number of worries that students might have on questions relating to languages in education.

With the aim of filling current gaps between the description of languages and the provision of intercultural bilingual education, the Colombian Ministry of National Education and the National University have for two years been negotiating the establishment of a postgraduate course in ethnic education for students with experience of intercultural bilingual education. It is hoped that this new programme will start in 1995, training the co-ordinators and area organizers of the Ministry's ethnic education programme.

Consideration is also being given in Colombia to the possibility of arranging undergraduate training programmes for ethnolinguists. That of the University of Amazonia is the furthest advanced in its planning, and it is likely that it will very soon offer specialization in ethnolinguistics combined with primary education for indigenous young Amazonians.

In Peru, out of six universities providing undergraduate courses in any branch of linguistics, only two are considering specializations or courses directly related to the issue: the Greater National University of San Marcos (UNMSM), which trains students in Andean, Amazonian and Hispanic linguistics; and the Pontifical Catholic University of Peru (PUCP), which includes courses in Andean and Amazonian linguistics in its linguistics syllabus. UNMSM also offers Master's level courses in linguistics relating to indigenous languages. There are, additionally, courses in descriptive linguistics, ethnolinguistics and sociolinguistics as part of the postgraduate provision in Andean linguistics and education at the National University of the Altiplano in Puno, to which we referred in the previous section. Also within this general area are the summer courses which have been offered for two years by the University of Lima, with the support of the Summer Institute of Linguistics – an institution which belatedly remembered the obligation into which it entered with the Peruvian Government in 1946 to train linguists specializing in the description of Amazonian languages who could take the place of its own specialists based in the region.

In Brazil and Mexico interesting developments can also be observed, among them the Master's and doctoral programmes in descriptive linguistics offered by the University of Campinas (São Paulo) and the Master's programme in Indoamerican linguistics of CIESAS (the Centre for Higher Research and Studies in Social Anthropology). The latter has been operating since the end of 1990 in collaboration with the Indigenous National Institute (INI), largely serving indigenous or vernacular-speaking professionals and already with its second intake.

The CIESAS programme is based on the experience of the two first-degree courses in ethnolinguistics developed in 1979 and 1983, and arises out of the observation that 'in other institutions there have been higher education programmes, both at first degree and at Master's level, aimed at indigenous sectors, but none of them has been particularly concerned with indigenous languages. Moreover, although postgraduate programmes in linguistics are offered in the country, none of these brings together the two basic features of the programme . . . that is, a central interest in Indoamerican linguistics and a commitment to the training of indigenous professionals' (CIESAS/INI, n.d., p. 2-3).

As will be appreciated, national-language linguists, who are in many cases indigenous, are being trained throughout the region to take up the descriptive and planning tasks carried out for many years exclusively by foreign professionals and not infrequently by missionaries who combined evangelism with work in linguistics. The instability of the programmes, caused by their dependence in many cases on foreign personnel and capital, is a cause for concern. Unless the home States and national institutions, such as university councils and councils of science and technology, play their part, we shall be unable to meet the challenge now posed by our own indigenous populations: the stable and continuing functioning of an intercultural bilingual education system.

NEEDS VS. PROVISION IN HUMAN RESOURCES TRAINING
FOR INTERCULTURAL BILINGUAL EDUCATION

As has been seen, while there is a growth in current opportunities to pursue studies related to intercultural bilingual education, these remain insufficient to meet the demand for such programmes and the needs of that methodology. There are still only a few centres of professional training which have begun to consider the indigenous issue, and especially about questions directly linked to intercultural bilingual education. Institutions such as CIESAS and the National Pedagogical University in Mexico are exceptions, as are some sections of the Rafael Landivar University and the University of El Valle in Guatemala. In Colombia, the University of the Andes stands out, and to a lesser degree the National University; in Ecuador, the University of Cuenca is on its own, and in Chile it is only the 'Arturo Pratt' University of Iquique and the Catholic University in Temuco. In Peru, the Greater National University of San Marcos and the National University of the Altiplano stand out. It is interesting that, with the exception of Colombia, this list contains countries with a significant indigenous population.

Table 1 enables us to identify the types of programme which currently exist. If we compare existing provisions with the needs which we established in the first part of this paper, we see that at a global level there are

Table 1: Types of provision of human resources training for intercultural bilingual education

Orientation	Agent	Method	Country
Training in use of intercultural bilingual education materials and methodology	Ministries of Education	Face-to-face NGOs	All those having intercultural bilingual education projects or intercultural bilingual education programmes
Certification of serving teachers	Ministries of Education through teacher training centres	Partly face-to-face Distance education	With specifically intercultural bilingual education orientation: Mexico, Guatemala, Colombia, Ecuador, Peru
Training of intercultural bilingual education teachers	Universities Institutes of Education or Teacher Training Colls	Face-to-face	Mexico, Guatemala, Colombia, Ecuador, Peru, Chile
Training of trainers	Universities	Face-to-face	Ecuador, Peru, Bolivia (in preparation)
Training of 'specialist' researchers in: · descriptive linguistics/ ethnolinguistics	Universities	Face-to-face	Mexico, Guatemala, Colombia, Peru
· sociolinguistics			Guatemala
· linguistics appl. to intercultural bilingual education			Ecuador, Peru
· school administration			Guatemala

still significant gaps. Such lacunae are most noticeable in a number of major academic fields which could contribute to a better understanding of bilingualism and intercultural bilingual education, such as psycholinguistics, sociolinguistics and applied linguistics. With regard to the first of these, it has been observed that no university in the region offers courses in this area as a specialization and that the discipline is more or less absent from the syllabuses of the few specialization programmes which currently exist. Only one university in the entire region offers a specialization in sociolinguistics related to the indigenous issue, and two in linguistics applied to intercultural bilingual education.

It may be that one of the areas which needs greater attention and receives little concern is the training of trainers. As has been pointed out, there is still a lack of that intermediate level of professionals able to organize, plan and direct bilingual education activities, and to take on tasks of far-reaching importance for the future of the method such as the training of teachers. This lack may also account for the fact that there are still insufficient programmes devoted to the preparation of the next generations of teachers required by intercultural bilingual education.

While this is the overall situation, there are further worries at the level of each country involved in intercultural bilingual education activities. In no country in the region is there provision for all the specializations needed to ensure the effective launching of intercultural bilingual education and to help in meeting the basic learning needs of indigenous learners.

LESSONS FOR BOLIVIA

Now that Bolivia is entering a process of integrated education reform, which gives a prominence to intercultural bilingual education never before accorded to it in the country, thought has to be given to the implications of such political decisions for the area of human resources development. On the one hand, we have to ask whether the country already has enough professionals, beginning with the teachers, of sufficient quality to meet the challenges posed by the new legislation. On the other hand, we have to consider the professional programmes provided in the country and the requirements of ensuring that new educational policy decisions can be put into practice in the classroom and do not merely remain good intentions.

With regard to the first question, it should be remembered that while the country has a high percentage of primary and secondary teachers, both urban and rural, who speak an indigenous language,[15] few teachers have received any type of training in using a teaching method that employs the indigenous language as the oral or written medium of education, in order to serve children who speak an indigenous language and are to varying degrees monolingual or bilingual. Although it may be stating the obvious, it should be reiterated that it is not sufficient that teachers should speak Quechua, Aymara, Guaraní or any other indigenous language. A fluent speaker of any of these languages does not automatically become a teacher of that language. For this to happen, it is necessary not only to study and find out how the language works, but also to learn how to teach it. If we add to this that the teacher also has to help the students to learn Spanish as a second language, we shall realize that the challenge facing Bolivian teachers is far from easy.

It is estimated that at the present time only some 400 teachers are implementing bilingual programmes of education in primary school and using Aymara, Guaraní or Quechua to carry out the programmes devised as part of the two intercultural bilingual education projects developed in the Andean region of the country. If we add the approximately 200 teachers working in indigenous communities in the eastern province of Oriente or in Amazonia, then we have a body of no more than 600 teachers with a knowledge of this methodology who could begin to fulfil what is laid down in the new law; and they represent less than one per cent of the total number of serving teachers. It is true that not all of the 90,000 teachers in the country will have to teach bilingual education programmes, but in a country where over sixty per cent of the population speak a vernacular language, at least fifty per cent of teachers, if not more, should be able to serve the vernacular-speaking children living in rural and marginal urban areas of the country and needing relevant and equitable educational provision. Hence, one of the tasks to be undertaken as soon as possible is that of teacher training, meaning both preservice training and training for those already working as teachers. For some, the syllabus should cover the effective use of the alphabet and orthographical rules of the indigenous language, so that they are able to improve the way in which their bilingualism evolves and can really become involved in a methodology which requires the use of the written, rather than merely the spoken form, of the language predominantly used by their pupils, viz. the indigenous. By making use of this tool – writing – teachers could also begin to think about the indigenous language and the mechanisms which govern its functioning and use.

Besides this new principle of teacher training, another should be to encourage teachers to unlearn, indeed to reject what they were taught during their professional and social education which, unfortunately, will only have filled them with a negative attitude towards indigenous pupils and those pupils' individual abilities, and towards the possibility of survival of the peoples to which the pupils belong. Just as from a linguistic point of view teachers have to be encouraged to begin a process of rediscovering the richness and potential of the language which may have been their mother tongue or which they learnt from older family members, in the area of culture this process is no less important and is another precondition for the 'professional' training of teachers. It is therefore imperative to bring teachers to question all the 'truths' they possess about the Andes and indigenous affairs in general, so that they can learn to value the skills, knowledge, attitudes and beliefs of peoples who have always been thought backward and were therefore to be assimilated into the Western, Christian mainstream.

In order to accomplish this wide array of tasks and to provide guidance to policy-making, further support will have to be given to developing a number of studies to ascertain the training needs of teachers in the skills and theory of intercultural bilingual education. These studies will have to involve not only the existing staff of teacher training colleges but also the teachers conducting intercultural bilingual education programmes, including young people studying at teacher training centres. An example of such research is that just completed, with the support of UNESCO, in six of the country's teacher training colleges with a view to determining attitudes to questions relating to interculturalism, bilingualism and intercultural, bilingual education.[16]

As will be appreciated, the teacher training demands placed on the country are on such a scale that they need to be addressed by a range of actors: teacher training colleges, universities, NGOs, etc. And it should be noted that we are referring to the teachers needed in intercultural bilingual education to serve only the vernacular-speaking learners. If we consider that intercultural bilingual education should also reach Spanish-speaking pupils, the requirements will be greater as it will also be necessary to prepare teachers and materials for the teaching of indigenous languages as second languages.

This is a goal shared by all those who believe that the only way to really change the relationship between the indigenous and the non-indigenous is by encouraging *two-way* bilingualism. However, if we pause to reflect on our technical limitations and the little that has been done to ensure the effective and adequate learning of indigenous languages by the Spanish-speaking population, even though the majority of the population speak vernacular languages, we shall see how far away we still are from turning this social goal into practical action.

Fortunately, the high proportion of the population speaking indigenous languages in the country, and a change of attitude among the Spanish-speaking population brought about by far-reaching changes in plans and syllabuses, which are today imbued with a spirit of interculturalism as a result of the law, will help in this difficult task of awakening among Spanish-speaking pupils curiosity and interest in indigenous peoples, their languages and cultures. The media, which have such influence in the country, have an enormous role to play in strengthening this unaccustomed and incipient re-encounter of the country with itself. In the field of languages, they will have to stimulate the learning of indigenous languages by organizing radio and television programmes, initially in Aymara, Guaraní and Quechua as second languages. This leads on to the training of good radio presenters and speakers as second language teachers, using educational television broadcasts of the highest possible technical quality, guides and models in order to study the experience of similar programmes which have been successful in teaching foreign languages such as English, French and Portuguese.

However, besides all that has been suggested, we should not lose sight of the requirements and challenges which the new national socio-educational context poses to the country's university system and research centres. University-level professional programmes urgently need to be organized, together with serious planning for linguistic, sociocultural and educational research, in order to provide the country with answers to the many questions today associated with intercultural bilingual education. Bolivia needs whole armies of professionals able to make fresh input into teacher training, and this requires that a number of the country's universities become involved in the training of human resources for intercultural bilingual education.

One of the priorities will be the training of trainers, and to this end it may be possible to adopt the Mexican model by organizing courses offering degree qualifications to the staff of existing teacher training colleges. Equivalency systems could also be established to give at least partial recognition to studies at such colleges and accumulated teaching experience. In the curricula domain, use should be made of what has been learnt through the development of the postgraduate programme in Puno, Peru, as intercultural bilingual education needs professionals trained in ethnolinguistics, anthropology and education to take on tasks such as teacher training, curriculum design, the preparation of educational materials, etc.[17]

But it would be a mistake to begin from scratch. It is imperative to examine what has been achieved, and to evaluate the country's few programmes on linguistics and native Andean languages in the light of the needs of the national education system, and to reorientate them, if necessary, in order to ensure that in the medium term there will be at least some groups of professionals with a good training in research and teaching who can in turn become involved in the teacher training plans for intercultural bilingual education which teacher training colleges will have to adopt in the institutional and curricula transformation imposed on them by the law. While this will be needed in places where there are at least some academic university programmes, such as the Andes, the requirements will be that much greater in the provinces of Oriente, Amazonia and Chaco.

One factor that might help in creating new programmes of professional training for intercultural bilingual education and in improving existing provision, may well be links and exchanges of experience with other higher education centres in the region which are successfully carrying out the training of human resources. It may also be necessary to institute a programme of bursaries for the training of Bolivian university teachers to specialize in work at first or Master's degree level.

One of the aims of this paper has been to provide information on the solutions found in other countries in the region that are also engaged in intercultural bilingual education, although on a smaller scale, so that those with the responsibility for planning, managing and implementing professional programmes for intercultural bilingual education can compare the Bolivian situation with what happens in other countries and can draw specific lessons for the Bolivian case.

Professional programmes such as those referred to throughout this paper are of key importance in launching intercultural bilingual education definitively and removing it from the limited experimental phase in which we have placed it. It is true that we still have much to learn about intercultural bilingual education and do not have all the professional programmes required: nonetheless, enough is known in Latin America to take a firm and decisive step forward in designing it so that we can go on learning from practice and from life: activities which necessarily go hand in hand with the training of new professionals who will take up this challenge.

It is impossible to imagine expanded intercultural bilingual education coverage in Bolivia or any other country in the region unless time, effort and money are invested in the training of human resources alongside the development of what happens in the classroom. As has been repeatedly pointed out, educational provision in indigenous areas is among the poorest there is in the region's education systems. Although this impoverishment is due to innumerable factors, among which the failure of those systems to respond to their own linguistic and cultural diversity stands out, it is also related to our inability to improve qualitatively the situation of teachers working with indigenous learners. In fact, the situation of the personnel engaged in intercultural bilingual education is the most critical element of this impoverishment (Tedesco, 1990) and endangers the sustainability of intercultural bilingual education on the continent.

NOTES

1. This paper is based partly on an earlier paper published in 1990 in Paris, in *Prospects*, the quarterly education journal of UNESCO. On this occasion I have updated the information and added three new sections, the first and the last two.
2. I use the term *indigenous* in the sense in which it is used by the continent's ethnic organizations; that is, to designate the peoples descended from those who had arrived in America and were living there before the arrival of the Spanish. As is pointed out by the highest officer of the Confederation of Indigenous Nationalities of Ecuador, Don Luis Macas: 'While we suffered oppression under the term indigenous, with the same term we shall liberate ourselves'. By extension, I therefore speak of indigenous language, indigenous culture, indigenous education, etc., but I avoid using the expression *original*, which is frequently employed in Bolivia.
3. What is understood by intercultural bilingual education today is an educational approach that confirms the ethnic, social, cultural and linguistic identity of the learners with the intention of encouraging a reflective and critical dialogue between elements of their culture and others from different cultural spheres, so that learners may decide, where appropriate, to adopt and incorporate into their culture alien elements that are nonetheless necessary to improve the current living conditions of the people to which they belong.
4. In this paper, I use the term *vernacular* as a synonym for indigenous language. By vernacular, according to the international convention approved by UNESCO, I refer to a language spoken by a people oppressed by another people, whose language has the status of official language. By extension, then, I also use the term *vernacular speakers*. By *normalization*, on the other hand, I refer to the sociopolitical intention of changing the social status of the vernacular languages in order to make them as 'normal' as any other. In this sense, the term is associated with processes such as standardization and the development and cultivation of the written form of these languages, although it also involves an enlargement of the social domains of use, going beyond personal and family relationships and the community of origin and entering areas and contexts of greater formality and abstraction.
5. In principle, the use of this term is to be eschewed. It is used in inverted commas because the speakers of native languages are still often thought of as individuals who 'only' contribute information to the development of research or the preparation of educational materials. But, even if this were their only contribution, it should be realized that without them the work of the professionals could not be accomplished. Fortunately, an increasing number of researchers therefore regard the ill-named 'informants' as collaborators. Moreover, it should be noted that readings and interpretations of reality arise from the exchange of skills and knowledge and the communication associated with the frequency of interaction between researchers and collaborators. Such an exchange leads to learning which enriches the views of both sides.
6. Accounts of such situations sometimes reach the press: 'In some places in the Altiplano, girls and young women are forced to undo their plaits and not to wear the *pollera* (full skirt)'. See the 'Ocurrencias' supplement of the *Presencia* newspaper, p. 8, La Paz, 28 August 1994.
7. We prefer to term training programmes for serving teachers who lack professional qualifications *certification* rather than *professionalization* programmes as we consider it necessary to recover the notion of professionalization for plans of a different type and broader range which aim to raise the professional level of every teacher, whether or not formally qualified. We reach this view from the consideration that all teachers need to put aside their status of technicians to which centralizing and homogenizing systems have

reduced them, so that they gradually assume greater autonomy in their work and are able to decide – as would any other professional – how to handle in the most appropriate and satisfactory manner every situation and case which they have to address. Plans and programmes which aim to raise teachers' level of self-esteem and to create greater managerial autonomy could be termed professionalization.

8. Personal communication from Mary Martínez, SEIC specialist.
9. In Mexico, out of 39,360 teachers serving in indigenous areas, only 608 have primary education, 8,029 secondary education, 6,331 the *bachillerato* secondary leaving certificate, 12,731 have studied at a basic teacher training college and 2,561 are graduates of a higher college of education.
10. For lack of space we do not refer here to some of the most significant programmes in anthropology, which have also made a notable contribution in staff and ideas to the development of intercultural bilingual education programmes in the region.
11. The programme receives financial support from several non-governmental organizations and from European cooperation agencies, as well as from the Centre National de Recherche Scientifique (CNRS) of the French Government.
12. An additional characteristic of this scheme which is in line with what we have been discussing relates to the links established between the training programmes and those for the professionalization of teachers.
13. Of the eighty-seven graduates of the National University of the Altiplano in Puno, eight gained degrees of Master of Science in Andean Linguistics and Education, four gained professional certificates in minor specializations, and some thirty have current research projects.
14. The programme has a team of linguists exclusively attached to the project by CNRS.
15. It is estimated that in Bolivia over fifty per cent of teachers are bilingual in Spanish and an indigenous language.
16. We refer to a study being conducted in eight countries throughout the world, of which two are in Latin America: Mexico and Bolivia. In Bolivia the study covers six teacher training colleges, three rural and three urban, and it has been carried out using surveys, the organization of focus groups, and observation of classes. In that country, the study is being conducted by Luis Enrique López, Luis Antonio Rodríguez and Oscar Chavez, with the collaboration of Enrique Herrera (see chapter IV).
17. We welcome the joint initiative of the Education Department of the Greater University of San Andrés in La Paz and the Teacher Training Colleges of Huata and Warisata in arranging a two-year educational extension course permitting teachers to acquire a specialization in intercultural bilingual education leading to a university degree.

REFERENCES

Amadio, M. 1989. Progresos en la educación bilinge en situación de escacez de recursos. Experiencias y perspectivas de Nicaragua [Progress in bilingual education in a situation of scarce resources. Experiences and perspectives from Nicaragua]. *Boletín del proyecto principal* (OREALC, Santiago), no. 20, p. 71–84.
CIESAS (Centro de Investigaciones y Estudios Superiores en Antropología) (Mexico). 1983. *Plan de estudios del programa de formación profesional de etnolingistas* [Syllabus of the programme of professional training for ethnolinguists]. Mexico City. Mimeo.
Colombia. Ministry of National Education. 1988. *Seminario para la elaboración de material educativo para la etnia sikuani y una propuesta de programa de profesionalización para maestros bilinges sikuani* [Seminar to design educational material for the Sikuani people

Teacher training and multiculturalism

and a proposal for a professionalization programme for Sikuani bilingual teachers]. Bogotá. Mimeo.
Directorate General of Indigenous Education (Mexico). 1987. Mexican Secretariat of Public Education. *Propuesta Curricular del Bachillerato Pedagógico Indígena y sus Modelos de Operación* [Draft curriculum of the indigenous teaching *bachillerato* and the ways of implementing it]. Mexico City.
Directorate General of Indigenous Education (Mexico). 1990. Mexican secretariat of Public Education. *Consideraciones para la licenciatura en pre-escolar y primaria de maestros en servicio en el subsistema de educación indígena* [Considerations for the first degree in pre-school and primary education for serving teachers in the indigenous education subsystem]. Mexico City. (Working document.)
Jung, I.; López L.E., eds. 1993. *La formación de especialistas en educación bilinge intercultural en América Latina (Subregión Andina)* [The training of specialists in intercultural bilingual education in Latin America (Andean subregion)]. Lima, GTZ. (Working document.)
Larson, M., et al. 1979. *Educación bilinge: una experiencia en la Amazonía peruana* [Bilingual education: an experiment in Peruvian Amazonia]. Lima, Ignacio Prado Pastor Publishers.
López, L.E. 1989. *El desarrollo de recursos humanos para la educación bilinge en los países andinos* [The development of human resources for bilingual education in the Andean countries]. Quito, CEDIME/Research Council of the University of Cuenca. (Working document.)
López, L.E. 1990. El desarrollo de los recursos humanos desde y para la educación bilinge intercultural en América Latina [Development of human resources in and for bilingual intellectual education in Latin America]. *Prospects* (UNESCO, Paris), vol. 20, no. 3, p. 349-58.
Montoya, V. 1983. La educación bilinge en proyectos integrados [Bilingual education in integrated projects]. *In.* Rodriguez, N.J.; Masferrer K., E.; Vargas Vega, R., eds. *Educacíon, etnias y descolonizacion en America Latina: una guia para la educacíon bilinge intelectural,* vol. 1, p. 57–82, Mexico, III; Santiago de Chile, OREALC.
National Pedagogical University of Mexico (Mexico). 1990. Secretariat of Public Education. *Proyecto: Licenciatura en educación prescolar y en educación primaria dirigida a docentes del medio indígena* [Project: First degree in preschool education and primary education for teachers from the indigenous environment]. Mexico City.
National University of the Altiplano (Peru). 1993. *Proyecto: Curso de postgrado en lingistica Andina y educación* [Project: Postgraduate course in Andean linguistics and education]. Puno, Peru. (Working document.)
Peru. Peruvian Ministry of Education. National Directorate of Educational Technology. Directorate of Educational Resources. 1993. *Modelo curricular para la formación y profesionalización docente en educación bilinge intercultural* [Curriculum model for teacher training and professionalization in intercultural bilingual education]. Lima.
Scanlon, A.; Lezama, J., eds. 1982. *Hacia un México pluricultural* [Towards a multicultural Mexico]. Mexico City, Joaquín Porrua & Co.
Tedesco, J.C. 1990. Introduction. *Prospects* (UNESCO, Paris), vol. 20, no. 3, p. 301–03. (Open file: Intercultural bilingual education in Latin America.)

56

CHAPTER IV

Interculturalism, technical education and teacher training in Bolivia

Luis Antonio Rodríguez Bazán and
Oscar Chávez Gonzáles

INTRODUCTION

In Bolivia, the teacher training institutions are called the 'escuelas normales'. They are either 'rural' or 'urban', and provide training for all future professional educators. There are twenty-seven teacher training colleges throughout the country: ten urban and seventeen rural.

All rural teacher training colleges are situated in the territories of indigenous peoples, such as the Quechua, Aymara, Guaraní and/or peoples of the eastern Amazon; nonetheless, no teacher training college trains teachers in intercultural bilingual education. All aim instead at homogenization and at assimilation to the dominant language and culture. Although in some colleges the concepts of bilingual education and familiarity with native languages have been introduced in the last few years, true teacher training in intercultural bilingual education is not yet a reality. The efforts that have been made, with a few honourable exceptions, have not even aroused interest among students.

Everyday life in a teacher training college is of interest both from the point of view of the general question of interculturalism in the country and, in this instance, of the issue of interculturalism in relation to technology.

In this paper we intend to explore the perceptions of future teachers with regard to interculturalism, teacher training, technology and technical education, and science. We shall analyse their opinions on issues such as the relationship between interculturalism, technology and science, and how training for intercultural bilingual education might take into account this relationship.

This will allow us to establish an effective method of diagnosis, which will then allow us to put forward suggestions for improving coherence in teacher training policies for true intercultural bilingual education; this in turn implies productive education.

We do not intend to carry out a full analysis, or to conclude with a specific proposal. We aim only to offer information to help us to visualize certain problems, and to provide various points of reference for the development of intercultural bilingual education programmes. We hope this will be a step towards the formulation and implementation of effective teacher training programmes.

PRESENT-DAY EDUCATION AS A POINT OF DEPARTURE

Much ink has been spilt in criticism of current teaching practices, sometimes obscuring and unnecessarily polarizing discussion rather than shedding light on real problems, so that the debate frequently becomes sterile. Our discussions with students and teachers have started with the identification of educational difficulties.

Starting points for our focus groups have included the quality of training received, and how and to what extent the system alienates them from their own cultural identity, so that the school becomes part of a web of domination.

'In Bolivia there is almost no complete education of the personality; so that some people come out hardly able to read . . . They cannot complete their education . . . can't achieve a, let us say, more or less rounded culture. That is why they even drop out and become ashamed of their origins.'

Education thus appears to be increasingly remote from reality, and does not enable the learner to face up to the demands of society.

'These textbooks don't have anything to do with our national reality . . . It's another culture.'

One frequently-repeated demand is for 'education for life'. This is mentioned not only by our interviewees but also by parents. One of the components of this educational option is technology.

CULTURE AND INTERCULTURALISM

Current conceptions of culture in Bolivia are closely linked to the everyday interculturalism typical of the population, i.e. of constant contact between individuals from societies as different as the indigenous and the creole-*mestizo* urban. Culture is here interpreted as the intercultural environment and its potential, although the idea of culture as a mark of social differentiation is still present, if much diminished, and in contrast to the reality and discourse of multiculturalism.

'Culture is the learning of each person, his or her degree of culture, so to say.'

'Culturally we are hardly at the level of other countries; our culture is still backward in science.'

These conceptions correspond to a colonial view that sees culture as a mark of social and essentially ethnic differentiation. Hence, 'cultured' is perceived as 'educated', without a precise definition of what this means, although it is evident from the last remark that it is associated with Western scientific and technological development. Whoever does not conform to this set of values is seen as comparatively uneducated.

In this context, education is one way of acquiring culture, as it is seen as forming the ideal 'educated man', which is simply a synonym for 'Western man'.

'Culture is everything that one learns, but *how* one learns varies from place to place; for example, if someone lives in the countryside, they will certainly have a culture, but it will be static . . . but a lot of people who live in cities, they get more culture as they learn, because in the city there is the chance to learn. There are institutes, media and the chance to raise the level of culture of a group.'

As is evident here, there is an order of hierarchy between the creole-*mestizo* and the indigenous, and between urban and rural environments. What is curious is that such conceptions contradict the notion of culture as the customs and traditions of indigenous peoples, although this interpretation is also present in what students and teachers say.

'We have a different culture, our ancestral culture, which was left to us by, let us say, the Inca empire; perhaps that culture is more valuable.'

'In another sense culture can be, well, a people's whole tradition, maybe their customs too.'

The contradiction apparent here is of significance because it can be present in single individuals as well as society as a whole. On the one hand, the different conceptions of culture are present in individuals who act in accordance with those conceptions; and on the other, within the same group of persons more than one conception can develop, which besides being contradictory may also have other dimensions. Statements such as 'in another sense culture can be' or 'but we have a different culture' lead us to think that in some way we possess various cultures and notions of cultures, which relate us to the multiculturalism that typifies the country but which manifests itself in cultural dualism or biculturalism. These are two different concepts, but the second is applicable to all oppressed cultures. We may also be led to think of the notion of movement, particularly taking into account the developmental dynamic of society, which is abandoning colonial, hierarchical ideas that were destructive of the 'other' culture.

The presence of limited conceptions of culture is very widespread.

'Culture is the tradition and customs of a people, of what has been preserved, of what is preserved nowadays.'

In these limited notions there is a tendency to fall into cultural romanticism, which can nonetheless become a route to the restoration and reaffirmation of one's own culture.

For the students of Cororo, the idea of interculturalism has two primary meanings: one as a synonym for bilingualism, and the other as a wider process of recovery. What is certain is that bilingualism, being a more concrete category and a more 'observable' and familiar practice, tends to dominate the intercultural content in education; that is, under a limited version of interculturalism we only take into account the incorporation of mother tongues and second languages in education.

'Intercultural means to me that the teacher can speak two languages, Spanish and Quechua; and then the teacher has to think about this when he teaches the pupils in both languages.'

Interculturalism as a process of recovery is generally based on the limited view of culture, and proposes the readoption of traditions and customs.

'Intercultural means cultures that we must not lose. In every region that we have . . . we should not lose our cultures, clothing, our traditions in our communities.'

What is important is the notion of ownership, since customs and traditions are generally referred to in such comments as 'ours'.

When a reference to interculturalism indicates a linking of different cultures, especially of the modern to the traditional world, the modern world represents progress, and the traditional backwardness, and interculturalism is a process in which the backward can acquire the advantages of the advanced.

'Intercultural is not losing our culture but also accepting progress . . . not staying still with our culture because if we stay as we are we shall go on being backward . . . because the world is evolving we have to go at the same speed.'

The non-hierarchical conceptions of culture make room for conceptions of interculturalism, although still with the notion of integration.

'Keeping our culture, not letting it disappear . . . but not standing still with our culture because our culture is also being rejected according to the values of the world . . . So we must also integrate with the other culture.'

A widening of the discussion, an examination of our practices and our future options will show us how we may, on the basis of our everyday individual and social practice, construct broader conceptions of culture and interculturalism.

TECHNICAL EDUCATION AND INTERCULTURALISM

Intercultural education, as an alternative to traditional education, can also be seen as a key cross-curricula dimension of education for life, since technology, science, and the general accumulation of technological and scientific knowledge are almost inevitable consequences. The field becomes more complex if this type of education is understood to include respect for differences and the strengthening of cultures, because this respect and strengthening will manifest itself in the possibility of cultures developing their own perceptions of reality in relation to scientific and technological knowledge.

Intercultural education programmes, because of their needs and their own dynamic, very quickly tend to put into effect, or to associate themselves with, productive projects. While efforts in the early stages may be concentrated on launching the programmes and influencing traditional teaching processes, changes in the science and technology of different people and cultures soon occur.

A first examination of indigenous science and technology warns us that these do not have a 'scientific' character at all and that, unlike the Science with a capital 'S' of the Western world, indigenous science is empirical. It is often forgotten, however, that empiricism implies trial and error, observation and constant experimentation, and that observation and experimentation form the basis of that very Science to which we accord a higher value.

Other conceptions of science and technology, also obviously ethnocentric, even include the indigenous science and technology of superstitions and beliefs. Some, however, admit the value of empiricism.

'Our cultures have their good sides, too; they do. For example, empirical healers too, they cure using herbs . . . Doctors too, use medicines based on herbs. So I think they have their own value.'

Although for reasons of space, we shall not go into a discussion of science and scientific method in this paper, thought should be given to the relativity of 'true' science and to the possibility that different conceptions of science may exist, just as there are different cultural matrices relating to ways of perceiving reality.

In this context, it is relevant to ask how science should be conceived in intercultural education programmes or, to put it differently, what type of teacher training would provide for a diversified development of science and technology.

The points of view of learners would seem to refer to stereotyped and traditional images of technology.

'In this college, at least in my field—domestic education—there are a lot of shortages; we do not have enough materials to learn with, for example in textiles we do not have machines, we do not have sewing machines either. I think that will make it very difficult for us when we leave.'

Moreover, requirements centre on an urban conception of technology.

'But I do not think we are learning what we should be learning . . . because if this college is technical it should have the machinery and all that . . . at least better than what it has. So how are we going to become technical teachers if we are not learning something that is vital: how to operate machines that we may be faced with in a few years? We shall make mistakes.'

In rural environments where technical teacher training is introduced, demands are thus made which relate to an image of development, industrialization and urban life. Students refer to practical action and to making education more than theoretical.

'I am specializing in agriculture . . . We are doing well in science, but in terms of practical application, for example, we have nothing to work with. We have not even got tools, so that we get the theory but nothing to work with in practice . . . We do not have the materials we need.'

But these needs refer to industrial agricultural technology; tractors and spraying are still the favoured images of development.

'I should like it to be mechanized . . . We have land here but we do not have a tractor . . . In animal technology we would like now to have shears for castrating . . . We still do things the empirical way. We need so many things . . . We need sprays.'

These trends even occur in subjects such as domestic education, in which an urban image of the home is popular and local resources are not used.

'I am specializing in domestic education. We need sewing machines, and a kitchen where we can do our practical work.'

Conceptions of craft work also refer to urban rather than rural workshops, to foreign rather than indigenous technology.

'I am specializing in craft, and we need machinery . . . We have a mechanical plane but we need a circular saw too . . . We have an industrial drill . . . but each machine can only do one thing and that is not enough.'

There is little room for the notion of differences between science, technical equipment and technology, or for the idea of appropriate technology, or to be more precise, indigenous technology, which the various technological and scientific models of intercultural education might offer us.

In this respect, it should be remembered that technical education is not the same as technological education. 'Technical' refers to the use of procedures and tools or instruments designed by someone else; while 'technological' means the design of procedures, including the making of tools and artifacts to solve problems previously identified and analysed. Technology thus refers to a way of thinking and to finding solutions to problems of everyday life; that is, to the development and exploitation of the innate creativity in every human being.

'We have to teach children to do something useful, to use the materials which they can find in their environment. For example, in crafts it might be earthenware or ceramics . . . similarly in agriculture, instead of using fungicides they can use something that is available: by collecting the resin of certain trees. Also, instead of using chemical fertilizer, they can use the manure from their animals, or vegetable compost.'

Opinions such as these have a link with some of the efforts made in development programmes, especially those run by non-governmental organizations, to use technologies that fit the thinking of indigenous peoples. On the basis of experiences such as these, interculturalism should set out to restore and enhance original technological approaches, and to stimulate the adoption of those elements of technological products which, although alien, can be used to strengthen a people's own cultural fabric, and especially to improve the conditions of life of indigenous peoples. Technological education, in an intercultural context, should set out to enhance human capacity to confront new situations and to solve problems.

'It would be good to learn using my own resources; where I am going to work, for example, to use wool instead of cotton . . . something local . . . but I would like to learn on a machine, even though not everyone uses a machine. We are now seeing machines even in the mothers' centre – weaving machines, sewing machines . . . and in any case I shall be working where there are machines and they are going to need me. I think that our country will make progress with time, and new machines will appear. Of course, it would be good to learn to use our own original materials too.'

Moreover, we have to consider the possibility that new technologies may be developed which will enable us to confront the problems facing the whole of humanity, and indigenous peoples in particular, so that basic needs can be satisfied and everyone can exercise the rights of social and cultural reproduction. In this context, education will have a predominant place and function.

Another of the questions asked of the focus groups was the relationship between technical education and migration.

'If they learn all this and go home and do not find the necessary materials there, then they will have to migrate to the city.'

Certainly, if students are trained in techniques which cannot be applied in the rural environment, they will have no option but to migrate, but if the technology that they learn to use can be applied in rural areas, they will have less motivation to migrate.

TEACHER TRAINING, INTERCULTURALISM AND TECHNOLOGICAL EDUCATION

Without going into an exhaustive examination of teacher training and its relationship to interculturalism and technical training, let us begin to identify sets of problems which reveal the complexity of the issue and the starting points for a consideration of technology and science as a key cross-curricula dimension of intercultural education programmes.

The quality of training is related to the infrastructure and equipment of the teacher training centres. The capacity of the installation is related to the choice either to establish teacher training centres specializing in technological education, or to make technological education a component of all teacher training centres. A related question is whether to have teachers specialize in technological education or to require every teacher to have some training in this field, or both.

The way in which technological education is incorporated into the curricula of training centres will also have to be looked at. It will be necessary to define whether it is a matter of cross-curricula subjects or of incorporation in a number of subjects, and time will have to be made for discussion of technological issues, especially the possibility of identifying, exploiting and improving indigenous technologies.

Programmes to train trainers will have to address the needs arising from technological aspects of teachers' professional practice. That is, the teachers of the future teachers will need to guarantee that graduates of teacher training centres will have the capacity to handle technology packages appropriate to the reality outside their schools. New teachers also have to possess the ability to develop technological strategies in co-operation with the communities themselves.

The curricula of the teacher training centres must respond to the needs of the curricula of primary and secondary schools, and hence the training curricula must contain a technological component. To omit this would lead to breakdowns which, in the most extreme cases, would lead to technical teachers having to cope like grade teachers, for example, being asked to teach reading and writing without proper preparation.

'For example, the students who have left this college are not now working in their field of expertise. Why not? Because the field does not exist . . . and if it does, not many have adapted, because it is not the same as what they are teaching us.'

'There are not many schools offering their field [technical studies] as a course. Therefore, most go and work as grade teachers in primary school . . . We are trained to be technical teachers, and they send us to be grade teachers . . . There are a lot of shortages here.'

CHAPTER V

Training in intercultural education for primary school-teachers in the Czech Republic

Jirí Kotásek and Richard Růžička

THE PROBLEM OF INTERCULTURAL EDUCATION IN THE CZECH REPUBLIC:
SOCIAL AND POLITICAL CONTEXT

After the collapse of the communist system in Central and Eastern Europe, the former Czechoslovakia and other formerly communist States in that region faced a complex of novel and difficult questions concerning nothing less than the transformation of the political, legal, social and economic map. One of the most pressing was the problem of relations between nations, nationalities and ethnic groups, both inter- and intra-State. Czechoslovakia's first attempt at a solution was to change the constitution. By 1990, modifications to this had allowed for the federalization of the State, wherein Czechs and Slovaks had fully equal rights. One year later, the Charter of Fundamental Rights and Freedoms was passed in the Federal Parliament and fixed, besides human, political, economic, social and cultural rights, the rights of ethnic minorities. Citizens from minority groups were guaranteed free development and the rights to develop their own culture, to distribute and receive information in their own language, and to meet freely in their nationality associations. They were also given the right to be educated in their own language, to use such language in official contacts, and the right to participation in solving problems involving ethnic minorities. The most significant problem of constitutional law, concerning relations between Czechs and Slovaks, was peacefully resolved in 1992, by the agreement to create two fully sovereign States—the Czech Republic and the Slovak Republic—and to co-operate further in the economic and cultural spheres.

The Czech Republic, as an independent State, has a relatively homogenous structure from the point of view of ethnicity. Ninety-five per cent of the population are Czechs (formally, those identifying themselves as Czechs, Moravians or Silesians) and 3.1 per cent are Slovaks. There are, according to the official census, also small numbers of Poles (0.6 per cent), Germans (0.5 per cent) and Romanies (0.3 per cent). There is also a negligible number of immigrants, whose stay in the country is temporary. Nevertheless, the question of the co-existence of the Czech majority with the minorities has been considered relevant in so far as the Council for nationalities has been established, headed by a government minister who develops legislation and co-ordinates activities relating to ethnic co-operation based on the principle of the protection of human rights.

The Czech Republic did not, however, entirely avoid the influence of national and racial prejudices and xenophobia. Some research has sounded warning bells; for example, one survey asked students in secondary schools what they felt about selected ethnic groups (Arabs, Jews, Blacks, Romanies, Vietnamese, Germans). Most sympathy was directed towards Blacks, Jews and Germans, but most antipathy towards Romanies and Vietnamese. There is also the alarming phenomenon of the 'skinhead' movement and its connections with neo-Nazism.

These problems have inspired much research and action. Some has dealt with anti-Semitism, which is in fact less prevalent in the Czech Republic than in many other countries. More significant has been the question of relations between the Czechs and Germans, a problem exacerbated by memories of the German occupation during the Second World War and the evacuation of the very numerous pre-war German minority. At the present time, the most numerous minority, the Slovaks, do not regard themselves as being problematic because of their close linguistic and cultural affinity to the majority, and they are not, in substance, marginalized by the Czechs—despite some lingering resentment of the Slovak initiative in separating Czechoslovakia.

The most considerable problem seems to be the relation of the Czech population to the Romanies. Experts calculate the Romany population in the Czech Republic at 300,000 persons. The relative largeness and the cultural disparities of this group—as well as the fact that some refuse to be regarded as its members—indicate the necessity of realizing a new political, social and educational solution.

Multiculturalism is becoming the solution at both philosophical and political levels; this view was expressed in influential addresses given by President Havel, who encouraged the 'peaceful co-existence of cultures'. In his view, 'the creation of a new model of co-existence of all cultures, nations, races and religious streams, in the framework of a unique, mutually connected civilization, is becoming a cardinal political task of the end of this millennium'.

In recent years, the idea of intercultural education has gradually penetrated the Czech environment. It is, to an ever more frequent extent, utilized and understood by the community of research and development specialists and also by schools and teachers who use it in innovative programmes. At another level it also concerns the development of minority schools. Finally, the efforts of trainers of future primary school-teachers to teach the principles of intercultural education are gradually bearing fruit.

INCLUSION OF INTERCULTURAL EDUCATION IN THE ACTIVITIES OF TEACHER TRAINING INSTITUTIONS

In the Czech Republic, the training of future primary school-teachers (i.e., teachers of the first four or five years of the basic nine-year school curriculum) takes place exclusively at the Faculties of Education, which together represent a fully-recognized and largely independent institution with university status. Their mission comprises not only the training of primary school-teachers but of all teacher categories and also, to an extent, of social services staff. Some of the faculties are responsible for postgraduate studies in the sciences and for conferring postgraduate doctorates. The inner departments of the faculties consist of humanities, social sciences, mathematics and natural sciences, and cover technical as well as aesthetic education. Also important are the departments of education, special education, psychology and philosophy, which influence the overall orientation of a future professional teacher's studies. The number of university faculties has risen from the initial three established in 1946 to nine today. They are located in various regional centres and their network effectively covers the entire territory of the Czech Republic. The faculties maintain close links with their own regions.

For the purpose of identifying, analysing and evaluating positive experiences identified by the faculties in the field of intercultural education, we collected relevant data using the following methods:

1. A questionnaire was distributed to the deans of all faculties of education in March 1994 with open, uncensored questions concerning the implementation of intercultural education in various fields of the faculties' activities. We had obtained written responses to our questions from all the faculties by May 1994.

2. Interviews were held with the heads of the departments most influencing the professional training of future primary school-teachers at the four faculties selected for distribution of the questionnaire to students.
3. An analysis of documentation was carried out in October 1993 for the Governmental Accreditation Commission, which is evaluating the faculties.
4. A study of all the faculties' research and development projects submitted to and approved by the grant agencies of the Ministry of Education, Youth and Sport, was carried out, and the research projects and reports referring to intercultural education were selected and assessed.
5. On the basis of a search into material published on multicultural/ intercultural education, the activities developed by the faculties in this field were identified and evaluated.
6. The position of intercultural education within the activities of the faculties, as institutions for initial training of teachers, was determined and evaluated with regard to the following aspects:
   - How the aims of intercultural education are reflected in the mission statement of the respective faculty and to what extent the academic staff is interested in the issue.
   - Whether the faculty has established an independent unit or research team for intercultural education, and whether a research project subsidized by grant agencies is being carried out.
   - To what extent and in what way intercultural education is applied in academic teaching and the teaching practice of student teachers.
   - To what extent the efforts concerning intercultural education have an effect on students.
   - Whether the research and teaching programmes dealing with intercultural education carried out by the faculty are familiar to the public and what response there is to them (possibly even within an international context).

The authors assessed the implementation of intercultural education in teacher training, which enabled them to classify the individual faculties of education according to the extent of their involvement in this field.

Intercultural education and the institutional aims of the faculties of education

After the great political upheaval in our country—then the Czechoslovak Republic—the first issues from the faculties' point of view were: the establishment of an autonomous system of management; the avoidance of totalitarian ideology and indoctrination in teaching; raising the academic level of teaching staff as well as the quality of teaching; and the assimilation of teachers to change.

However, the transformation of the faculties had to be achieved in the face of restrictive budgets and serious difficulties with the recruitment of qualified new staff. In these circumstances, it may be understood why intercultural education was not given first priority. Even if the majority of the faculties and their staff, under the influence of the changing political and social situation, began to appreciate the importance of intercultural education, their feelings were rather implicit than explicit. In only three of the faculties, located in the borderland regions with more pronounced ethnic differences, can the objective be considered as officially sanctioned and publicly announced. The academic staff of these three faculties is largely aware of intercultural education and the problem of the adaptation of teaching to the needs of minorities.

A long tradition of both research and practice in the field of educating the Romany ethnic group may be observed in a further three faculties, which are located more centrally (in Prague, Brno and Olomouc). Their establishment of contacts with countries which are more advanced in the theory and practice of multiculturalism suggests increased interest in the subject.

The following opinion was heard at one of the faculties with an active group of researchers in the field of intercultural education: 'We assume that the teaching staff of our faculty is not fully aware of the importance of multicultural education. The reasons may be various, but it seems to us that the essentials are an information insufficiency, here as elsewhere, and an aversion to this problem area'.

It is evident that interest in intercultural education is much more pronounced in the disciplines relating to a professional aspect of teacher training (education, special education, psychology and social sciences). In all the faculties which declare a stronger involvement in intercultural education the point is, first of all, that Romany children and youths are involved. It is a conspicuous fact that, besides some negligible attention devoted to the small Polish minority, no indications of any interest exist in the issue of Slovak children in Czech schools.

Research and development activities of the faculties of education in the field of intercultural education

The mission of the faculties of education comprises, besides the proper education and training of student teachers, research and scientific activities, particularly in the field of interdisciplinary research into systems of education, teaching and learning. Research and development in the faculties has a great influence on the quality and practical relevance of teacher training. This general statement is also valid for the specific field of intercultural education.

More than half the faculties claim to have systematically planned and positively evaluated scientific and developmental activities related to intercultural education. One set up an independent research unit to examine the issue; a further four have research teams working on the basis of approved projects. The establishment of units and teams is assisted by the grant agencies of the Ministry of Education, Youth and Sport, namely, the Fund for the Development of Higher Education and the Programme for the Development of Basic and Secondary Schools; these agencies finance and control the realization of projects. They support intercultural education and have included it among research priorities.

The research projects carried out at the faculties of education, or at other university faculties, are oriented partly to the general issues of education for citizens, partly to the status of national minorities as well as their education, and partly to the specific problem area of the Romanies–of training teachers for the education of Romany children and youths.

Thanks to the scientific interests of some members of their staff, and/or thanks to the joint research intentions of several departments, research into intercultural education exists at the faculties of education of the Universities of Ustí nad Labem, Prague, Olomouc, Brno and Ostrava. The research carried out at these faculties is nonetheless a function of the fact that in their respective regions the issue of national and ethnic minorities, especially of Romany children, has become an urgent socio-political problem.

The Institute for the Study of Romany Culture has been established at the faculty of education of the J. E. Purkynì University in Ustí nad Labem (North Bohemia). The institute is involved in systematic research of the social conditions, behaviour and educational difficulties of the Romany ethnic group which is, as a consequence of migration, one of the most numerous in the North Bohemia region. The activities of the institute are represented partly by the projects 'Education of teachers for the Romany population' (1992) and 'Multicultural training for the teachers of Romany pupils in North Bohemia' (1993), under the leadership of the Prorector of the University, J. Vomáèka. These projects are being followed-up by a new developmental project 'Programme of multicultural education of ethnic Romanies in North Bohemia' (1994) submitted by J. Balvín. The key aims of these projects are 'a systematic forming of consciousness and sense of own value in the youngest ethnic Romanies', and 'to contribute to the self-identification of Romanies, both inner (identification with themselves and with their own culture), and external (identification with other cultures, mutual understanding and respect, dialogue and communication as elements of a democratic and humanist culture)'. The authors of the projects consider education as a major element in the process of Romany self-identification and in their social integration. Within the framework of the projects, a sociological research activity dealing with Romany families is taking place, as well as the preparation of special textbooks for Romany pupils at primary schools, and consultative and educational activities for the public at large. The research work carried out at the faculty also represents a basis for the education of student teachers.

Anthropological and socio-educational research into Romany youth has a long-term tradition at the faculty of education of the Charles University in Prague. Since the 1970s, anthropological and health research into Romany children has taken place at the Department of Human Biology and Health Education, together with study of the conditions and methods of their schooling. The research work is reflected in university textbooks intended for future teachers at primary and special schools. The work is concerned with the principles of educating Romany children and reflects the socio-political and educational approaches of that time, i.e. in the context of an assimilationist theory.

A record of the attention given by the Prague faculty to the problems of the development and education of Romany youth was preserved, even after 1989, in for example 'Pilot theoretical study of the problem area of the development of the functional characteristics of the Romany children'. General principles for assimilation of the term multicultural education into the Czech environment have been elaborated in the Institute of Educational and Psychological Research. However, while drafting the research, the changes of 1989 occurred, resulting in more emphasis on the multicultural theory. The project 'Education of national minorities' issues from an assumption that 'as a consequence of the lack of tolerance, understanding, knowledge, of various dubious efforts at assimilation, of insensitive administrative interference and also of unjustifiable outrages committed against this ethnic group in both distant and recent history, the Romanies are currently the least educated and weakest social group of inhabitants in which insufficient motivation and interest in school and education still dominate. Changing the curriculum so that it would correspond not only to the needs of the majority but also to other groups of society might help; another form of help may come from the personality of the teacher him/herself'. The author is thereby emphasizing the importance of training future teachers at primary and special schools to be tolerant and to respect distinct cultures, to be prepared to adapt the curriculum to the needs and potentials of the Romanies and to raising their awareness concerning the history, culture and spiritual diversity of this people. A component of the project is also teaching the Romany language to future teachers who are going to work with Romany children.

Another project is being realized within the Prague faculty by researchers from the Institute for the Development of Education. Its title is 'Educational programmes for the Romany population'. The project is oriented towards the design and implementation of out-of-school educational programmes for Romany children aged 6-14 years (for example, art education in the mother tongue with orientation towards Romany folklore), for youths aged 15-18 years (for example, care of family and child) and for Romany mothers who propose to work in kindergartens with Romany children as ancillary personnel. Faculty students are involved in all these programmes.

The research work carried out at the faculty of education of the Masaryk University in Brno has a psychological orientation. The intercultural area became a matter of interest to the Department of Psychology, which entered into co-operation with the Museum of Romany Culture in Brno, one of the most advanced Czech centres of ethnographic and folklore study concentrated on Romanies. The project 'Some psychological aspects of the education and cultivation of Romany children and youths in school' ascertained the psychological premises of their capacity for education, and analyzed socio-cultural factors which had influenced their ontogenesis and socialization. The hypotheses arrived at on dissimilarities in the Romany children concentrate on emotional areas, but rationally cognitive processes have also been identified by means of psychological tests. The knowledge acquired has clarified the specific behaviour of Romany children in the school environment in comparison with the majority, and indicated the possibilities of the adaptation of teaching to the needs of this ethnic minority.

Further follow-up research work was also done, e.g. 'Psychological training of teachers for educating Romany children'. The aim was 'to collect information on Romany youths that have or would like to have primary school-teachers who in their work meet Romany pupils'. The authors are aware that 'within the changed political conditions some of the old problems are resurfacing'. The research summarizes the knowledge of 193 teachers at basic schools for Romany children. In conclusion it is stated: 'The dissimilarities characterizing Romany children are often more reflections of social, school, cultural and health negligence of varying extents, than of an expression of ethnic traditions and the way of life following from them. Other factors leading to the problems of upbringing and education of Romany pupils are insufficiently developed language skills −as a rule due to bilingualism (Romany-Czech, or Romany-Slovak) as well as the dissimilar style of family upbringing which may be, according to current Czech standards, characterized as inadequate and based upon a different type of value orientation'. The knowledge acquired from this research should became a basis for drafting a basic compendium of knowledge that may serve in training student teachers. The report also comprises the programme of action in the field of teacher training and planned future activities of the faculty, as concerns the Romany population.

The research work at the faculty of education of the Palacky University in Olomouc is oriented towards study of the broader consequences of intercultural education. One of the projects is called 'Education towards citizenship and Europeanism' and should be able to provide information on the conditions necessary for creating a comprehensive lecturing system at the teacher training faculties. The project is oriented to the area of political and cultural pluralism and human rights.

In connection with the hitherto single-university-based actions related to the Romany issue, a complex new project has been submitted, 'Equal access to education—training the national minorities', which may be realized by an inter-faculty interdisciplinary team. Its objective is 'to improve the access of the Romany minority to education through education and training of teachers for this minority as well as through sociological and psychological research, selective educational practice and publishing activities'. The project involves the following five linked areas:

1. Designing lectures and establishing a team of experts for training primary school student teachers.
2. Researching the opinions of members of the majority society towards Romanies and vice versa.
3. Researching the cognitive and personality properties of Romany children.
4. Overcoming the language barrier of Romany children of pre-school age through preparatory classes at primary school.
5. Publishing original literature on the needs of Romany children and translation into Czech of a publication by Agnus Fraser, *The gypsies*.

The new project will contribute to better awareness in primary school student teachers of the problem of minorities, as well as giving them new teaching experience. The publishing activity is intended not only for students but also for the broader public. Interdisciplinary research in the field of Romistics is being established.

The question of the Polish minority, which is concentrated in North Moravia and Silesia, and of training teachers to understand the particular issues involved in their education are dealt with at the university in Ostrava.

The broader framework of intercultural education is under examination by some researchers here in their work on the European dimension of education and on the 'European teacher'.

Training in intercultural education for future primary school-teachers

Primary school-teacher training is regarded as an independent discipline in the Czech Republic. Courses usually last four years and culminate in a final examination. The qualified primary school-teacher may then go on to take the academic degree known as the Magister.

Preconditions for admission to the course are to have finished upper secondary school with the secondary school certificate, and to pass an admission examination at the chosen faculty of education. In his/her admission examination, the applicant should demonstrate knowledge at secondary school level of the Czech language and Czech literature, an adequate knowledge of mathematics, skill in music, art and sport and, last but not least, evidence of a suitable personality for the teaching profession and a positive attitude towards children. The admission examination is demanding and selective, due to the high level of interest in this field (particularly among women).

In spite of the fact that, since 1990, the faculties of education have been allowed to draft their curricula entirely independently, the basic subject structure of the studies has not changed—apart, of course, from removing the totalitarian ideology. At primary school (i.e. first four or, in the near future, first five years of education) the same teacher teaches all subjects and, at the same time, is responsible for the physical, mental and social development of the children, as well as for cooperation with their parents. Therefore, initial teacher training is of a multi-subject character and, in some of its features, reflects the secondary school curriculum. The possibility of optional specialization has been mooted.

The curriculum is thus divided into a complex of disciplines intended for all future primary school-teachers and to special studies in music, art, physical and dramatic education. Some special studies in foreign languages (English, German, French), have also recently been established.

The common core of the studies is formed by educational, anthropological and psychological disciplines oriented to the issues of educating the children up to ten or eleven years of age and to the methodologies of teaching the various subjects. The optional courses of philosophy and social sciences are closely linked. Essential parts of the curriculum are the Czech language, Czech literature, mathematics and primary social studies. Teaching practice is included from the first year, culminating in four to six weeks of continuous practice in the third and fourth years. For the final examination, a student submits his/her diploma work based upon simple research, study of literature and practical experience.

The overloading of the curriculum as well as the insufficient co-ordination of individual courses is a subject of criticism and discussion. However, no faculty has yet developed a universally acceptable alternative. The current pilot projects put emphasis on optional courses and on efficient linkage between academic teaching and systematically planned practical training.

From the curriculum, it is evident that the question of intercultural education should be of considerable import in the initial training of primary school-teachers. On the basis of the questionnaire, interviews and analysis of documentation, we cannot state that this is in fact the case at all faculties. A major reason for this may be the present overwhelming orientation of society towards economic transformation, as well as the general attitude of the public, which is not yet fully aware of the changing social conditions within an integrating Europe. Nevertheless, it is possible to present several positive experiences.

Intercultural education has been most reflected in training for the teaching and psychological disciplines, particularly at those faculties which have studied minority education in their own official research programmes. To a lesser extent, it is also present in the teaching of philosophy, ethics and social sciences, even at those faculties which did not apply for research grants in this field. The departments responsible for teaching the Czech language, history and civic studies, art, music and foreign languages are not involved. However, the data cannot be considered as entirely reliable due to less than total knowledge of the activities of the faculties and their departments.

The most important positive experience at several faculties has been the realization of a cycle of lectures and special independent courses devoted to general and specific issues of intercultural education. They have usually had an interdisciplinary character, and some outstanding external specialists have been enlisted. The objectives are to raise awareness, to weaken prejudices towards minorities, and to solicit the provision of social care for members of minority groups.

Organized on a university-wide basis and intended for the public, academic staff, teachers and student teachers, is a lecture cycle at the University in Olomouc which covers:
- The substance of racism, and the question of human rights and tolerance.
- Political and cultural pluralism.
- The democratic State and national minorities.

- Ethnic Romany identity.
- Socio-educational work with Romany families.
- Specific problems of a Romany child in school.
- Criminal activity in youths, and drug abuse.
- Assistance to Romanies.

An optional course intended for primary school student teachers has been established, derived from the lectures and seminars, a research work concerned with the problem area of Romanies in the Czech Republic, and experience from field activities. The course is especially oriented to the specificities of the education of Romany children. It is completed with seminars presenting the suggestions of students on how to solve specific issues. Both at the beginning and at the end of the course, the attitudes of the students to this ethnic minority are ascertained.

The faculty of education in Brno has a course, elaborated in co-operation with the Museum of the Romany Culture in Brno, included in its curriculum for future primary school-teachers. The course has the following content:

- Historical development of the Romanies in the world and in our country (up to 1948, and to the present time, respectively).
- Family and social relations in past and present times; the structure of a family.
- Traditional folklore, religion, superstition and healing; the system of Romany values and its dissimilarities in comparison with the majority culture.
- Romany folklore (with an exhibition), cultural life and artistic creation; Romany subjects in art.
- The anthropological characteristics of Romanies/state of health of the Romany population.
- The substance, reasons for, and development of criminality in Romanies.
- The current situation in the social, associative and political life of Romanies.
- Characteristics of the Romany language.
- Educational/psychological problem areas relating to Romany children and youths.

A course teaching the principles of the Romistics is also being introduced at the faculties in Ustí nad Labem and in Prague. At the same time, courses in the Romany language for primary school-teachers are being established.

The principles and knowledge connected with intercultural education are gradually penetrating some other faculty study programmes, most frequently in the courses concerned with the aims of education, the social determination of the education system, implementation of human and civic rights and the rights of the child in education, education in favour of tolerance, education and minorities, etc. A considerable role in developing the conception of intercultural education has been played by domestic articles and publications, and basic foreign literature. The fast-developing contacts of the faculties with foreign countries have also contributed. Even United Nations documents concerning human rights, and the Charter of Fundamental Rights and Freedoms—which represents the basis of the constitution of the Czech Republic—have influenced the content of courses. There are even new university textbooks concerned with the subject. The elaboration of special learning aids related to intercultural education is also occurring, especially the making of video programmes (particularly at the faculty in Ustí nad Labem).

A remarkable tradition in the Czech Republic is the attention given to Romany children by Special Education programmes involved in the education of handicapped individuals. The reason is that a considerable number of Romany children, in consequence of communicative difficulties and cultural dissimilarities, were, until recently, in special schools for the mentally handicapped. For this reason, special education for future primary school-teachers includes recommendations for educating such children. In this field, the faculties in Prague and Olomouc have considerable experience.

In the complex of the Sciences of Education, social education is increasingly a field of study, presenting to future primary school students knowledge about the consequences of the political and social transformation of Czech society. Multiculturalism is becoming one of the primary tenets of that discipline.

The knowledge acquired from psychological, anthropological and sociological surveys of the children, youth and families of the Romanies has also influenced courses on developmental, educational and differential psychology at some faculties. Psycho-social characteristics of Romany children were the focus of psychological courses carried out by some faculties. Students are becoming aware of appropriate tools for identifying the individual dissimilarities of this group of children and are learning specific procedures for working with them in schools. It seems to us that the most advanced faculties here are in Brno and in Ustí nad Labem, where training for students in the field of intercultural dialogue with the adult Romany population is being developed.

An effort is made at several faculties to influence the attitudes and sensibilities of future teachers towards ethnic minorities in special workshops. The faculty in Ustí nad Labem, on the basis of current research, is introducing an exercise to overcome psychological and language barriers. The faculty in Olomouc is 'clarifying which elements condition irrational behaviour towards ethnic minorities and the formation of racist prejudices'. In the exercises, an analysis of emotional behaviour and projective techniques is utilized. The faculty in Brno has elaborated a programme of psycho-hygienic training for future students, which comprises aspects of coping with irrational ideas, including racist prejudices. Members of the academic staff consider simulation and role-playing to be effective tools in this arena.

Besides the educational/psychological disciplines, philosophy, ethics, aesthetics, sociology, cultural anthropology and politics also give consideration to intercultural education. But little data is yet available. Journalism, naturally involved in the problems of nationalism, xenophobia, racism and anti-Semitism in the Czech Republic, penetrates academic teaching.

One positive example of intercultural education in training of primary school-teachers is the study programme of an obligatory subject, Principles of Aesthetics, which is taught at the faculty of education in the West Bohemia University in Pilsen. 'The principle of tolerance towards all aesthetic views and stimulation of aesthetic perception is being viewed here as a basic problem; it is not only a question of tolerance towards the opinions of ethnic minorities, but also of the exclusion of persons manifesting distinct tastes and differences from normal aesthetic values. One study unit directly explains the multicultural dimension of post-modernism'.

Another example from the same University is the course on comparative religion. The students are acquainted with types of religious systems (e.g. Buddhism, Christianity, Islam, Hinduism, Judaism, etc.) and learn about the relation between specificities of the systems and indigenous ethnic culture. An in-depth analysis of Christianity is comprised in the programme. The objective of the course is to inculcate tolerance towards all religious systems, based on understanding dissimilarities in cultural environments. Courses of this type have become popular at many faculties during recent years, filling up the gap left by the official ideology of the former regime.

As concerns departments which provide future teachers with the knowledge necessary for teaching, several attempts have been made to implement intercultural education at the departments dealing with the Czech language and Czech literature (Ustí nad Labem and Brno). Attention is devoted to Romany culture when teaching literature. The Music departments are covering Romany musical folklore. In history and social studies, the issue of the relation between Czechs and Germans has gained in importance. Faculties located in borderland regions where this question, thanks to tourism and journalism, is penetrating everyday life, are particularly concerned (Liberec, Ustí nad Labem, Ceské Budìjovice, Pilsen).

The number of seminar works and theses with connections to intercultural education is gradually increasing, according to reports from the faculties in Olomouc, Brno, Ustí nad Labem and Prague. The faculty in Brno refers to the diploma theses of primary school student teachers who are examining the efficiency of given training methods in the development of certain mental operations in Romany children.

However, intercultural education is not found merely in academic teaching, workshops and diploma theses. Some faculties have included it in programmes of teaching practice. The students teach not only within the network of their faculty schools, but also in schools with a high representation of minority pupils. The faculty in Ustí nad Labem, in whose region there are many Romany families, is one such example. The faculty in Ostrava sends students to teaching practice at schools where Polish is the language of instruction. The other faculties involve students in the activities of the Romany population outside school. Prague students, in the framework of the project of M. Rauchová, participate in cultural/educational activities with Romany children. These activities are primarily oriented around artistic, musical, physical and dramatic education in the form of games developing attention spans, memory, and perception. Some groups of students look at the development of the lexicon of the Czech language; where possible, a basic teaching of the Romany language has been included. Further, the students become involved in talks with Romany adolescents about the problems of drug abuse and sexual education. Another practical activity for students is taking care of Romany children whose mothers participate in educational activities on family education. The project is reported to have been very useful for gaining an understanding of the Romanies. Z. Jaåabová, from the university in Olomouc, has also promoted a project in which students have been included as educators of Romany children in holiday camps, and have observed preparatory pre-school classes for these children.

In some faculties, attempts have been made to create a special file of reference on intercultural education and, particularly, on the Romany problem area. Success in this field has been recorded, especially by the faculties in Ustí nad Labem, Olomouc, Prague and Brno. The other faculties mostly state that their libraries are not yet sufficiently stocked with the necessary literature; they consider literary sources as essential for raising interest in the area.

Student response to faculties' efforts to implement intercultural education

In their reports, the faculties mostly state that the responses of students to educational activities generally, and especially intercultural activities, have not yet been systematically observed and analyzed. The IBE's project represents one of the first attempts at ascertaining students' views on the education of minorities.

In the faculties not involved, or only marginally involved, neutral or sceptical standpoints were found. For example, one stated that: 'Aversion or unconcern towards these issues was not expressed, but individual attitudes were complex; some students have not yet formed strong views, and it is not possible to exclude the existence of non-tolerant attitudes'. The following statement has a general validity for the whole Czech Republic: 'At a universal level, a rejection of nationalism and racism is manifested; however, in everyday life, an aversion towards Romanies often exists'. Another faculty, involved especially in the question of Czech-German relations, states: 'Besides a good knowledge of the history of Czech-German relations found in some students, real analysis does not yet exist. Neither positive nor negative attitudes towards ethnic groups have yet been manifested'.

However, even in faculties where multiculturalism is a research and teaching priority, conclusions are restrained. The faculty in Ostrava says: 'Nobody here has ascertained the state of student opinion, so that it is not possible to present positive or negative examples. However, the uneasiness of students towards teaching in classes with numerous Romany children is well known'. From the faculty in Brno: 'The work done so far may be rather called an orientation. Real analysis will not be feasible without the application of methodologically proved procedures. We have not yet reached that stage'. The faculty in Olomouc is more optimistic, though with reservations: 'Some positive results of multicultural preparation of students certainly exist. Bogard's scale of social distance and Lickert's scale of ethnic attitudes showed a slight positive shift after completion of the cycle of lectures. Seminar work and diploma theses demonstrate the same effect. But besides a mild positive shift towards interest in the Romanies, it is also possible to observe negative attitudes being manifested, e.g. by limited participation in the lectures as well as by certain forms of aversion'. Analogous results have been achieved also in Prague where the active participation of students has led to positive attitudes. A genuinely optimistic standpoint appeared only in the faculty of Ustí nad Labem, and was due to the more extensive voluntary activities of the students under the influence of the Institute for the Study of Romany Culture, and to the close regional links to the Romany community.

National and international publicity concerning intercultural education at the faculties of education

The faculties, in their efforts to implement intercultural education, have not confined themselves merely to teaching. This is true especially of those which have adopted research and development projects and gained finance for them from grant agencies.

At some of the faculties, specialist seminars and conferences are available for academic researchers, in-service teachers and school administrators (e.g. at Brno, Olomouc, Prague).

The Institute for the Study of Romany Culture in Ustí nad Labem has created a complex of alternative textbooks for Romany children. Consultative activity, carried out on the basis of gathering information and professional literature, is covered in the projects of the faculties at Ustí nad Labem, Olomouc and Prague.

Considerable publishing activity in the field of the Romanies is being executed by the university in Olomouc.

The faculties are initiating and advising on innovative projects for basic and secondary schools in the field of intercultural education, particularly in the regions of Ustí nad Labem, Prague, Brno and Olomouc. Close contacts exist between the faculties, the public administration, minority communities and interest groups.

Some professional activities have involved foreign partners. Contacts have been made by the faculties in Olomouc, Ustí nad Labem, Prague and Ostrava.

CONCLUSION

The decision of the IBE to effect an international comparative research project on training in intercultural education for future primary school-teachers has become an important stimulus for analysis of the activities of Czech teacher training institutions. This endeavour, to describe and analyze the issue in the international context, is in fact the first domestic research project concerning the whole area of Czech primary school-teacher training.

It has been ascertained that the concept of multiculturalism has penetrated the public and also influential political leaders and experts. Intercultural

Implementation of intercultural education into the activities of the faculties of education in the Czech Republic

Faculty of education	Reflection of intercultural education in the institutional aims	Research and development activities in the field of intercultural education	Application in academic teaching and in teaching practice	Response of students	External influence	Evaluation of the faculty involvement in intercultural education
Masaryk University in **Brno**	2	3	3	1	3	12
South Bohemia University in **Ceské Budìjovice**	0	0	1	0	0	1
College of Education (with a university status) in **Hradec Králové**	1	0	1	1	0	3
College of Mechanics and Textiles (with a university status) in **Liberec**	2	0	2	1	1	6
Palacky University in **Olomouc** *	2	3	3	2	3	13
Ostrava University, **Ostrava** *	2	2	2	1	1	8
West Bohemia University in **Pilsen**	2	1	2	1	1	7
Charles University in **Prague** *	2	3	3	2	3	13
J.E. Purkynì University in **Ustí nad Labem** *	3	3	3	3	3	15

System of points: 0–not mentioned; 1–sporadic extent; 2–some extent; 3–considerable extent. / * Faculties selected for the international questionnaire survey of the IBE.

education—despite the unitary structure of the Czech society—has emerged as one of the priorities of educational policy.

The majority of university faculties of education—four in Ustí nad Labem, Olomouc, Brno and Prague—have taken up the issue. They have initiated projects in intercultural education and research into teacher training. Grant agencies of the Ministry of Education, Youth and Sport have given important financial backing.

Awareness of the problem has been also discovered at the level of student teachers. Their answers to the questionnaire have shown considerable understanding of the situation of Romany children. It is not clear, however, if the knowledge and attitudes of future primary school-teachers are the product of faculty academic teaching and managed teaching practice, or of social tension and media influence.

It is expected that international comparative research will stimulate broader implementation of intercultural education concepts in teacher training courses, and further domestic research.

CHAPTER VI

Training programmes for the teachers of tomorrow: intercultural education in Jordan

'Ebeidat Zouqqan

This study is a survey that analyses the curricula for training primary school teachers for intercultural education in Jordan. It required analysis of the cultural groups prevailing in Jordan as well as of curricula intended for teacher training. National bibliographical sources covering teacher training were also examined to discover the extent of concern with intercultural issues.

The study deals with Jordan's experience which was supervised by the Ministry of Education in collaboration with UNICEF. It also deals with universal education in its direct relationship with intercultural education.

EDUCATION AND JORDANIAN SOCIETY

Jordan counts 4 million inhabitants, mostly concentrated in the cities of Amman, Irbid, az-Zarqa'a and al-Balka'. Forty-two and a half per cent of them are below 15 years of age. The population is characterized as follows: a high fertility rate of 5.6; a high birth rate of 34 per 1,000; a high rate of basic education enrolment at 95 per cent; a high rate of population growth at 3.3 per cent.

Jordanian society is comprised of demographic groups with different religious leanings. The Arabs constitute the majority, and Circassians represent 2 per cent. The majority of the population are Muslims while Christians constitute about 8 per cent.

Seventy per cent of the population live in urban areas. It can thus be seen that Jordan suffers from a demographic concentration in cities, with an imbalance in geographical distribution as the population is dispersed in southern parts and concentrated in the central and northern parts.

Jordan has witnessed several strong migratory waves, the most notable of which was the migration of Palestinians in 1948 and in 1967 and the migration in the aftermath of the Gulf War in 1990. These migrations led to changes in the demographic situation in the country and caused the geographical imbalance in the population distribution, culminating in the concentration of population in major cities. In spite of the Arabic and Islamic identity of most of these migrants, their values and social and cultural traditions differ in certain cases with those of the original inhabitants—a justification for their being considered a specific cultural group.

To examine Jordanian society more closely, a summary of the society and its education-related problems will be given; they are as follows:

1. An increasing infant and child mortality rate caused by environmental threats such as polluted air, water and habitat and by social attitudes and behaviour related to early and consecutive pregnancies;
2. A rising mortality rate of mothers due to poor health care, repeated pregnancies and insufficient pregnancy care;
3. Poor health services in rural areas and lack of information, awareness or means of mass dissemination through organized health information programmes;
4. An increasing population of school age; it is now estimated that children attending schools constitute a third of the population. The high dependency rate (5 to 1) reflects a number of difficulties, especially of an economic and educational nature. It also indicates a diminishing level of female education and status;
5. A decreasing level of female participation in the labour force—only 13 per cent—and an increasing illiteracy rate in the labour force now reaching 7.6 per cent; sociologists claim that this trend is caused by discrimination against women's employment as well as increasing fertility and dependency rates;
6. An increasing unemployment rate among women which has reached 34 per cent as opposed to 14.4 per cent among men. This has ever-increasing negative social and economic impacts;
7. A mounting family size of 6.9 persons per household, urban explosion and a vertical instead of horizontal expansion entailing expense, waste, loss of agricultural lands and an increasing number of sparsely-occupied luxury housing;

It is important to note that the aforementioned demographic situation has a direct impact on the educational situation as every rise in population has its cultural, socio-economic and educational effects.

It is of prime importance to highlight the following indicators and phenomena:

1. Basic education in Jordan is mandatory and free in accordance with the Jordanian constitution and the Education Law No. 3 of 1994;
2. Basic education lasts ten years;
3. There are 1.2 million students in the Jordanian education system;
4. Basic education attracts 95 per cent of children of school age while the drop-out rate is at 5.2 per cent;
5. There is an average of thirty students per classroom with the ratio of students to teacher being 25 to 1;
6. There is no gender-based distinction in education;
7. Illiteracy is 13 per cent in rural areas which is much higher than in urban areas. Illiteracy is also higher among women than men. This is explained by the discrepancy in educational and socio-economic levels between the sexes, the need to employ children to make ends meet, an inability to pay education expenses, and early marriage among rural women.

Education is regulated by Education Law No. 3 of 1994 which outlines the philosophy of education, its policies, phases, objectives and different mechanisms. It also outlines all the characteristics of the educational system in Jordan.

In this context, several points need to be highlighted. There are twelve years of learning: ten in basic education and two in secondary education. Learning starts at the age of six. The philosophy of education is inspired by the Jordanian constitution, Arab and Islamic civilization, national experience and the principles of the Arab El Nahdda, all of which constitute a cluster of educational, intellectual, national, human and social factors. The aim is to raise a citizen who believes in Allah, who is dedicated to his/her country and its security, and is endowed with humane virtues.

According to Education Law No. 3, the minimum requirement for a teacher at the kindergarten and primary levels is a Baccalaureate degree, while for a teacher at the secondary level a diploma in education is required in addition to a Baccalaureate degree.

In accordance with this law, the Ministry of Education has reached an agreement with Jordanian universities on preparing teacher training programmes in the primary and secondary phases. This requires an initial training of 25,000 teachers of both sexes who are not holders of a Baccalaureate degree but rather holders of a diploma or its equivalent enabling them to enrol at a university for a degree. This in turn will qualify them as primary level teachers.

There is a number of teacher training programmes: at the University of Amman in central Jordan; at the University of Yarmouk-Irbid in northern Jordan; at the University of Moaata- Al-Karak in southern Jordan. These universities offer the following courses:

- A training programme for teachers of Grades 1-4. Each teacher will teach all subjects to one class;
- A training programme for teachers of Grades 5-7;
- A training programme for teachers in the higher grades of the primary and secondary levels;
- A training diploma programme for teachers holding a Baccalaureate degree.

The United Nations Relief and Works Agency (UNRWA) Faculty of Educational Sciences offers similar training programmes for teachers who will work at schools of relief agencies in Jordan or in Palestine.

EDUCATION AND CULTURAL FACTORS

This section deals with education and cultural factors stipulated in Education Law No. 3 of 1994 and more specifically with the paragraphs on multiple cultures and its position towards human culture. It will also give some indicators on different cultures.

Article 3 of this law stipulates the foundations on which the educational philosophy is laid. Its intellectual foundations are represented in belief in Allah, in the lofty principles of the Arab Omma as well as in Islam as an intellectual and behavioural system, respectful of humankind and the supremacy of the rational mind.

The educational philosophy also has national, patriotic and human foundations based on Jordan being a monarchy and the Jordanian people being one complementary unit, with no place for ethnic, regional, sectarian or family discrimination. The social foundation is reflected in Jordanians all being equal in their rights and social, political and economic obligations, to be distinguished as citizens according to the extent of their devotion to their society.

Society's cohesion and survival is in the interest of every individual. Social justice, through bringing a balance between the individual and the group and the cooperation of all its citizens, is a social necessity.

As to the overall objectives of education, Article 4 of the same law stipulates the following:

1. A conscious understanding of the realities, concepts and links related to the natural, geographical, demographical, social and cultural environment, whether nationally or internationally, and using it effectively in daily life;
2. An openness to human culture with its values and positive trends;
3. Shouldering any responsibility resulting from citizenship and its rights;
4. Working towards the building of positive values and attitudes towards the self and others, towards work and social advancement as well as adopting democratic principles in individual and collective behaviour.

Article 5 of the same law defines the principles of educational policy and highlights the following:

1. Directing the educational system toward striking a better balance between the needs of the individual and those of the society;
2. Stressing the importance of political education in the education system, and the consolidation of principles of sharing and justice.

Article 11 defines the objectives of secondary education with a focus on the following:

3. Trainees should have a culture based on their country's civilization both in the past and present, and be aware of the importance of being open to all civilization;
4. Trainees are required to interact with their society's culture while working towards its development;
5. Trainees need to adapt themselves to changing circumstances in their country as well as to natural, demographic, social and cultural conditions;
6. The trainee is required to be rational in any discussion, tolerant and polite when listening to others.

The philosophical preoccupation with culture can be deduced from the above. The fact that the educational philosophy is based on belief in Allah and in Islamic thinking means that any contribution made by Islamic thought to life in general has an impact on the educational system. Islam is a religion that believes in a deity; its religion is that all human beings are creatures of Allah, and have the right to live in accordance with their cultural, moral and social values. It can be seen that through history and through the development of the idea of Islam, Muslims in their contacts with different communities have been open, respectful, recognizing the cultural identity of different peoples whether inside their own country or outside it.

The fact that the Education Law stresses that the Jordanian people are a complementary whole implies a recognition of the status of the multiple cultures complementing each other in one people. Complementarity is thus multiplicity and harmony. Refraining from discrimination in any form signifies that there is complete trust between different religious, regional, sectarian or tribal groups.

The fact that the Education Law underscores equality in rights and obligations, and sets out social justice for all citizens and groups of the Jordanian society, signifies that there is full appreciation for the various individuals and categories.

Concentrating on solidarity as a necessity in the interest of every individual is but a reflection of the importance given by educational thinking to the dignity of individuals and the need to establish a network of mutual relations.

Lastly, understanding the changes related to the demographic, social and cultural nature of the Jordanian environment indicates the right of each community of any religious, social or cultural affiliation in any geographical area to safeguard its own culture and values while working towards its development.

It can be seen that the Education Law does not clearly mention the division of the Jordanian society into categories or communities. In the interpretation of the author, who has witnessed the background and formulation of this law and the subsequent discussions, this law is characterized by the following points:

1. The nature of the political phase through which Jordan is passing is reflected in the mounting political risks which threaten Jordan's security and the safety of its territory, and even its mere existence. This has resulted from armed military conflicts in the Middle East, especially Arab-Israeli conflicts and post-Gulf War international relations;

2. The authorities' intention in highlighting trends that discourage disunity is to support unity, harmony and complementarity based on the democratic system adopted by the country in 1988. This has laid the democratic and humane foundations needed for multiplicity, be it political, intellectual or socio-cultural;

3. The majority of Jordanians are Muslims and Muslim culture is the culture of all Jordanians, including Christians who have been greatly influenced by Islamic concepts, values and principles. Also, the use of the Arabic language has dissipated any differences, leading to an intermingling of the various cultural aspects in the same crucible. Circassians, for example, are Muslims who speak Arabic, work in all fields and participate in all social, cultural and technical institutions in the country on the same footing as the Christians;

4. The authorities' intention to avoid any regional or sectarian strife has directed the country to adopt unity and solidarity, especially among

Jordanians of Palestinian origin. Thus, the term 'Jordanian of multiple origins' has become widespread so as to avoid distinguishing between a Jordanian of Palestinian origin and a Jordanian from East Jordan.

In spite of all of the above and for the purpose of this study, more than one culture can be mentioned while stressing the common factors that bring together all cultures. These cultures can be found among: (i) inhabitants living in heavily populated urban areas such as Amman, Irbid, az-Zarqaa and al-Balqaa which represent 87% of the population; (ii) inhabitants living in southern areas such as al-Karak, Ma'an and al-Tafila; (iii) inhabitants of Palestinian origin who cannot be distinguished from inhabitants living in densely populated areas.

Though there are common cultural factors in these categories of people, they have special traits—even if limited—that justify their being considered culturally distinct groups.

It is noteworthy to state that teacher training institutions follow this classification. Teachers under (i) attend the Universities of Yarmouk and Jordan while teachers under (ii) obtain their training at the University of Moa'ta. As for teachers under (iii), they receive their training at UNRWA's Faculty of Educational Sciences which is restricted to Palestinian teachers.

A glimpse of the programmes which are offered is given below. Teacher training programmes given at Jordanian universities resemble those given at UNRWA's Faculty of Education Sciences; each programme is composed of the following:

1. General requirements or disciplines attended by all students, be they teachers or not;
2. Educational requirements, which is a cluster of disciplines attended by all teacher trainees from various specializations;
3. Specialized requirements, which is a cluster of disciplines attended by teacher trainees from the same discipline.

The minimum requirement for obtaining the Baccalaureate degree is 128 hours.

It is important to point out that the Faculties of Educational Sciences at Jordanian universities have not integrated culture- and geography-specific teacher training programmes into their curricula. However, there is a concern for the fulfilment of local needs and universities see themselves as playing a role in the development of local society through Centres for Educational Advisory Services.

With the exception of UNRWA's Faculty of Educational Sciences, Jordanian universities do not train teachers to be specialized in a specific culture nor are they trained to work in a given environment. In comparison, UNRWA's Faculty of Educational Sciences stresses the training of teachers qualified to teach at the international relief agency for Palestinian refugees and other schools. This faculty serves the local and Palestinian society in particular, and strengthens the cultural identity of the Arab Palestinian people, its development and its protection.

Studying at this faculty is restricted to Palestinian teacher trainees. It can also be said that the approaches adopted by the majority of faculties resemble one another, for there is hardly any difference among the disciplines taught at the different teacher training colleges. Any difference would be in the general atmosphere prevailing in each college and in its student activities.

The Centre of Educational Training of the Ministry of Education endeavours to organize well-developed in-service programmes. To this end, it deploys modern training strategies and methods different from those practised by university lecturers or at colleges of education in Jordanian universities.

Lecturers at Jordanian universities resort to traditional methods such as lectures, and trainers at the Ministry of Education use modern methods such as brainstorming sessions, small group and workshop training in addition to other methods which will be mentioned later.

Multiculturalism in Jordan

Based on the aforementioned details and on the fact that the Jordanian people are Arabs — 90 per cent of whom are Muslims — ethnic and religious minorities do not represent organized groups within institutions, and only a small number work in the field of education. The team of researchers believed it was necessary to organize a brainstorming session to determine the different cultural categories involved in teacher training.

The brainstorming session discussed this subject for over three hours during which different ideas were expressed. This led to the rise of a general trend showing that for the purpose of this study, there are three categories:

1. Teachers representing the majority of the population, who attend the Universities of Yarmouk and Jordan;
2. Teachers who teach at schools of the relief agency for Palestinian refugees who have received their instruction at UNRWA's Faculty of Educational Sciences;
3. Teachers who work in the south and who have received their training at the University of Moa'ta.

This study demonstrated that every group in this classification has a specific culture distinguishing it from other prevailing cultural traits.

CURRICULA FOR TRAINING TOMORROW'S TEACHERS

Teacher training at the University of Jordan

The University of Jordan offers two teacher training programmes: a training programme for the class teacher and a training programme for the subject teacher.

The training programme for class teachers. This aims at training a classroom teacher qualified to teach in grades 1 to 4. The plan consists of the following:

1. A course that fulfils university requirements, with a total of 21 registered hours during which the trainee receives training in Arabic, English, Islam, the history of Jordan, the environment, the Palestinian cause, food security, human rights and development;
2. A course of special requirements at the Faculty of Education whose total duration is 18 registered hours, during which the trainee receives a training in psychology, education, statistics, growth psychology and biology;
3. A course of specialist requirements whose total duration is 48 registered hours, during which the trainee receives a training in Islamic education, social and natural sciences, mathematics, gymnastics and technical education.

Trainees are also taught other courses whose total duration is 40 registered hours during which the trainee receives training in a number of subjects such as curricula, teaching methods, appraisal, analogy, production of teaching material, methods of teaching academic research, practical and civic education, curricula of education research and class management.

The training programme for subject teachers. Here the aim is to train teachers to teach one of the following subjects: Arabic, Islamic education, English, mathematics or science and social sciences. The plan of this programme consists of:

1. A course that meets university requirements which resemble those found in the class teacher programme;
2. A course of special requirements at the Faculty of Education which resemble those found in the class teacher programme;
3. A course of specialist requirements whose duration totals 93 registered hours divided among educational subjects reaching 40 registered hours such as curricula, teaching methods, appraisal, material production, methods of subject teaching and practical education.

Other academic subjects are also taught according to the specialization of the trainee. They take up 53 registered hours.

Teacher training at the University of Yarmouk

The University of Yarmouk offers the same programmes given at the University of Jordan. The trainee is taught 128 registered hours in each specialization, distributed as follows:
– university requirements totalling 27 registered hours;
– college requirements totalling 17 registered hours;
– specialization requirements totalling 84 registered hours.
The similarity between both universities is due to the fact that these programmes are disseminated in agreement with the Ministry of Education. Courses taught at both universities are also similar.

Teacher training at the University of Mo'ata

The University of Mo'ata offers a classroom teacher training programme and another for subject teachers. These are the same programmes given at the Universities of Jordan and Yarmouk, though the latter differs by its military aspect.

The class teacher-training programme. The aim is training the class teacher in grades 1-4 at the primary level. The programme consists of 130 registered hours divided as follows:
1. University course requirements of 31 total hours during which trainees are taught military history and sciences, weaponry, Islamic culture and sociology, Arabic and English.
2. Educational college course requirements of 18 total hours during which trainees are taught educational psychology, appraisal, analogy, production of educational material, the place of the school in society, curricula development, behaviour modification and psychic health;
3. Specialized course requirements totalling 81 registered hours, during which trainees are taught language and literature, child literature, social and natural sciences, and mathematics in addition to teaching methods for the different subjects.

The training programme for subject teachers. This aims at training subject teachers from grades 5 to 10 at the primary level. It is similar to the programmes offered at the Universities of Jordan and Yarmouk.

Teacher training at UNRWA's Faculty of Educational Sciences

This faculty started operation in 1993/1994 with the purpose of training academically and educationally qualified teachers to teach at the primary level at the international relief agency schools. The faculty concentrates on the use of several means whose objective is to serve the local and Palestinian society and strengthen the cultural identity of the Arab Palestinian people.

The Faculty of Educational Sciences offers one programme which is the class teacher training programme. Its academic plan is as follows:

1. General cultural requirements totalling 21 registered hours during which trainees are taught Arabic, English, the Palestinian cause, Islamic civilization, and the history of thought, in addition to contemporary problems, principles of logic and management, sociology and the relationship of humankind with its environment;
2. Educational training requirements whose duration totals 54 registered hours during which trainees are taught psychology, history of education, childhood, educational psychology & research, class management and the educational system in both Jordan and Palestine including teaching methods, group dynamics and school health;
3. Specialization requirements whose duration totals 48 registered hours during which trainees are taught different courses in addition to practical education.

Criteria related to intercultural education

A number of criteria outline the concept of intercultural education when studying multiculturalism and cultural identity themes. These criteria can be summed up as follows:

1. The course recognizes the multiplicity of cultures, their rich variety and their capacity of interaction and mutual reinforcement;
2. The course respects the cultural identity of each community or geographical entity be it religious, ethnic, racial, sexual or geographical;
3. The course includes incentives for such factors as cooperation, positive dialogue, exchange of information as well as free information flow among the different environments;
4. The course encourages self respect, respect for others and openness to all be they individuals or groups. It discourages partisanship, bigotry and any discrimination based on differences between human beings;

5. The course offers an opportunity to discuss youth, social and cultural phenomena as well as socio-political events, sport or cultural demonstrations;

6. The course encourages the principles of human rights as stipulated in different instruments such as the Universal Declaration of Human Rights and other related agreements;

7. The course promotes skills and attitudes linked to the mutual networks between individuals and collectivities;

8. The course deals with themes related to the definition of geographical and cultural environments, communities and categories composing the local, national, regional and international community;

9. The course highlights general humanitarian principles such as increasing the sharing of knowledge in developing human civilization and culture;

10. The course encourages celebrations held on local and national occasions, and develops customs, traditions and cultural traits specific to individuals and communities;

11. The course stresses tolerance, openness to civilizations and cultures without giving a precedence to specific cultural values;

12. The course ensures that minorities enjoy full respect and appreciation.

DESCRIPTION AND ANALYSIS

Description of the teacher training course involves an elucidation of its main objectives and contents. The course is divided into four categories: general, social, educational and practical.

General courses

General courses cover the following areas:

The Holy Koran and Faith. This deepens the ties trainees have with the Koran in their behaviour, work and intellect, consolidating monotheism and interpreting Koranic verses and provisions.

The Prophet's Hadiths. This deepens understanding of the Prophet's behaviour and intellect. The course includes the Prophet's sayings, his life and the sources of his Hadiths.

Islamic thought. The aim here is to explain the development of Islamic thinking over the centuries. The course is based on the psychological and social foundations of Islamic education, its aims and values, the factors that play a role in its development and the extent of the contribution made by various peoples in such a development.

Human biology. The trainee is made aware of the relationship between living organisms and their environment. The study components are those relating to the basic concepts of health through a study of the human body.

Child literature. The trainee is given some selected examples of child literature. The components include factors that increase linguistic potential to help them in expressing themselves, in defining their environment and the outside world;

Arabic language curricula and teaching methods. The trainee is made aware of the nature of language and its relationship with thought. Study components deal with curriculum units, curriculum development and ways of reading the written language. They also include an overview of the educational and psychological theories related to child development at the primary level. This course also has practical activities related to teaching strategies in the classroom.

Islamic education curricula and its teaching methods. Here the aim is to make the trainee aware of the Islamic education curricula used at the primary school level. Its components include the philosophy of Islamic education curricula, the different phases leading to its establishment and its teaching methods. There are also practical education activities.

Arab Islamic heritage. This increases trainees' awareness of the basic sources of their culture and the dynamic part played by heritage in shaping the intellect. Its components include an overview of the material and spiritual factors of heritage, the sources of Arab Islamic heritage and the extent of its relationship with Arab life, with Islam and the Arab environment.

Jordan's history and civilization. The goal here is to aid trainees to identify themselves with their history. The course deals with the political and civilization development witnessed by Jordan since its establishment, with highlights on Jordanian relations with both the Arabs and British and with international organizations.

Human rights. This informs trainees of their rights as set out in the Universal Declaration of Human Rights, and encourage their adherence to it. The course includes a description and an analysis of the concept of human rights.

Development in the Arab Nation. This involves study of the most important social and economic problems, the politics of the Arab Nation as well as the extent of its influence on development. It gives some development experiences while stressing the importance of interdependence in achieving this goal among Arab countries.

Nutrition and food security. This deals with problems of basic nutrition, the relationship between resources, environment and population. It puts forward the requirements needed for food security and the conditions needed to alleviate any imbalance.

Sociology. Trainees are introduced to sociology, its fields, its relationship with other disciplines. Study components include social theories and discussion of such topics as social change, social phenomena and methods of social research.

Hygiene. This aims at making trainees aware of public hygiene and its relationship to the environment. Study components include a definition of health concepts, conditions for school hygiene, scientific methods to improve the level of health and the foundations and principles of proper health education.

Health and Sports. Here the goal is to develop a positive attitude toward sports while showing its impact on fitness and hygiene. Study components include general athletic concepts such as speed, strength, resilience and fitness in addition to the rules governing professional sports.

Do these courses include intercultural education concepts?

Upon reviewing the objectives of these courses and their content, it can be seen that intercultural concepts have only been mentioned independently in a limited number of courses or in specific parts of the same courses. However, upon a closer look, a different observation can be made.

The fact that intercultural education is not mentioned independently does not mean that curricula do not relate to it. There are indeed courses that can be utilized and fully directed to serving the purpose of intercultural education. There are many examples such as human biology. The latter is based on harmony and complementarity of all organs in one and the same body and among its different systems.

The aims behind the studying of the Koran or the Prophet's Hadiths can be easily linked with ideas related to human dignity and the relationships among individuals and communities. This is precisely due to the abundance of concepts in religions which concentrate on cooperation, tolerance, mutual work and friendship as well as the development of humane trends which underscore peace and understanding.

Also, the curriculum on Jordan's history and its civilization depicts clearly Arab-Jordanian relations, Jordano-British relations, and Jordano-American relations.

The fact that subjects may not seem to be contributing to intercultural education does not mean they are ineffective. The right impact depends on teaching methods, strategies, means and aims. It also depends on the positive spirit permeating these courses.

A course such as human rights points clearly to intercultural education. If taught in the proper way, trainees can acquire values and a positive outlook regarding this issue. This would eventually lead them to respecting human rights regardless of the category or group they belong to.

An analysis of these courses reveals the degree of their contribution in developing values and principles related to intercultural education, provided that adequate teaching methods are used. These principles can be summarized as follows:

1. A respect for individual and community rights, be they cultural, social, political, religious or educational;
2. An awareness that each human being lives in a specific environment, though a network of relations is being entertained with others coming from different environments;
3. Every cultural environment plays a specific, active role whereby it can contribute through an interdependent relationship with other environments;
4. Every environment has a role to play in shaping individual and collective behaviour;
5. Respecting the culture of each environment does not at all mean the disintegration of society into many cultures; on the contrary, each group has its specific cultural traits in addition to cultural traits shared with other cultures.

Social courses

The followings are examples of the type of social courses offered in teacher training courses in Jordan:

Child social development during the primary level. This course aims at increasing the trainee's aware of factors that impinge on the social development of children, or on the relationship of youth with culture and education. Study components clarify the role of society, school and local environment, and provide information on child upbringing. This course also introduces problems and obstacles encountered in social upbringing;

Group dynamics. This course aims at making trainees aware of the importance of interaction between the individual and his/her community, as well as of the psychological and social consequences resulting from such interactions. The course also tackles the concepts of belonging, submission, control, social simulation and rebellion. It discusses behaviour modification in support of cooperation, competition, cultural dissemination and its methods.

The Palestinian cause. This course aims at making the trainee aware of the dimensions of the Palestinian cause from a political and socio-economic perspective. It indicates by the same token the relationship of this issue with international developments starting with the Balfour declaration, the British mandate, international resolutions and conferences and peace negotiations.

Education and society. This course brings the trainee's attention to the social dimensions and foundations of education and its process. Study components include the role of education in society and the factors that impinge on this role.

Methods of national education. This course aims at the creation of positive values and attitudes vis-à-vis the issues faced by the nation and the respect of its constitutional institutions. Study components include democracy, environmental education, sharing and thinking skills. They also address modern trends in social studies such as: health education; universal, ethnic and national education; ways of preventing drug use; the onset of disease; and deviation.

Do these courses include intercultural concepts?

These courses are interlinked with intercultural concepts by their objectives and components. This is due to their nature, which is to deal with society and its impact on individual and collective behaviour.

These courses include important indicators of intercultural education which can be described as follows:

Educators can highlight the impact of culture or social values of the family and local society in the shaping and development of children's behaviour as well as the differences in individual behaviour resulting from having different values and cultures. They also should determine the points of similarity and difference in the behaviour of individuals belonging to diverse cultural environments.

Examining concepts such as belonging, submission, control, rebellion, cooperation and competition provides a golden opportunity to mention multiculturalism and self-identity as well as the reasons behind different individual and collective behaviour. It has to be stressed that belonging to a specific, secondary culture does not mean rebellion, just as cultural dissemination of certain cultural values does not mean control or submission.

The curriculum of national and civic education includes all the positive concepts needed to model the citizen's behaviour. Through this the trainee learns course skills and values that uphold the local and national environments, the constitutional institutions in his/her region or in the nation. He/she learns the skills of dialogue, participation, thinking and cooperation in working towards the development of the local or national environment.

The Palestinian cause can reflect the extent of the race between civilizations, as it can reflect the most recent peace efforts, demonstrating the importance of a meeting point for civilizations and their interaction for the sake of consolidating peace. The Palestinian cause is a lesson to every trainee as it points out that a clash of values can bring about disasters and wars and that a harmonious relationship between values can bring about peace and affluence.

Educational curricula

Teacher training curricula in Jordan include the following:

The sociology of education. This course aims at teaching the sociology of education as well as the relationship between the education system and other systems prevailing in society. Study components include the examination of educational and social phenomena, customs, traditions, values, social interaction, and cultural behaviour. Other components deal with social discipline, the relationship of education with social change, the meaning of democracy, and equality of opportunity in addition to the relationship of education with social classes and mobility.

General teaching methods. Here the aim is to make trainees aware of the methods of imparting knowledge and related skills. It includes the underlying principles in the planning of classes, ways of presentation through lectures and discussions, and dialogue, methods of imparting knowledge, values, observation and other skills as well as using several reference sources in research.

Organizing teaching in group classes. The aim is to make trainees aware of the cultural, social and democratic factors which impinge on the form of the school and its group classes. Study components include examination of social, economic and demographic problems as well as of teaching methods in group classes.

Class management. Here the aim is to provide trainees with the necessary skills for class management such as planning, interaction, retribution and punishment, and the respect of individual differences among students.

General psychology. This course aims at defining the concepts of psychology and its relationship to human behaviour. Its components include the relationship of psychology with other disciplines, the study of psychic phenomena such as intelligence, memory, amnesia, realism, conflict, frustration, means of defence and methods of psychic healing.

The science of psychic growth. The aim is to provide trainees with information on the factors influencing child growth. Its components include the impact of genetic history and environment, the specific traits of the different growth phases and studying methods of growth in addition to requirements of sound growth.

Appraisal at the primary level. This course aims at making trainees aware of the importance of analogy, appraisal, its methods and general principles. Its components include the determination of educational objectives, measuring means, tests, observation, records, interviews, appraisal, final appraisal, feedback and conditions for the preparation of good tests.

Teaching techniques. This course aims at increasing the efficiency of trainees in using educational techniques and tools. It addresses their conditions of use and the most appropriate circumstances for such use in addition to any consequences arising from such use.

Organizational behaviour and leadership in teaching. Here the aim is to make each trainee aware of the various concepts and theories of leadership in education. Its components include leadership patterns and behaviour, conditions for effective leadership and ways to prepare educational leaders.

Special education. This aims to teach trainees how to behave with students with specific learning problems. This includes the teaching of the special education concept, tools and means of diagnosis of special cases as well as those means used in teaching this category of students.

Guidance and orientation. This course aims at teaching the skills for orienting and guiding students. Its components include the means of orientation and guidance, theories of orientation, individual and collective orientation and student problems.

Do these courses include intercultural education concepts?

These courses differ according to the extent their objectives and contents are linked with multicultural or intercultural education subjects. But they can provide an appropriate forum for the discussion of intercultural education if taught with the appropriate educational methods and strategies.

When trainees are taught modern teaching methods, they can dispose of an excellent possibility for dialogue, as well as developing positive attitudes and values.

Individual differences among individuals and communities and the need to adapt teaching methods so as to meet people's differences constitute fertile soil for the introduction of intercultural concepts. Individual differences should thus be respected, accepted and considered by teachers, and teaching methods and strategies adapted to suit these differences. The course on leadership in both education and organizational behaviour provides an adequate opportunity to deal with individuals and communities. Each leadership pattern has its own cultural and social factors in addition to the most appropriate structures which can ensure its success. Also, the course on special education requires the use of various ways of dealing with the special education student; this could be linked up to the concepts of intercultural education.

Courses on practical activities

The practical side of teacher training is addressed in the following courses:

Physical education. This aims at the acquisition of concepts and skills of physical education. Its components include the concept of movement, children's specific movement characteristics, activities best suited to children and safe sports.

Technical and group education. This aims at developing the trainee's taste, and helping him/her acquire the skills of artistic work. Its components include artistic expression and composition, appreciation, meditation, free art and its role in shaping the personality of the child.

Musical education. This aims at helping the trainee acquire the first skills in reading musical notes as well as playing a few instruments. The course also includes expression through rhythm, popular songs and musical instruments specific to the local environment.

103

Professional education. Here the trainees learn the most importance aspects of professional work. It ensures that they acquire agricultural, household, carpentry and other skills.

Do these courses include the concepts of intercultural education?

These activities provide many opportunities to tackle the concepts of intercultural education since they offer various subjects such as musical, artistic, physical and professional education. They can all be fully used to further the concept of intercultural education, as described below:
1. Each structure has its particular traits:
   - Each environment has its sports, games and popular dances;
   - Each environment has its musical instruments, popular songs and specific art;
   - Each environment has its popular dress and jewellery designs;
   - Each environment has its works. Agriculture has its specific characteristics, the Palestinian cause has its particular concerns, even household utensils differ from one environment to the next. This can allow us to speak of a multiplicity of cultures;
2. If these curricula are to be implemented in a modern fashion through exhibitions, sport galas, folk and art evenings, fashion shows, competitions and symposia, the above-mentioned subjects could be considered an important focal point for the enrichment of the cultural life in each environment and at the national level.

METHODS OF TRAINING TEACHERS OF TOMORROW

Teaching plans

This is an analysis of all teaching plans used by lecturers at Jordanian universities, the College of Educational Sciences and UNRWA in teacher training programmes intended for Jordanians and Palestinians.

The similar approach used in all the teaching plans can be explained by the close relationship of these universities and the fact that its lecturers work in more than one university.

A review of the contents of such plans shows that studying at such universities is of a purely academic nature. Furthermore, the manner whereby student performance is evaluated follows in most cases the following pattern:
1. Programmes or teaching plans are carried out through lectures;
2. Trainees are required to participate in the discussion of lectures and they are graded according to the extent of their participation;

3. Trainees are required to prepare a brief report or paper on one of the subjects of the course;
4. Daily, three- and six-month tests are given. Trainees pass their course when they have attended all lectures, prepared a report and passed their exams;
5. According to some teaching plans, trainees are required to prepare before each lecture.

Courses on teaching methods

Trainees learn the methods of teaching their specialization in six registered hours. The trainee specialized in teaching Arabic has six registered hours of the course covering its teaching methods. As for the trainee specialized in teaching English, he/she has six registered hours of the course covering its teaching methods, etc.

Teaching plans for these courses share the same type of student performance appraisal. Upon reviewing the student performance appraisal in the course on teaching methods, it can be noted that appraisal of student performance in the English-teaching course includes: preparing the mid-term test (30%); class activity and attendance (25%); final examination (50%). Appraisal of student performance in the Arabic-teaching course indicates that trainees are evaluated according to grades obtained in the following tests: first test (25%); second test (research and reports) (25%); final examination (50%).

Thus, the plans for teaching the methodology course resemble the plans for teaching theoretical courses, as they are both based on lectures and written examinations. The author is of the view that the teaching of the course on teaching methods should not be conducted in the same way as the other courses. It must involve practical tools that aim at giving skills and strategies in addition to teaching communication and interaction, as opposed to a theoretical background. Teaching the practical methods through lectures does not allow trainees to perfect the various communication and teaching skills.

The following conclusions can be drawn from the above-mentioned points:
1. Methods used for teacher training are based on lectures;
2. Trainees' success depends on his/her ability to pass theoretical exams;
3. Trainees do not get practical training to perfect their teaching skills.

Courses on practical education

Some colleges of education give courses covering general teaching methods and twelve registered hours are allocated for this. It is during this allotted time that trainees learn to make practical applications in classrooms. They observe examples of teaching and actually teach during a limited time. This course also involves television viewing of some teaching situations.

Some universities offer a theoretical course on practical education for three registered hours and a second practical course on practical education for six registered hours. In the theoretical course trainees are taught theoretical considerations in teaching methods and skills, and academic planning. In the second course they visit schools and try out practical applications.

The author has noted, in his work in training and in practical education programmes at the Universities of Jordan or Yarmouk, that trainees undergo life-like teaching situations but these experiences do not go beyond the mere exercise of an adequate method in teaching the subject of study. The same can be said for training in academic planning and class management.

Thus, it can be noted that teacher training methods in education colleges are theoretical. Trainees acquire a theoretical training and sit written exams, while training methods focus on lectures for the most part, though discussions may be allowed during limited hours. It can be said that teacher training in Jordan does not pay sufficient attention to modern teaching methods which foster interaction among trainees and which allow room for increased attention and understanding as well as the establishment of networks among all participants.

MODERN METHODS: THE EDUCATIONAL TRAINING CENTRE

As stated earlier, teacher training programmes at Jordanian universities concentrate on methods that depend on the trainer, like lectures, overviews and exams. These are not apt to give trainees the skills they need, or the required values and attitudes.

Multicultural and intercultural education requires the use of training methods based on interaction, communication, exchange, listening and dialogue. It requires accepting and respecting others, and trusting their ideas and cultures, for any method can be proactive in teacher training through providing the following skills:
– listening and receptive skills;
– skills in reading body language;

- communicative and interactive skills instead of isolation and uniqueness;
- mutual dependence skills instead of independence;
- network relations skills instead of vertical, horizontal relations;
- skills based on cooperation instead of competition;
- skills based on trust in others and appreciation of their achievements;
- work skills instead of those based on exploitation and superiority;
- skills based on accepting criticism;
- skills based on harmony with others instead of conflictual relations;
- skills based on multiplicity instead of bilateral or unilateral ones;
- attitudes of openness and not of discrimination.

Educating or training teachers of tomorrow from a multicultural perspective requires the use of modern strategies and training methods aimed at developing the aforementioned attitudes and skills.

The Educational Training Centre of the Ministry of Education uses training strategies related to intercultural education. A number of teacher trainers have been taught at the Training Centre and use these strategies. Some of the most important are discussed below.

Workshops

A number of training workshops have been organized to make trainees aware of the importance of relationships among individuals and understanding the nature of such relationships. In these workshops, several activities took place. They include:

Web and billiard ball models. These aim at developing trainers' awareness of the mutual relationships among different individuals and that every individual is enmeshed in a 'web' of relationships. Messages are sent through these relationships.

'The world in the classroom'. The idea here is to make trainees aware that there are objects and tools in the classroom which have been made by different peoples and thanks to distant ideas. Trainees learn that in their group there are 18 countries represented in addition to ideas, tools and objects of various Jordanian environments.

'It's a small world'. This activity aims at facilitating the task of trainees in expressing their views abroad and in geographically distinct areas in Jordan, as well as organizing correspondence among them.

'I am counting on your cooperation'. In this activity, trainees face seemingly unresolvable situations unless they communicate with each other and benefit from one another's papers.

'Globingho'. Here, trainees learn the importance of relationships in different parts of the globe. They fill out forms describing any travels they have made abroad or those made by relatives or friends. They describe tools they themselves use or those used by foreigners living in their districts, etc.

'Fruitful cooperation'. This activity aims at making trainees aware of the characteristics of different cultures in the world and of the differences in cultural values among local communities.

'Identity auction'. In this activity, trainees learn of the differences among themselves in their personalities, interests and cultural values.

Training in specific skills

Specific skills are taught through such activities as are described below:

Attribute linking. This activity encourages trainees to join different groups such as the under 25 age group, the group working in rural areas, that which has graduated from a specific school, or trainees born in the same year, etc.

Diamond ranking. The idea here is to help trainees arrange ideas, objects or values according to their cultures in such a way that every trainee is able to discover a special pattern by organizing a cluster of ideas. A discussion then follows based on the foundations of such arrangements.

Alternative pathways. This activity increases trainees' ability to seek solutions and alternatives according to a determined situation or factors.

'Woolly thinking'. The aim here is to make trainees aware of the extent of interdependence or interlinkage between different subjects.

Importance of intercultural education

The Ministry of Education is interested in the concept of intercultural education as it is in conformity with the implicit and explicit references set out in the education law of Jordan. The Educational Training Centre of the Ministry of Education is responsible for the training of all teachers in Jordan; consequently, it has a global, comprehensive view of teachers from all local environments in contrast to universities which work in a specific local context.

Colleges of education at universities in Jordan pay heed to academic and theoretical subjects rather than to practical issues. In contrast, the Educational Training Centre is free from such academic and theoretical constraints.

JORDAN'S EXPERIENCE WITH COMPREHENSIVE EDUCATION: INTERCULTURAL EDUCATION ISSUES

The first National Conference on Educational Development was held in 1987 to meet the future ambitions of Jordanian society. The ambitions of Jordanian society are to enable its sons and daughters to enter the twenty-first century safely, equipped with knowledge, skills and attitudes adaptable to the requirements of the epoch and to any creative changes. This will help them distinguish themselves on the basis of their abilities so as to benefit the most from available human and natural resources.

The conference resulted in Education Law No. 3 of 1994 which is the major reference point in the process of education development and its multiple programmes. The aim of such programmes is to ensure a qualitative leap in the march towards Jordan's development and progress as well as the revival of its society and its speedy improvement.

The above-mentioned law includes the foundations of educational philosophy in Jordan which are national, patriotic, human, social and intellectual. These foundations and intercultural education are highlighted in some articles among which:

- Article 13, item 1c: Jordanians are equal in their political, social and economic rights and obligations. They are distinguished only by the extent of their contribution to society and their belonging to it;
- Article 23, item 5c: Social and political participation within a democratic system is the right of the individual and his/her obligation to his/her society;
- Article 23, item 6c: Education is a social necessity; it is the right of each individual according to his/her potential and abilities.

To this end, the Ministry of Education has introduced education innovations in different fields. This includes educational experiments addressing intercultural education.

This comprehensive education adopted by the Ministry of Education on an experimental basis is one of the programmes that deal with the intercultural aspect in the Jordanian society. This society is composed of rural and urban inhabitants of both Arab and non-Arab origin, Jordanian and/or Palestinian origin, Muslim and/or Christian, Bedouins, etc..

The absence of cultural differences in the field may be due to social, economic and historical events witnessed by Jordan since the establishment of its state in 1921.

Some of the most important factors in comprehensive education dealing with intercultural education will now be mentioned. These are the same factors that were included in the programme for in-service teacher training which the Ministry implemented in response to the recommendations of the National Conference on Educational Development.

Why is comprehensive education included?

It has been noted that pre-service teacher training programmes launched by Jordanian universities aim at providing tomorrow's teachers with academic knowledge, educational methods and education- and research-oriented skills enabling them to deal with their society's culture in a traditional fashion. This means that the trainer and academic syllabus are the only sources of culture being used. This was evident in the previous analysis of the contents and methods of pre-service teacher training programmes.

Thus, the in-service teacher training programme as well as the subsidiary programme for comprehensive education implemented by the Ministry of Education on an experimental basis aims at helping teachers acquire interactive teaching methods and develop techniques which foster critical and creative thinking. This will also give them skills and knowledge in desirable and accepted behaviour.

This will eventually bring each trainee to the required level based on his/her experience, potential and ability, with trainers playing a facilitating role in the educational process, organizing the environment and stimulating learners into generating ideas and results.

Some of the most important objectives sought by comprehensive education are as follows:

Learning to live together: this includes cooperation and solidarity among the various participants in society, teaching them to avoid conflicts by resolving differences in addition to participating in decision-making and consensus-building regarding views, rights and obligations.

Appreciation of the self and others: developing self respect, avoiding a negative outlook toward the self and others and consideration for their cultural specificity. Learning to avoid partisanship in the various societal situations.

The future: envisage a possible, a probable as well as a preferred future at the individual, category and society levels. A better understanding of multiculturalism can be reached by following in practice the preferred individual and collective future within the various natural and social environments.

EXPERIMENTAL APPLICATIONS IN JORDAN

The programme on comprehensive education lies within the initiative taken by UNICEF in collaboration with the International Institute for Global Education of the College of Education at Toronto University in Canada as well as the Ministry of Education in Jordan.

To carry out this initiative, the following activities have been carried out and implemented as of 3 May, 1993. They have not as yet been finalized.

An educational workshop in preparation for the programme was held. It was attended by educational supervisors and distinguished teachers from selected schools. The workshop included various activities on global education. Also, two experts from the International Institute for Global Education at the University of Toronto elucidated related concepts and various dimensions of the initiative. The aim was to see how these activities might be accepted and suited for curricula and schoolbooks as well as to identify local suggestions to help in achieving the programme objectives.

A national team was selected from among those both participating in the experimental workshop and obtaining training. A training session was organized to teach them the preparation of interactive training material.

An analysis of school curricula and books was made under the Educational Development Plan of 1989-1998. The aim was to determine teaching activities which can be developed to increase the impact of school curricula and books, and which will realize objectives within social education research, science, mathematics and health education. The intent is to harmonize these activities with the education development trends prevailing in Jordan as well as with the plan for developing education frameworks.

International criticism of problems was taken into consideration, including various issues at stake in Jordan such as freedoms, peace and human rights, discrimination and environmental pollution, etc.

A field test was carried out for teaching activities and material which had been developed and modified in the light of observations made by students, teachers and members of the technical team. Fifty-one educational activities were developed during this phase.

Local trainers chosen from among education supervisors and distinguished teachers were trained to lead education workshops and to apply approved teaching and learning activities. This enabled them to use interactive methods in education.

From March 10 to April 17, 1994, the teachers in question tried out these activities in the field, in schools of four educational areas: Amman, al-Balkaa, al-Zarqaa and Maadba. UNICEF supported the programme by fulfilling material and educational requirements.

The experiment was modified by using various tools developed by the programme's technical team with the support of two Canadian experts, David Sully and Graham Bank. These tools were questionnaires and interviews with an overall aim: to gain a clear picture of what actually happens in learning and teaching, especially the latter's impact on trainees' skills and attitudes. The following is a definition of the most relevant improvement tools:

1. A teacher's diary containing the teacher's record of observations, personal feelings, expectations and fears related to daily training and to every educational activity carried out by the teacher (prior to, during and after implementation) and at any time the teacher believes it useful to put down his/her observations.

2. Observation of the educational situation (the implementation of the activity) which involves questions posed by either the supervisor or teacher. It deals with all aspects of the educational situation including the teacher, trainee, learning environment, etc.

3. The feedback related to the trainee. Students indicate their likes, dislikes, any surprising elements and modifications they would like to add or delete.

4. A model interview sheet for teachers and/or a questionnaire seeking information on the experiences of teachers and their attitudes. It is filled out prior to and during the programme's implementation and upon its finalization. Fifty per cent of teachers were interviewed while the other 50 per cent filled out the questionnaire.

5. A model interview sheet for students. The supervisor is in charge of recording students' responses and observations regarding the implementation of activities, what they have learnt and their suggestions related to the educational situation, its different elements and whether activities are suitable. In addition, students' responses are gathered during implementation and after its finalization.

6. A model for measuring trends which is tried out on students prior to the beginning of the programme as well as upon the finalization of activities. The measurement covers various aspects such as the extent of listening, partisanship, confidence in others, dialogue, democracy, self-esteem and social responsibility.

Educational activities positively influenced students' attitudes by making them opt for cooperation, self-esteem and respecting the views of others in addition to listening. Opportunities arose to show decision-making skills, thought development and group work during the implementation of activities.

The classroom environment was active. It was distinct from the traditional environment, and was marked by students' participation, interaction and the discovery of their experiences and preferences.

The education environment did not raise any administrative problems in schools as expected by education supervisors and school directors.

Parents showed their preferences for such activities since students apply their skills and knowledge in their family life or in society.

The cost of materials was relatively high because of their excellent quality and the limited number of students. It was felt that such a programme would be within the financial and technical means of schools.

In the light of the meeting of the Committee in charge of programme follow-up, and the brief overview made by both Canadian experts on the results of reform, it was decided that the experiment would be extended until 1994 so as to include 20 schools from ten educational regions representing teachers and trainees from both sexes, from both rural and urban areas. Eighty teachers from men's, women's and mixed schools will thus be called on to participate.

The technical team will be in charge of developing educational activities in Arabic, social education, sciences and mathematics for grades five and six.

CHAPTER VII

Teacher training for intercultural education in Lebanon

Nabil Nicolas Constantine

Education, the conquest of space and computers: three fields that remain mysteries and sources of complications for modern man. The main characteristic of a myth, according to Roland Barthes, is to 'turn fiction into reality', so that things take on the shape of their own meaning; thus it can be said that education in general, and the training of teachers and supervisors in particular, is a myth and remains the most complicated unsolved mystery.

Education is, therefore, a complex phenomenon with its own rules and prior considerations, both real and unreal; its values are both disconcerting and confusing at the same time.

Rapid changes in the field of knowledge, the growth of technological progress, adjustments to economic and political norms, the complexity of social appearances, relations between religious, cultural or ethnic groups–all these factors indicate that the process of training at all levels (rehabilitation, refresher courses and basic training) is still virgin territory, just like any other form of futuristic planning or any development project.

The International Bureau of Education's choice of Lebanon as an example of a country with multiple cultures, languages, religions and ethnic groups is proof of UNESCO's interest in understanding the true nature of Lebanon's education system, including the weak and strong points that this plural system might create.

To a certain degree it is possible to describe Lebanon as a multi-cultural, multi-linguistic, multi-religious and multi-ethnic country, despite its reputation as a multi-religious country that stands out due to the large number of religious groups within its population, as well as the events experienced from 1840 until the most recent episodes of war between 1975 and 1989, when religious factors were important and sectarian factors often played a role.

As for the multiplicity of cultures and languages, this became evident with the arrival of foreign missionaries, the establishment of schools during the Ottoman occupation, the foundation of the Maronite School in Rome in 1584 and the Congress of Louwaizeh in 1736. It is worth noting that the Maronites closed the doors of their villages and regions to the American and English missionaries, fearing the expansion of the Protestant and Evangelical Churches on the one hand, and to safeguard their relations with France on the other, thus creating a bitter quarrel between the French-speaking and English-speaking communities.

In Orthodox and Druze villages, however, these missionaries were welcomed and there was an increase in schools using English as their first language. A large proportion of the Orthodox community was converted to Protestantism, while schools of French missionaries were established in Maronite villages and regions. Meanwhile, the members of the Muslim communities were divided between the missionary schools on the one hand, and the Turkish schools on the other, where the foreign language taught was Turkish, alongside French and Arabic. The syllabuses and books that were adopted covered, of course, the subjects of literature, history, geography and science, just as in the countries of origin of the missionaries, and the spread of the culture of those countries was a natural process.

Students became known as 'Jesuits' or 'Americans', according to their syllabuses and the languages used in their schools, and these labels still exist today, although they gradually began to disappear as the Lebanese University developed and as other universities of a sectarian nature were founded, a subject that was discussed in the previous paper by this author entitled 'Religious teaching in Lebanon'.

The term 'multiplicity of ethnic groups' covers a large section of the Lebanese population, including Armenians, Syrian Orthodox and Catholics, Nestorians, Chaldeans, Kurds and other minorities living in Lebanon, most of whom hold Lebanese nationality and are represented within the legislative and executive authorities and the official administration; e.g. out of 128 members of the Chamber of Deputies, seven are Armenian and two represent the remaining minorities. Ethnic multiplicity is evident in the languages, private schools, customs, traditions, social institutions and political parties of the ethnic communities, which continue to operate as if they were still part of their countries of origin. Thus, in spite of their loyalty to Lebanon, they have two distinct personalities, one permanent and the other temporary.

Yet, in spite of all this, it is the description of Lebanon as a multisectarian country that stands out, to the point where it is the six main communities, i.e. Maronite, Greek Orthodox, Greek Catholic, Shiite, Sunni and Druze, which jointly hold the reins of power and the State, since these communities form the majority of the Lebanese population, i.e. over 94%.

Because Arabic is the official language of Lebanon, because the deputies of Lebanon came to an agreement at the Congress of Taëf (1989) on the distribution of the three presidencies—the first for the Maronite community (President of the Republic), the second for the Shiite community (President of the Chamber of Deputies) and the third for the Sunni community (President of the Council of Ministers)—because the same agreement shared out ministerial portfolios, parliamentary seats and first grade administrative posts equally between Christians and Muslims and because of all the outward signs that make the Lebanese State a sectarian state, people of good will try to eliminate sectarianism, either by calling it 'political sectarianism' or by asking for it to be permanently removed through a separation of religion and State and by proposing a secular system.

In general, though, Lebanon today can still be described as a multisectarian country. For this reason, it is essential to study the phenomenon and to place special emphasis on the consequences of this plurality on the education system in Lebanon.

POSITIVE EXPERIENCES IN TEACHER TRAINING FOR INTERCULTURAL EDUCATION

The CRDP (*Centre de recherches et de développement pédagogiques*) is the institution responsible for training teachers for State primary and middle schools. The authorities at the Centre are aware of the importance of this role in the process of education.

From the beginning, they have tried to improve the practices and procedures within this process, by improving teacher training colleges and working out legal texts and internal regulations. The office responsible for training and refresher courses at the CRDP published most of the texts concerning regulations on the work of teacher training colleges between 1973 and 1974. The most important of these are:
– Regulations concerning educational assessment;
– Regulations on student affairs;

- Teaching syllabuses leading to the various branches of the Baccalaureate in education;
- Regulations concerning the teaching staff in teacher training colleges;
- Regulations concerning educational seminars;
- Regulations concerning medical services;
- A teacher-training college prospectus.

The office responsible for training and refresher courses is similar to a technical and administrative institution which, on a permanent basis, trains teachers for the various branches and cycles of education, apart from the secondary and university levels. In addition, it adopts modern methods and techniques of teaching, as well as advanced syllabuses based on modern educational principles and guidelines.

The primary and middle school teacher training colleges are places where educational concepts can be tried out directly under the supervision of education specialists and research workers in the different fields of education. This is the main reason why the teacher training colleges have become affiliated to the CRDP.

In the light of what has been said, we should ask what the CRDP has achieved at the level of teacher training colleges and which projects have been completed to further the training, preparation and empowerment of good teachers. Among these achievements and projects, are there any positive experiences which serve intercultural education in the country?

Events in Lebanon paralysed the activities of the CRDP and disrupted the process of training and refresher courses for several years: in 1976, 1979, 1982 and from 1984 to 1991. The Ministry of National Education tried to fill the void within the ranks of the teaching profession by employing teachers with the Lebanese Baccalaureate or its equivalent, without putting them through training sessions.

At the beginning of the 1970s, i.e. during the first few years after its foundation, the CRDP tried to improve the branches of general teaching in primary teacher training colleges by creating specialist branches, including: foreign languages (French or English), fine arts (drawing and music), pre-school, general and physical education.

Through its training office, the CRDP achieved a number of projects aimed at improving the general level of teachers, such as:

1. The creation of teaching workshops in all teacher training colleges.
2. The encouragement of activities.
3. Provision of psychological and educational guidance services for pupils in teacher training colleges.
4. A study of the situation of teachers in teacher training colleges.
5. A study of the situation of students in teacher training colleges.

As part of its task of training teachers, the CRDP prepared a ten-year plan which was adopted in 1973. The plan dealt with the different divisions and subjects taught in the pre-university cycle of general education, starting with pre-school education and finishing at the end of the secondary cycle. Under this plan, over ten thousand teachers from the private and State sectors were trained. In addition, specialized training sessions were organized in the field of educational guidance and in the preparation and improvement of teaching methods. These sessions were organized especially for teachers in teacher training colleges with the aim of improving their level of teaching.

To complete its task of training teachers, and in addition to its projects aimed at improving the various branches of general education and the level of training, a group of subject specialists at the CRDP created special courses for teacher training colleges which would be adopted by teachers during training. Fifty-nine such courses were created, covering all the subjects included in the syllabuses of teacher training colleges.

Out of all these achievements, which of them can be called positive experiences that serve intercultural education?

If 'intercultural education' in Lebanon indicates the plurality of cultures of the Lebanese people, i.e. a basic plurality and not one that is taught or learned through imitation, we must state here that the Lebanese State considers the Lebanese people to be ONE people, multi-sectarian, but not multi-cultural.

The Lebanese Constitution, amended on 9 September, 1990 following the Taëf summit and the document on national accord, confirms what has just been stated in the following way:

1. Lebanon is a sovereign, free, independent state, a permanent homeland for all its people and UNITED, with its borders defined in the Constitution and internationally recognized.
2. Lebanon is an Arab country with Arab identity. It is a founding member of and active in the Arab League and is a founding member of and active in the United Nations Organization.
3. Lebanon is a parliamentary, democratic republic, based on common freedom, starting with the freedom of opinion and belief.
4. Freedom of thought is absolute and the State, in reverence to the Almighty, respects all sects and guarantees the free exercise of religious beliefs.
5. Education is free, as long as it does not infringe on public order. There will be no limitation of the right of communities to have their own schools, provided they abide by the laws of the State.

By simply reading these statements, it is obvious that sectarianism is the most important area. Paragraphs c, d and e deal with freedom of thought, respect for religions and sects, freedom to hold religious services and the right to found religious schools.

The right to found private schools is written into the Constitution with the aim of protecting religious customs and traditions. Freedom of teaching is conditioned by the application of official syllabuses and State control.

All of this arises from the Constitution. So from where does the interest in multiple cultures arise? Is it the responsibility of the CRDP to train teachers who are specialized in the teaching of students from multiple cultures?

Neither the old nor the new syllabuses relevant to the training of teachers today contain chapters, books or themes on the diversity of cultures within the Lebanese people. The concept of cultural plurality in Lebanon, as seen by the State, applies to the diversity of foreign cultures. The CRDP, therefore, tried to fill the gap in primary schools with teachers specialized in foreign languages (French or English).

This attempt could have been considered to be a positive venture if it had been carried out as the officials at the CRDP intended. But while the centre tried to provide French language teachers to schools which needed them, the teachers themselves requested transfers to schools closer to their places of residence, and, unfortunately, the administration usually satisfied their requests because successive ministers at the Ministry of Education were, above all, politicians interested in satisfying the voters rather than working for the common good. Consequently, foreign language specialists did not work in their own field and the level of foreign language teaching in State schools fell.

At another level, the CRDP tried to train specialist teachers for pre-school education, which until that time had been limited to one class known as the 'preparatory class'. When the CRDP was founded, it introduced a two-year pre-primary cycle instead of one-year, for pupils between three and five years of age.

This cycle required special attention. For this reason the CRDP founded specialized sections to train teachers, in which the students were from different family, social, economic and sectarian backgrounds. Syllabuses for this cycle included various activities in languages, mathematics, science and education, etc., in the form of dance, songs, drawing, modelling and all kinds of educational games. This venture suffered the same fate as that experienced by the language project and the problem of a lack of teachers specialized in pre-school education remained acute. It was very rare to find teachers specialized in the teaching of preparatory classes.

As for those subjects which include in their syllabuses themes related to culture and civilization, such as history, school and society, and civic education, the CRDP tried, through those subjects, to introduce the student to his cultural heritage and civilization, his environment and society, with the aim of allowing him to acquire the experience, skills and values that would lead to national loyalty and civic behaviour. Even this type of training did not lead to the desired results.

Even if we remain optimistic about our ability to change these facts and if we consider that events in Lebanon were the main cause of the paralysis of educational progress and the failure of the CRDP's ventures, the cloud that lies over the nation's education system remains and we can only hope for those improvements on the political and education scenes in Lebanon which should come with the Middle East peace process.

SYLLABUSES FOR TRAINING PRIMARY SCHOOL TEACHERS

In the past, the Athenians attributed the victories of Sparta to the education system adopted by this 'city-state'. At the beginning of the last century, when the Prussians were defeated by Napoleon, they blamed their failure on their education and the philosopher Fichte declared: 'Burn the teaching syllabuses and find something better!'

Even today, the education system can still be said to be responsible, through its syllabuses, schoolbooks, teachers, school buildings, equipment, methods and aims, for any progress or decline experienced by a given society. The fact is that this system is the most important factor in the life of an individual or a group; the individual is the product of the system from the day he is born, in the context of his family, his school, his society and his life-long education.

The education system takes on great dimensions through its responsibility for the foundation and development of societies. The CRDP is responsible for educational planning, syllabuses, the 'national schoolbook', school buildings, equipment, teaching methods and the training of teachers. These and other responsibilities led to the establishment of an education system based on Lebanese values that take into consideration all the characteristics of the Lebanese individual and groups, whether natural, social, sectarian, cultural, linguistic or ethnic.

Following the war's destruction of the infrastructure of the country and of the State, and in particular the structure of the education system, the officials at the CRDP worked out an educational plan aimed at solving the following problems:

1. The absence of a global educational policy in harmony with State policies, with the aim of establishing a long-term Lebanese strategic philosophy.

2. The lack of clarity in objectives of the teaching syllabuses through which this educational policy would be applied, and which thus remains at present detached from reality and only weakly linked to the job market. This has resulted in a decline of the educational level among academic and vocational employees. This confusion was caused by constant disagreements over certain subjects (especially history and civic education) and over objectives and purposes. This in turn led to the paralysis of teaching syllabuses from 1968 onwards and a decline in scientific and technological levels.
3. The difficulties experienced by the administrators of the education system and teaching staff caused by:
   (i)   The lack of competent administrators in the education and school system, a fact made worse during the war;
   (ii) An excessive number of teachers who are non-specialist and lacking in quality, caused on the one hand by the gaps left by displaced groups, and on the other hand by the halt in training and refresher courses for practising teachers;
   (iii) Unequal distribution of skills (needs and specializations) or unequal geographic distribution, which led to a surplus in some villages and towns and serious deficiencies in others.
4. Disregard for the architectural, sanitary and educational requirements of schools and school equipment.
5. The numerical imbalance between general education and technical education as a result of the lack of educational and vocational guidance.
6. The absence of any firm relationship between university teaching and pre-university teaching, as well as between teaching and the needs of society.

All these problems concerning education led to the establishment of an educational plan entitled 'Educational recovery in Lebanon'.

THE PLAN FOR RECOVERY

The specialists at the CRDP prepared a draft plan. A preliminary reading of the plan and its contents concerning teaching syllabuses leads us to the following observations:

The main aims

The plan stressed the intensification of national feelings of belonging and unity, and spiritual and cultural openness through a revision of syllabuses (including teacher training syllabuses). In our view, the expression 'spiritual and cultural openness' is vague. Does spiritual openness simply mean the acceptance of the religions and sects of others? Or does it mean the study of other religions and sects through a single schoolbook on the subject of religions? Are the authors aware of the importance of spiritual openness in the scientific and objective sense rather than its sentimental and superficial meaning, which, after all, led us to the present state of affairs?

The basis of the plan

The draft plan is based on human, national, social and educational factors, especially where educational policy is concerned. What matters to us is that the plan makes a point of considering the plurality of religions in Lebanon as a precious heritage which should be protected and enriched and which can help us to fight social discrimination and religious fanaticism. In addition, the plan stresses faith in human values and openness towards international cultures, as well as everything that is linked to the sovereignty and identity of the country, human rights, freedom of education and the need for education.

Concerning the social dimensions of the plan, the relevant paragraph recommends 'the constant evolution of teaching syllabuses in accordance with the skills and special gifts of the citizen, on the one hand, and the needs of society, the marketplace and the job market on the other, until medical, ecological and demographic studies also find their place in the syllabus'.

We note that this paragraph and the following ones contain no reference to the theme of the multiple cultures of the Lebanese people, and when speaking of cultural openness, they only mention foreign cultures, for example: French, English or American culture, etc.

As far as ethnic groups and languages are concerned, the authors of the plan adopt the basic idea that the Lebanese people are ONE people, with Arabic as their language, without taking into consideration the different groups within that people, such as Armenians, Syrian Catholics and Orthodox, Assyrians, Chaldeans, Kurds and others who have recently grown in numbers since a decree was passed giving Lebanese nationality to almost 130,000 residents, 44 per cent of whom are Christian and 56 per cent Muslim.

The paragraph entitled 'political-educational fields' was devoted to the evolution of teaching syllabuses and stressed the following points:

– 'Formative education' through the introduction of modern technology in schools;
– Education assessment in school examinations, through the use of tests;

– The unification of history books and civic education books for use in schools.

Another paragraph is devoted to the strengthening of the teaching profession; it stresses the need to treat teachers justly.

The paragraph entitled 'Changes in the level of teaching at all stages' deals with changes in teacher training syllabuses, as well as refresher courses for teachers working at present in the private and State sectors. As far as training courses and refresher courses were concerned, the authors of the plan did not take account of the need to train teachers for Armenian, Syrian Orthodox or Kurdish schools, for example, by means of special programmes to prepare the student for his future role as a teacher, or a refresher course for teachers to make them more aware of the history, customs and traditions of these groups, thus making their task easier.

Even in the training syllabuses currently in use, there are no articles, chapters or books on the subject of the special characteristics of the groups that make up the Lebanese people, nor even of the majority Christian and Muslim groups.

The educational plan

As far as teaching syllabuses are concerned, paragraph 2 is a repetition of the main objectives of the plan, to which are added practical procedures corresponding to the general aims. The most important points of this paragraph are the following:
– The establishment of a definite structure of teaching cycles.
– The development of new ideas for syllabuses, with well-defined objectives for each subject.
– The training of specialists with enough experience to assess syllabuses on a permanent basis.
– Changes to teaching syllabuses in order to integrate specialist teaching.
– Training teachers to adopt new methods of examining, such as assessment and tests.

In paragraph 5, entitled 'The teacher', and especially in the first part, the authors of the plan mentioned several procedures that could be adopted in order to develop the system of training and retraining. These include: a revision of the educational rules on the subject of training and retraining; the development of new texts on the admission of students to teacher training colleges; the establishment of new syllabuses and courses at teacher training colleges; and finally, the launching of a project for continuous assessment.

These articles, like so many others, remain theoretical, and will remain so until the specialists take action to put them into practice. It is at this level that sectarian fanaticism comes into the picture to apply its own criteria in accordance with the interests of each sect, thus leading to vague, superficial decisions, far distant from the essence of the problem.

Even the practical procedures suggested by the plan do not show, for example, how the new syllabuses and courses at teacher training colleges will be carried out, or if this development will take into consideration the problems of the Lebanese child or of Lebanese youth, together with many other subjects which even today are ignored by our educational syllabuses.

What good is the subject of psychology if the student at teacher training college learns nothing about the Lebanese child, his social, economic, educational and psychological circumstances, etc., which would enable him to solve his problems once he finishes his training? The CRDP's research on the Lebanese student, entitled 'The Lebanese child between six and seven years of age, his problems and needs', was in vain because it has still not been integrated into courses at teacher training colleges and has not been distributed to those schools which might benefit from it.

Unfortunately this research remains insufficient because the world of the child requires serious attention, particularly that of the Lebanese child who has not been seriously considered with a view to solving his problems, and ultimately those of Lebanese society.

If our analysis of the plan appears pessimistic, this is because of previous negative experiences concerning the subjects of history and civic education. The present situation serves to deepen the roots of sectarianism within the higher ranks of the administration, thus making scientific, objective solutions more and more inaccessible.

The organization of the plan, its execution and approximate cost

The management of the plan is in the hands of a consultative committee named by the Minister of National Education, who specifies its prerogatives. Executive administration is by top officials at the CRDP.

The plan is executed in three stages, each of three years. The preparatory studies suggested for the plan are of great importance, as shown by their titles: 'structures of teaching cycles'; 'general statistics on education in Lebanon'; 'a social survey in Lebanon'; 'the job market in Lebanon and its requirements'; 'problems of the Lebanese child and his needs (consequences of the war)'. All these studies are directly or indirectly related to the following educational factors: syllabuses, teachers, educational administration, schoolbooks, teaching methods, school buildings and school equipment.

We should point out here that before the war in Lebanon, during the academic year 1973-74, the CRDP produced the only general education statistics to include all sectors of education, which covered 95 per cent of establishments, thanks to excellent co-operation with the government. The remaining 5 per cent represented a few schools which were inaccessible to the CRDP's representatives; these were private schools charging fees and legally unauthorized religious schools. Legal and administrative measures were taken against them.

During the war, in 1977-78, a similar but unsuccessful attempt was made. Following this, for several years the CRDP ceased to publish statistical bulletins containing global figures. When publication was resumed, it was done simply as a matter of continuity.

The most reliable statistics are those produced by State schools whose directors are obliged to present annual reports to their superiors, or whenever requested to do so.

Several factors prevent the production of global statistics satisfying scientific principles, such as the mistrust of State educational institutions, weak State control and the freedom granted to private education in Lebanon by the Constitution. To this, we must add the fact that the Lebanese do not cooperage with research workers in the kind of serious manner required. For example, as far as the cost of education is concerned, parents give exaggerated figures for their expenditure, far beyond their modest monthly salaries, and this invalidates research and prevents any study from achieving its objectives and finding adequate solutions. We hope that the necessary steps will be taken to avoid the production of misleading figures and results, which only serve to complicate the situation.

In any case, there is nothing which gives rise to the hope that in the very near future it will be possible to carry out scientific and objective studies. Proof of this can be seen in the difficulties met by research workers working on the cost of education in Lebanon or those filling in questionnaires on annual statistics for the academic year 1993-1994, as well as the difficulties of access to most free and fee-paying private schools. Statistics concerning these schools remain estimates only and consequently they invalidate statistical analysis and research.

If the authors of the plan insist on carrying out the studies, we hope that they will take into account the special characteristics of the Lebanese child and his background, not only sectarian and social, but also cultural, linguistic and ethnic, together with his customs and traditions, because the fact of giving a child Lebanese nationality, in accordance with the criteria for granting nationality, is not enough to make him Lebanese.

The granting of a nationality recognized by all countries of the world presents the individual with certain rights and dictates to him certain duties which put him on an equal footing with all his co-citizens. But in Lebanon, obtaining nationality means being automatically included among the ranks of the sect to which he belongs; thus he becomes Lebanese Maronite, Lebanese Sunni, Lebanese Druze, etc. There is nothing to indicate that this double identity will be eliminated in the near future.

As for the terms, slogans and suggestions in this plan, they can be of no significance before there is agreement by all sides on State policy. All other policies will be based on this policy, and that applies in particular to the education policy illustrated by this plan.

But in the present situation, the plan can only be based on general subjects which have nothing to do with the heart of the problem, and in our opinion can only make matters worse. When we read the various stages of execution of the plan and its methods, it becomes obvious that its authors are unaware of the Lebanese problem and are only seeking to satisfy the Minister. For example there is the proposal to establish 36 teacher training colleges in all regions of Lebanon, including 27 for primary education (pre-school, French, English, general), five for middle school education, two for fine arts, and two for physical culture, with the aim of training in the first instance 3,000 teachers (within a period of three years) and 3,000 others at the second stage (within a period of three years).

At present, the CRDP is training 2,000 students in teacher training colleges, but colleges for fine arts and sport have still not been established.

The plan did not explain the reasons for deciding to open this large number of teacher training colleges, nor the statistical information that indicated the need for them. Moreover, any proposal of this nature requires in-depth research before it can be adopted, together with the scientific and objective will, precise statistics, and, finally, a clear outline of the policy that would be best suited to Lebanon.

As far as teaching syllabuses are concerned, again we find the same general terms, such as 'the establishment of a developed structure of teaching cycles'. How? Who would be in charge of such a task? According to which criteria? Or, for example, 'the determination of new formulae for teaching syllabuses'. How? Would specialists be consulted? According to which criteria? According to which policy would these specialists work? Is it enough to improve the level of subject content? Or to introduce new technology? Or modern methods of assessment?

Important problems are forgotten: the priority given to nationalism; citizens whose sect is of primary or of secondary importance; the problem of history books, civic education books, the Arabization of syllabuses, etc.

The results foreseen

We quote the results foreseen by the authors of the plan:
1. Improvement of the level of productivity within education administration and an increased level of experience.
2. Improvement of the level of teaching and training.
3. Decrease in the amount of waste of education resources by improving the efficiency of education procedures.
4. Improvement of the social and economic level of the individual and of the group.

PROGRAMMES ADOPTED FOR TEACHER TRAINING

During the Ottoman occupation and French occupation.

In 1516 the Ottomans occupied the territories south of what is known as Turkey today, together with the Lebanese coast. In order to reward the princes of Lebanon who had helped them march along the coast towards Palestine and Egypt and the other countries of the Middle East, the Ottomans gave the chief of the Lebanese princes the right to govern directly over his own territories, in return for a tribute to the Ottoman Sultan. This region, known as Mount Lebanon, comprised the Lebanon of today, without the regions of Tripoli, Sidon, a large part of the interior of the country and the city of Beirut. These towns and regions were governed directly by the Ottoman government in Istanbul and came under the Ottoman system of education. For the Lebanese in Mount Lebanon, under the power of their local prince, teaching was in the hands of European missionaries and Lebanese congregations and individuals.

This state of affairs continued until 1918 (end of the First World War). But this long period of 402 years was interrupted in Mount Lebanon by two decades (1840-1860) of bloody conflicts, followed by a system of autonomous government (1860-1915) known by the name of Moutassarifia under the control of six European powers. During this period, there were numerous European and American missionary schools and universities in the towns and villages of Mount Lebanon, as well as native colleges. The syllabuses of these schools were based on those in the countries of their founders, and also on the needs of the local population. After 1918 and until

1943, Lebanon was under a French mandate—on 1 September, 1920 the French representative declared the creation of Greater Lebanon, including Mount Lebanon and the Lebanese regions formerly under direct Ottoman control.

These four centuries had a deep influence on the Lebanese people and left their mark in the field of education and teaching.

During the Ottoman occupation, future teachers were trained in schools for schoolmasters and schoolmistresses. These schools were considered to be institutions of higher education, just like the School of Applied Arts, the offices of earth and maritime engineering, law, medicine and agronomy. To be nominated in Ottoman schools, known as Roushdiye, a teacher had to hold a diploma from the teacher training college; teachers were all considered to be State employees, and came under the retirement system.

In view of the importance and impact on the lives of the Lebanese of the Ottoman occupation, which lasted over 400 years, we feel it is necessary to take a brief look at the syllabuses, especially those which are directly related to teacher training, i.e. the upper degree of the secondary cycle. We stress that this syllabus was only applicable to State schools; as for private schools, each had its own syllabus, proposed by the school and approved by the relevant authorities.

The syllabuses imposed by the Ottomans included the following subjects: the Turkish language and certain notions of the Arabic and Persian languages; the French language; general history and Ottoman history; general geography of the great Ottoman dynasties. Mathematics, science, agronomy, law and other specialist subjects required at the time were added to the above subjects. In addition, especially in schools which were not under Ottoman domination, the syllabus could include languages such as Greek, Latin, English, Italian, Bulgarian and Armenian.

Because nobody could teach in the State schools unless he possessed the diploma of the teacher training college, and because there were not enough teacher training colleges to satisfy the needs of the schools, these schools did not evolve and the syllabuses were not always applied in practice. It is worth pointing out that these schools were only attended by the sons of the poorest social class, while wealthier people educated their children in private schools which were reputed to have a better academic level.

During the French occupation of Lebanon (1918-1943), known as the French mandate, several changes were made in the field of education. Teaching of the French language was imposed in private schools. It became compulsory to consider the French language as an official language, along with Arabic, and the French flag was adopted with the addition of the cedar in the middle. Teaching of the Turkish language was eliminated. Official examinations were organized for the award of diplomas, which became an important element in nominations for posts in the State administration. Several measures, considered to be positive, were introduced on the organizational level. In general, the Lebanese education system evolved in a positive manner, thus preparing the way for work undertaken in this field at a later date by independent Lebanon.

But since this study deals with teaching syllabuses and in particular the training programmes of the teacher training colleges, we shall not examine the education system of this period, but only what concerns the teacher training colleges.

During the French period, teachers were trained for the primary cycle only, contrary to the system in France where a higher training college trained teachers for secondary education, separate from the training of university teachers. The training of secondary teachers came about later, in 1951, at the higher teacher training college, which was to become the Faculty of Education of the Lebanese University. In the past, the diplomas of the teacher training colleges were the upper levels of State education; they retained their importance until the foundation of the Lebanese University in 1951. Decree No. 2823 of 25 November, 1924, issued by the governor of Greater Lebanon, created two teacher training colleges: one for schoolmasters and the other for schoolmistresses. One week later, the primary teaching syllabus was issued. Graduates of both teacher training colleges had to teach according to this syllabus in the State primary schools.

The same decree determined the teacher training college system by allowing one year for general education and one year for vocational training.

It also specified that the following subjects would be taught in Arabic: history, geography, ethics, civic education, social sciences, administrative law and literature. All other subjects were to be taught in French.

The teacher training college awarded diplomas to 60 students per year; they were expected to teach in State schools for five consecutive years. From 1964 onwards, this period was doubled. One of the most important events in the training of teachers was the publication of a monthly bulletin entitled 'Education Bulletin', which in 1887 published the French instructions on secular State schools and compulsory education in France. These instructions are still valid today, in particular because of the emphasis they place on the relationship between moral guidance at school and the educational role of the family, in addition to religious education. Here, the teacher does not replace the priest, nor the father of the family, but he complements them with the same objective of guiding the child towards virtue and creating a balance within him between his spirit, his heart and his soul.

This bulletin was distributed to teachers as a model to be followed, especially as it published methods of teaching French, literature, mathematics and science, etc.

The period of independence (1943 to 1971)

The process of training teachers was linked organically to State education in the primary and middle cycles which the government of independence tried to spread to all Lebanese regions. The number of State schools, teachers and students increased: for example, between 1943 and 1971-1972, the number of schools increased from 348 to 1,338, that of teachers from 451 to 16,338 and that of students from 23,000 to 288,593.

Faced with this increase in numbers, it was essential to find teachers with a good level of education, yet these could not be found in sufficient numbers or of sufficient quality. This obliged the Ministry to nominate a category of teachers known as stand-in teachers with the aim of filling the gap, especially as the teacher training colleges could no longer satisfy the demand resulting from the increase in schools and students, and the preparation of teachers for technical and academic subjects proved difficult. In order to satisfy the demand, there should have been thousands of teachers, whereas the two teacher training colleges could only train 60 teachers per year.

Following the publication of Decree No. 26 dated 18 January 1955, on the organization of the Ministry of National Education and Fine Arts, the teacher training service took charge of the unified (boys and girls) teacher training college in Beirut-Bir Hassan, and the organization of refresher sessions. Decree No. 233, dated 1960, issued by the Ministry of Education, concerned the internal regulations of teacher training colleges, and indicated the needs to train students for primary and middle schools, to improve the level of serving teachers, to prepare the foundation of regional teacher training colleges and to develop the present teacher training syllabus.

Following the publication of Decree No. 570 on 20 July 1962 with the aim of realizing the above objectives, a teaching syllabus was established, spread over three years, that a student could follow after obtaining his middle school certificate ('Brevet') and after successfully taking written and oral competitive entrance examinations.

At the same time, there were now to be nine teacher training colleges, including two schools for male and female sports teachers. During the academic year 1971-72, the number of students rose to 952 for academic subjects and 45 for sports.

This programme, which remained valid until the foundation of the CRDP in 1972, stressed two types of training: academic and vocational. Academic training had three main aims:

1. To provide students at teacher training colleges with the knowledge and experience that are essential for their careers through different academic subjects, such as languages, science, mathematics, history, geography, etc.
2. To develop a scientific, logical and intellectual style of working.
3. To develop a spirit of research and discovery, with the aim of motivating the student to seek the absolute truth.

Vocational training consisted in providing the student teacher with the experience, technical skills and teaching style that would help him achieve the objectives of education, learn its principles, different concepts and other educational practices. This included knowledge of the psychological, philosophical and social principles on which education is based. For example, the teacher was made aware of the objectives of teaching a particular subject, why and when it should be taught.

He was also made aware of the relationship between the school and the environment and the effect of the one on the other. Vocational training also aimed to teach the student the general and particular methods of education which would help him to guide the educational process towards the desired objectives.

As for the subjects taught in teacher training colleges and the number of hours taught weekly, we can make the following remarks:

1. Training was academic and general, with no emphasis on specialization such as the pre-school cycle, languages, science and mathematics.
2. Twenty subjects were taught in a 33-hour week.
3. During training there was a clear distinction between male and female students, evident in the following subjects: household tasks and sewing for girls, agronomy for boys.
4. More subjects and more teaching hours were devoted to academic subjects than to teacher training. There were four educational subjects: child psychology, teaching in Arabic, teaching in French and the preparation of teaching methods. The number of weekly hours for these subjects in three years was 21, whereas academic subjects had 64 hours.

For this reason, we can consider that the syllabuses worked out by the teacher training service did not satisfy the strategic purpose of education and, consequently, did no more than skim over the problems of the

Lebanese child. In fact, questions concerning child psychology were limited to general matters concerning the child, as seen by foreign psychologists as a result of their experiments and studies of non-Lebanese children whose experiences are very different from those of the Lebanese child.

These syllabuses took no account of the plurality of cultures, languages, ethnic groups or sects. The teacher training college student became a teacher whose only role was apparently to confer knowledge, but with no efficient teaching role which would have made it possible to co-operate with the parents in order to educate the child first, and then to teach him. This deficiency was most strongly felt in poor regions where both parents and pupils needed the teacher to be a counsellor, an educator aware of the problems of the society and environment in which they lived.

In addition to this, there was the problem of primary school teachers being obliged to teach middle school classes, which obviously required a different type of training. It not only created problems at the level of academic subjects, but also at the level of the educational problems that the student could expect to have to deal with at this age, in particular the problems of adolescence.

A further, and even more important point, was that the syllabus did not take into consideration the question of training teachers to head a State school, and the choice of a headmaster was often subject to political, sectarian and other considerations unrelated to scientific and administrative conditions and qualifications. Even today, the situation remains the same in this respect.

With the CRDP

The CRDP was created in accordance with the law published in Decree No. 2356, dated 10 December, 1971, the Fourth Article of which emphasizes:
1. The training of teachers for all cycles and fields of education, with the exception of university education.
2. Suggestions as to the working conditions that should exist in all cycles and fields of education, with the exception of university education.

In Article 13, the same law abolished the teacher training service and the educational research service, both linked to the general administration of the Ministry of National Education. They were replaced by the Office of Training and Refresher Courses and the Office of Educational Research, linked to the CRDP.

Later, on 11 April, 1972, Article 15 of Decree No. 3087 concerning the organization of the CRDP requested the Office of Training, apart from its tasks previously defined by law, to:

1. Participate in the production of circulars and periodicals in order to improve the level of teachers and all employees in the field of education.
2. Include audio-visual techniques in the training of teachers.

In 1972, the CRDP started work on a complete plan for the training of teachers, based on global educational statistics using information collected from all types of schools and educational institutions in Lebanon, whether private, free or paid, technical, specialist, UNRWA schools for Palestinian refugees, teacher training colleges, universities or institutions of further education.

The aim of these statistics was to discover the facts on teaching and education in Lebanon in order to learn more about the conditions of the teaching body in Lebanon. This would lead to the determination of the problems experienced by schools, such as the lack of specialist teachers, the poor state of school buildings, equipment and teaching methods.

These statistics led to a ten-year plan for the training of teachers which was to become operational at the beginning of 1975. The plan included the training of 10,000 teachers for the State primary and middle school sectors and the training of a similar number of in-service teachers in the private and State sectors. In order to carry through the plan in its various stages, the CRDP undertook the following:

1. The establishment of an educational map aimed at distributing teacher training colleges throughout the regions of Lebanon, in accordance with educational needs and with the types of specialist branches they required: two preparatory years at the beginning, then, in the third year, specialization in the French or English language. Later, the CRDP created new branches: pre-school, general, French language, English language, arts and the branch of physical education which became the responsibility of the CRDP.
2. The organization of a study of the situation of students in teacher training colleges, their scientific qualifications and social and economic needs, aimed at improving their situation.
3. The establishment of specialist and general teaching syllabuses for teacher training colleges to satisfy the needs of primary and middle school education.
4. The creation of a Baccalaureate in education, separate from the Lebanese Baccalaureate, to allow students from teacher training colleges to continue their studies at the university.

5. A revision of the internal regulations of teacher training colleges, with the aim of improving them and bringing them up to date, especially on the subjects of examinations, the teaching staff and the student body, free activities and medical services.
6. The establishment of rules for training courses: the teacher training college should become a centre for training and make its training services accessible to teachers in the private and State sectors.
7. The publication of an education journal for Lebanese teachers, teachers at teacher training colleges and their students.
8. The use of educational radio and television broadcasts during training.
9. The production of a series of courses according to the different syllabuses, to be placed at the disposal of graduates of teacher training colleges to help them in their missions.
10. The adoption of a number of State schools close to teacher training colleges to be used for teaching practice.

Through this rapid assessment we can see that the attempts of the CRDP were seriously aimed at improving the education situation, in spite of the difficulties met by teachers during the war which began at the time of the foundation of the centre and became generalized on 13 April, 1975 when the CRDP was at the height of its achievements.

SYLLABUSES AND THEMES WHICH SERVE CULTURAL PLURALISM

Syllabuses for training courses

Teacher training syllabuses during the Ottoman occupation (1516-1918) were primarily interested in Turkish language, history and civilization, with Arab and French culture in second place. Foreign languages and cultures were taught according to need and the specialist branch. This applied only to specialist branches in higher education (languages, medicine, engineering, etc.), not including teacher training and only in those regions directly under Ottoman control.

Teacher training syllabuses during the period of the French mandate (Greater Lebanon and later, in 1926, the Lebanese Republic) allowed the Turkish language to be neglected as a result of the fall of the Ottoman Empire, and increased the level of teaching of French language and literature to bring them up to the level of Arabic language and literature. These two languages became the official languages of Lebanon.

During the period of Independence, from 1943 onwards, Arabic was the only official language in Lebanon. Syllabuses of teacher training colleges specified the number of teaching hours per week for Arabic language and French language: eight hours each. A single change was made to the syllabuses by Decree No. 36/74 of 4 October, 1974, in which the subject title 'French language' was replaced by 'Foreign languages'. In this way, the CRDP made it possible for graduates of schools whose main language was English to take the entrance examinations and continue their studies in primary and middle school teacher training colleges which began to give classes in English as the second language after Arabic.

This obliged the CRDP to found two branches for teacher training colleges: one that was general and another that specialized in foreign languages, i.e. French and English. Even new syllabuses in all branches devoted a larger number of hours to foreign languages and neglected Arabic in the foreign language branch.

The syllabuses adopted by teacher training colleges reflected, and still reflect, the politics of the government of Independence, the CRDP and consecutive governments, with Ottoman and in particular French contributions.

The importance granted to various languages and cultures led to open-mindedness concerning the cultures, civilizations and sciences of the outside world, but this was not the case with the various internal cultures (Syrian Orthodox, Armenian, Chaldean and Assyrian, etc.).

Openness to the outside world was aimed at the expansion of a particular language and culture at the expense of another language and culture. One example is the conflict between the French-speaking, English-speaking, Italian-speaking and German-speaking missions. The aim was to spread the sciences of the native language of the missionaries and to attract the largest number of Lebanese (to adopt a religious sect, to specialize abroad, etc.).

Authors of training syllabuses had problems not at the internal level over cultural pluralism, i.e. between members of the Lebanese people, but rather at the level of the plurality of foreign cultures in Lebanon.

The Lebanese system is known as a sectarian system and awareness of the problem of sectarianism led the authors of the 'Plan for educational recovery' to mention on every page sectarianism, religious fanaticism, coexistence and the holy religions. This is proof of the fact that the main problem is sectarianism and sectarian pluralism, and not cultural pluralism.

Lebanon's membership in the Union of French-speaking countries and the adoption of French in most State and private schools gave the impression that Lebanon's culture was French, but with time French culture has been weakened as a result of the competition provided by Anglo-Saxon culture, American in particular; this obliged the State to open State schools in which certain subjects were taught in English. The number of these schools has grown rapidly, in addition to the private schools which have adopted English as their second language, alongside Arabic; most Catholic and French schools, in fact, have adopted English as the third language, after Arabic and French.

The total number of schools in Lebanon in 1993-1994 was 2,361 schools in all sectors of general education, distributed in the following way:

1. State schools, including 14 pre-school, 329 primary schools, 735 middle schools and 155 secondary schools (55 per cent).
2. Private fee-paying schools (30 per cent).
3. Private non-fee-paying schools (15 per cent).

The latest statistics for the academic year 1993-1994 showed that there were 132 State middle and primary schools which had adopted English as the main foreign language alongside Arabic, i.e. 12 per cent of the 1,127 schools. This percentage represents a large increase compared with the early 1970s when there were still only a few schools with English as their main foreign language.

Let us stress that most subjects, other than languages, which are supposed to cover the topic of cultural pluralism, such as history, civic education, schools and society, and social culture, include general knowledge which has little to do with the complex demographic composition of Lebanese society and the cultures which are grouped within it.

TRAINING METHODS IN THE CONTEXT OF INTERCULTURAL EDUCATION

The teaching methods in the old and new syllabuses adopted in teacher training colleges aim to teach the student the importance of what is taught and its impact on the life of the individual and the group. This is done in the following ways:

1. By developing the national feelings of the student.
2. By teaching the student teacher how to select suitable methods to use with his pupils.
3. By teaching the habit of making objective assessments, using different tests and methods of assessment.
4. By teaching him how to use education methods in teaching.
5. By informing him of the importance of the mother tongue first, and then the use of foreign languages.

6. Other objectives can be added to these, depending on each subject of the syllabus. When the term 'multi-cultural' is used in the syllabus, it indicates foreign cultures.

7. The education methods taught to the student teacher through the different subjects such as child psychology, school and society, civic education, languages, science, etc., deal with the Lebanese student set in his own social, economic and cultural background. In this way, they help the student to become more aware of basic social, economic and cultural concepts, to discover the environment of the society, to study elements of discord and the elements that make up the society, and to acquire the ability to analyze the existing social background.

This is based on the idea that the individual's or the group's belonging to a particular religion is always based on the reality of a situation, as is belonging to a particular class, family or tribe within a given sect.

When the student teacher is made aware of social, economic and cultural concepts at the theoretical and academic level inspired by sociologists, economists and thinkers of foreign cultures, this is contrary to the true situation in Lebanon; consequently the student is not being helped to solve the problems he will meet during his career. It is essential to analyze the adopted training methods.

The CRDP divided up its training methods in the following way: methods based on the teacher, methods based on the student, and methods based on the teacher and student.

Methods based on the teacher. The teacher is the efficient critic and the student is the listener; the methods include the ways to recite and to speak.

Methods based on the student. At this level, the student is the efficient critic and the teacher is the guide. The most important of these methods is the method of planning. In this method we find several characteristics of good teaching, especially the freedom of the students to choose the objectives of their education and the characteristics of the various objectives, then to draw up plans that will lead to the achievement of their chosen objectives.

Methods based on the teacher and student. The most important of these is the method of collective discussion. Collective discussion between teacher and student is not simply an expression of different points of view, but a search for the truth. The teacher should be well-informed on the problem and on the ways of solving it.

If we return to the training methods adopted in teacher training colleges, it appears obvious to us that each teacher is free to choose the method that suits his students. The teacher also can, judging by his own wisdom and competence, vary his method according to the teaching situation.

We must stress that the work of the teacher remains unfinished if it does not complement the work of the student, and for this reason teachers in training colleges count on exercises and the practice of theories that the students learn.

In any case, the relationship between the teaching method and the desired objectives remains the basic purpose, especially as the educational process has to cope with the family and environmental factors that every pupil brings to school with him.

Several questions must be asked at this point: have the training colleges managed to train teachers capable of discovering these factors and the amount of influence they have on the lives of pupils? Have the methods adopted in training colleges helped the teacher to understand the dimensions of the hereditary, family and environmental problems that the pupils have to face? Have the methods helped to improve the competence of the student teacher in the field of intercultural education?

The answer, in short, is that the methods adopted cannot achieve their objectives for several reasons. They were not prepared with intercultural education as the main aim; in fact, intercultural education is not available in Lebanon in the sense specified for the purposes of this study. Even the methods adopted in training colleges for the teaching of foreign languages —French and English—use classical methods aimed at teaching the principles and grammar rules of the language in question.

Also, the academic period set for the training of teachers (one year after the Lebanese Baccalaureate) is not sufficient for training a competent teacher in the scientific subjects, nor in child psychology and sociology.

For this reason, changes in the content and teaching methods of training syllabuses in Lebanon are urgently needed. But any changes must take all aspects of the question into account, adopting new methods in order to find solutions to previously incurable education problems. Questions such as that of the multitude of channels directed towards foreign cultures and the opposition of these cultures to Arabic culture—the question of Arabization. Or the problem of cultural and linguistic pluralism within minorities such as the Armenian community, and the attempt to bring these minorities into the Lebanese education system, instead of hiding behind the veil of educational freedom which has made Lebanon into a group of education islands, between which the only link is the official diploma.

Yet even this diploma has been neglected during the past few years by most private fee-paying schools (especially the Catholic schools) because of the system by which foreign diplomas, even those earned in Lebanon, for example the French Baccalaureate or the American Sophomore, can be awarded the equivalence of the Lebanese Baccalaureate. This has caused fierce debate between those who want the equivalence system to be abolished and syllabuses to be Arabized and those who wish to maintain the present system of equivalencies together with the present syllabuses.

CHAPTER VIII

Teachers and multicultural education in Mauritius

P. Guruvadoo, A.C. Kalla, S. Thancanamootoo
and T. Veerapen

The objective of this paper is to examine the following issues:
- To analyze the curriculum for primary school teacher training in order to identify the components that are related to intercultural education.
- To analyze the methods used in the training of future teachers in order to augment their capacity for intercultural education.
- To identify and analyze successful experiences in teacher training for intercultural education.

An introductory section will describe the nature and evolution of multiculturalism at a societal level and from a historical perspective so that the reader can situate the specific context in which teacher education for the primary level is taking place in Mauritius.

MAURITIUS: GEOGRAPHY AND HISTORY

Geography

Mauritius is a small volcanic island 61 kilometers long and 47 kilometers wide, located in the south-west Indian Ocean some 800 kilometers east of Madagascar and 2,900 kilometers from India. Just over 1.3 million people, representing four ethnic and religious communities are crowded into its 1,865 square kilometers. Mauritius has several island dependencies, the largest being Rodrigues, lying 560 kilometers to the north-east and with an area of 104 square kilometers and a population of slightly more than 35,000.

Mauritius, situated near the Tropic of Capricorn, has a tropical maritime climate and a diversity of micro-climates due to the hilly terrain. Rainfall is ample, though it is useful to distinguish between a windward and a leeward side. The island is affected by tropical cyclones and occasional droughts.

While the rich volcanic soil can support a variety of agriculture, about 90% of its arable land is devoted to the cultivation of sugar-cane. The island is a classic example of monoculture within a plantation economy. Mauritius has no other natural resources except its beautiful landscape and excellent beaches, which make it attractive to tourists.

Historical background

When the island was discovered by the Portuguese in 1540 it was uninhabited. Between 1598 and 1710, the Dutch made two abortive attempts to found settlements and brought to the islands a handful of slaves – mostly Africans, but with some Indians. They introduced the cultivation of sugar-cane and destroyed the hardwood forests, killing off the dodo in the process.

The French took possession of Mauritius in 1715 and established the first permanent settlement in 1722, under the aegis of the French East India Company. The initial phase of French colonization proved difficult until the coming of Mahé de Labourdonnais in 1735, who transformed Mauritius from a mere stop-over place to a colony. He realized the importance of Mauritius in the grand design of controlling the Indian subcontinent and the Indian Ocean. He gave a boost to the cultivation of sugar-cane and cassava — the basic staple food of the African slaves.

The population of Mauritius prior to the coming of Labourdonnais consisted of some French and about 1,500 slaves — about equal numbers from West Africa, Madagascar and India. However, Mahé de Labourdonnais was to inaugurate the importation of slaves on a bigger scale from the eastern coast of Madagascar and East Africa, together with some free Indian artisans. At the time of the British conquest (1810), the population of Mauritius was made up of: 9% whites (6,227); 10.4% free coloured (7,133); and 80% black slaves (55,422) (Toussaint, 1974).

According to Baker (1976), by the beginning of the nineteenth century the Creole language — the lingua franca — was well established. This language had developed as a result of contact between the French colonialists and the mass of slaves. As in all slave societies in other colonies at this time, only white people were potentially full citizens. The first elementary school was created in 1764 (Brunot, 1935, quoted in Stein, 1982).

In the case of Mauritius, miscegenation became very prevalent and an intermediate coloured element was formed in the population through manumission of the illegitimate offspring of the white French elite. State and power were inversely related to group size. In 1809, some 6,000 whites controlled a colony of 63,000 slaves and coloureds.

Already at this time a small and growing number of Indians, particularly Muslims, and some Chinese had their own places of worship, thereby signifying the first sign of tolerance in this tightly ruled slave society. The emergence of this coloured class of Indians alongside the slave population in the town of Port Louis is worthy of note. The white population was divided occupationally into an elite and a lower class (Bernardin de St. Pierre, 1773). The elite class included planters, merchants, attorneys, surveyors, clergymen, doctors and army officers; the lower class comprised overseers, book-keepers, cleaners and soldiers. By the time the British conquered the island, Mauritian society was very much fragmented and internally differentiated by occupation, colour and place of birth.

In 1810 the British decided to take control of the Indian Ocean. First, they occupied Rodrigues Island, which had a small French settlement and some slaves of African origin. In December 1810 Mauritius fell and by the Treaty of Paris in 1814 Mauritius and Rodrigues became British.

The capitulation treaty of Mauritius in 1810 stipulated that the inhabitants would keep their religion, laws and customs (Napal, 1962, p. 80). The British were not to disturb the then Mauritian society to any great degree and, in this sense, a pragmatic policy was to prevail throughout the early years of British conquest. The British oversaw the administrative and military control of the island, while economic and social affairs were left to the white population. Obviously, imperial policies affecting other colonies were applied to Mauritius, such as, for example, the abolition of slavery.

During this phase, the major preoccupation of the British seemed to have been making Mauritius pay for its own upkeep. Hence, incentives were given to the plantation owners to cultivate sugar-cane and, in 1826, the United Kingdom granted the Mauritian sugar planters a privileged import duty, a status previously enjoyed by the West Indies. This was followed by a major revision of all the social institutions on the island and, in the wake of the Eastern Commission Enquiry (1829), the segregation affecting the coloured people, especially with regard to access to secondary education at the Royal College, was lifted.

The British rightly perceived the political power of the coloured population. In 1830, five years before the emancipation of the slaves, there were 18,019 'free coloured' citizens and only 8,135 whites (Simmons, 1976). This coloured community had arisen from liaisons between French settlers and their slaves — both Indian and African. Jumeer (1984) has argued that Indian slaves yielded fairer progenies and therefore phenotypically nearer to the whites, creating a substratum within the coloured community. This segment of the population adopted the customs and habits of the French-speaking Mauritian population and their goals became identical to those of the dominant whites. They were highly educated and occupied important positions in society and government. In short, 'they were Franco-Mauritian in all but colour' (Simmons, 1976). As in the West Indies, they were politically conservative and dominated the political life of the island until the 1930s.

The imposition by the British Government in the 1840s of English as the language of the law courts provoked uproar. In 1854, Beaton noted that Mauritius is 'in feeling, manners, and almost in language as much a French colony as it was fifty years ago and every Englishman resident in it feels himself a foreigner in a British colony'.

In 1838, as a result of the Slave Abolition Act of 1835, there were some 70,000 field slaves. The majority preferred to leave the plantations and settle on the coast or in the suburbs of Port Louis, even if the insalubrious conditions led to a high death rate.

Into this segmented society Indian indentured labourers were recruited from the mid-1830s onwards. Initially, these labourers were repatriated at the end of their five-year contracts, but later many of them settled permanently. By 1850, the total who had decided to stay was 55,700, and by 1860 it had reached 101,000. Thereafter, the influx of Indians tapered off rapidly and came to a halt completely after 1880, by which time the Indian population was in the absolute majority.

The Indians were mainly Hindus, but some 17% were Muslims. They also came from several different parts of India and spoke four different languages: Hindi, Telegu, Tamil and Marathi. Furthermore, there were free Indian immigrants who were mainly merchants from Gujarat.

Mauritian society was thus highly segmented and Governor Higginson in his annual survey of 1856 noted that 'the morbid antipathies of race and colour continue to be the source of frequent burnings and an undisguised animosity'.

Education was not seen as an integrating element, particularly since it was faced with the multiplicity of languages used on the island. The plantation economy largely dictated social and economic relations among the communities. This situation prevailed until the 1940s when the British colonial authorities established an Advisory Committee on Education under Sir Christopher Cox which gradually resulted in changes to the situation.

A PLURAL SOCIETY IN MAURITIUS

There is no need to delve into a lengthy analysis of the historical processes that account for the present situation. We shall concentrate on some factors which help us to understand facets of this plural society. The classic definition about pluralism in Burma and Java provided by J.S. Furnival (1948,) aptly suits the Mauritian situation: 'the medley of peoples . . . they mix but do not combine. Each group holds its religion, its own culture and language, its own ideas and ways . . . There is a plural society with different sections of the society living side by side but separately within the same political unit.' Furnival's ideas have been refined and amplified by various social anthropologists — of special interest to us here are the ideas of M.G. Smith (1965) and C. Jayawardena (1966, 1980).

The plural nature of Mauritian society is revealed by the 1972 census — the last one to enumerate the population according to ethnicity: Hindus, 428,167 (51.8%); Muslims, 137,081 (16.6%); Chinese, 24,084 (2.9%); general population, 236,867 (28.7%); total: 826,199. The composition has not changed dramatically since then.

FIGURE 1: The Mauritian population divided into ethnic and linguistic groups.

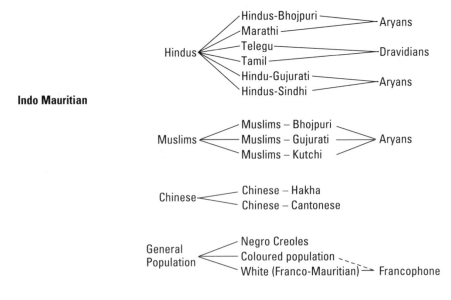

Source: Translated from Stein, 1982, Table 2.1.

It is surprising to note that Urdu, the ancestral language of the Bhojpuri Muslims, does not appear in Stein's list in Figure 1. It is certain that Urdu has been and is being taught in Mauritius, even appearing on the curriculum of the Royal College in the 1880s.

The retention of an ethnic identity, especially by the Asian immigrants, is an evident trait in Mauritius' plural society. The medium through which an ethnic identity exists is the awareness of sharing a common culture derived from a set of traditions arising from a common homeland. In Mauritius, the nearness of the Indian sub-continent has provided a direct link for retaining ethnic identity (Barz, 1980).

The decision of the Court of Governors of the India Board in 1857 to resist the implementation of compulsory education for Indian immigrants in Mauritius led to a considerable delay in the education of Indians, but at the same time gave rise to attempts at educating them in their mother-tongue.

The teaching of Indian languages — Hindi, Urdu and Tamil — received only slight attention in the nineteenth and early twentieth centuries (Ramyead, 1985), even though they were being taught in the fundamental social organizations of the Hindus and Muslims (Barz, 1980). Barz traces the vigorous teaching of Hindi to the Hindu Revivalist Movement which managed to permeate the official school system so that, by the 1950s, teaching in ancestral languages was well established in Mauritian schools. At the same time, training facilities were provided at the Teachers Training College for primary school-teachers. Nowadays, all the ancestral languages — Hindi, Urdu, Tamil, Telegu and Mandarin (but not Gujurati) — are taught in all primary and some secondary schools in Mauritius.

The teaching of oriental languages during the colonial period was an acknowledgment by the British Government of the rise in nationalist feelings among the Indian labouring classes in the island. The gradual introduction of these languages, alongside English and French, reveals the bargaining that characterizes Mauritian society to this day. The multi-ethnic society of Mauritius is a more positive experience than, for example, Guyana, Trinidad or Fiji.

Living space is very limited. Once Indians were allowed to own property, they were obliged to live in very congested areas. Following economic problems with the sugar industry in the 1880s and the parceling of the sugar estates — the Grand Morcellement Movement — villages were formed in the north of the island. Haraksingh's collapsing space theory (1988) is quite relevant in Mauritius: restricted space has forced different communities to tolerate each other. It should be noted that one ethnic group tends to predominate in some villages. Brookfield (1958) distinguished the predominance of Hindus in the windward and northern zones and Creoles to the leeward. Today, with increasing internal migration, there is more diversity. Most urban areas show a predominance of general population and Muslims. Rodrigues is inhabited exclusively by Creoles.

Thus, interculturalism in Mauritius means the application in schools of the principle of equity, which extends to curriculum content and school norms, values and standards. Minority children are not required to study those subjects or to participate in those activities that are against their religious beliefs, alienate them from their ancestral origin or create a gulf between them and their parents. Furthermore, the evolution of a set of shared values encompassing the various groups within the civic polity and the nation itself has been pointed out by Smolicz (1988). These values include the democratic and political tradition, the concept of each human being as worthy of freedom and respect, a degree of economic pluralism and English as the official language, despite the predominance of French in cultural affairs.

Today, with a major shift in employment from primary agriculture to manufacturing, tourism and other tertiary sectors, we are witnessing the emergence of new sets of values and the need for education to cater to the inculcation of those values that are being voiced related to multiculturalism.

TEACHER TRAINING AT PRIMARY LEVEL

The present situation

The training of all primary teachers was originally entrusted to the Teachers' Training College (TTC) set up in the 1940s. In 1982, however, this institution was dissolved and its staff diverted to other establishments, including the Mauritius Institute of Education (MIE). Set up in 1973, the main functions of the MIE were teacher education for the secondary level, research, curriculum development (both primary and secondary levels) and examinations (primary level). The latter two functions have recently been delegated to two specific bodies: the National Centre for Curriculum Development and Research (NCCRD); and the Mauritius Examinations Syndicate (MES) — although the MIE staff still provide consultant services to both institutions. With the dissolution of the TTC, the MIE was given responsibility for the training of all primary school-teachers as well.

Primary school-teachers fall into two categories: general purpose teachers (GP) form a heterogeneous cultural group and specialize in the teaching of English, French, mathematics, environmental studies, creative education and physical education; and oriental language teachers (OL) teach Hindi, Urdu, Tamil, Telegu, Marathi and Mandarin. In order to train OL teachers, the MIE works in collaboration with the Mahatma Gandhi Institute (MGI), which possesses the expertise in oriental languages. The MIE contributes to the pedagogical aspects of the course, as well as the general studies and physical education components.

This type of collaborative venture is typical of the official policy towards multiculturalism and has to a large extent determined its nature and evolution in relation to education: a dual strategy of 'separate but equal' and 'bridge-building'. The oriental language courses offered at MGI traditionally cater to a clientele coming from the specific cultural background of that language. They aim at consolidating the sense of identity and pride in one's heritage. The primary assumption is that respect for oneself is a prerequisite for respect of others (see Jeffcoate, 1976). However, trainee teachers from all linguistic groups follow together the educational studies and general education courses where they are able to share their experiences and work in an intercultural context. On the other hand, the general purpose teachers, consisting of students from most of the ethnic groups represented in Mauritius, all follow the same course taught mainly in English or French. Thus, they come into contact on a daily basis with a diversity of cultural experiences in both the overt and hidden curriculum and seem to assume this multicultural situation quite naturally.

However, among the general purpose students there is one group that appears to experience some difficulty in integrating into this multicultural context — the Rodriguans. Although situated some 350 miles (560 km) away, Rodrigues is considered as the tenth district of Mauritius, but has a very different cultural and economic reality. For instance, in 1994 there were about twenty students, all from the Creole ethnic group and all Catholics. They had not been exposed to a multicultural lifestyle and were educationally and economically disadvantaged. They may feel that the cultural reality of the teacher education courses provided by the MIE is alien to them.

Structure and organization of the courses

The Primary Teacher's Certificate Course is a two-year full-time course open to all candidates who possess a Cambridge School Certificate with five credits, although nowadays more and more candidates are Higher School Certificate holders. Recruitment is carried out by the Ministry of Education when it thinks fit. Two terms are devoted to teaching practice in various primary schools in Mauritius and Rodrigues, and four terms to actual training at the MIE. After their two years of training, successful students are immediately employed as permanent teachers, either by the government or by the Roman Catholic Education Authority schools in Mauritius and, for the Rodriguan students, in Rodrigues.

In 1994, there were some 383 general purpose students following the Primary Certificate Course. For teaching purposes, they are divided into eight groups each containing between thirty and sixty students, according to the size of the rooms available. All the major ethnic groups are represented, with the exception of the white (Franco-Mauritian) group. Teachers in this group usually work in private schools and rarely follow teacher education courses at the MIE.

As far as oriental language teachers are concerned, in 1994 there were twenty-eight students following MGI/MIE courses: seventeen Arabic, two Mandarin and nine Tamil. This was a rather exceptional situation; usually the Hindi students far outnumber the others. The intake for this group depends very much on vacancies available in schools. They follow courses for their own linguistic and cultural group taught by a staff member of that group at the MGI or as one group for such subjects as music, physical education, general studies and educational studies.

All general purpose students are taught by lecturers in the various departments of the MIE, who themselves arise from diverse cultural backgrounds. At present there are nine Muslims, forty-seven non-Muslims of Indian origin, and eleven from the general population (Creole and Chinese).

The following analysis will be concerned only with general purpose teachers, for the following reasons:
– at the time of writing the oriental language student teachers were carrying out their first term of practice teaching and were not on campus;
– the previous intake of oriental language teachers dates back to 1988 and the curriculum is now being revised. Because of this gap in recruitment and the new course material, some lecturers were not able to pronounce on the methods used.

ANALYSIS OF THE TEACHER-TRAINING CURRICULUM

Methodology

The analysis of intercultural components in the curriculum for teacher education at the MIE was carried out in the following ways:
1. An examination of the various components taught as expressed in the official handbook for the primary teachers' course, 1993-94.
2. Individual interviews — one to one-and-a-half hours — with a staff member from each of the departments providing part of the course.

3. Through participant observation.

Course description

General-purpose students follow courses on the following subjects: (i) English; (ii) French; (iii) mathematics; (iv) environmental studies I (social studies); (v) environmental studies II (science, consisting of pure and applied science; environmental science; agriculture; health and nutrition); (vi) creative education (art; design and technology; creative needlecraft); (vii) movement education; (viii) audio-visual education; (ix) music; and (x) educational studies (students are exposed to educational psychology; educational philosophy; educational sociology; the social psychology of teaching; comparative education; and curriculum studies).

Each of these ten main areas is allotted three hours per week. Twice a week, in sessions of one-and-a-half hours, students are also offered tutorials or 'activities' which may involve lectures by guest speakers on various topics, such as drugs, smoking, non-communicable diseases and the like.

An analysis of multicultural components

An analysis of the objectives and content of these various subjects in the training programme does not reveal a primary concern for multi-cultural education. The principal concern in most of those areas that will subsequently be taught in primary schools (languages, mathematics, environmental studies) is to equip trainees with knowledge about the content and methodology of teaching these subjects in order that they may function effectively as primary school-teachers. It is not surprising that multicultural components are more evident in the one subject where they also appear in the primary school curriculum — environmental studies I (social studies), known as EVS-I.

At the primary school level, one of the aims of this subject is to develop in students an awareness of the existence and the culture of the various groups existing in Mauritius, as well as encouraging a willingness to co-operate with each other through participation in various activities involving cultural events, customs and traditions.

To achieve this aim, the EVS-I course is offered to trainee teachers during four main components: (i) the EVS studies curriculum; (ii) geography; (iii) history; and (iv) sociology. Besides providing students with the knowledge and competencies needed to teach this subject, its main objectives are to help them develop a positive attitude towards the general environment and to adopt attitudes of openness and tolerance towards others through exposure to the rich heritage of the island, as well as to the ways and means by which culture is acquired and is at present being modified.

As the primary textbooks include components on religious festivals and the history of settlement in Mauritius and in the Indian Ocean in general, these topics receive specific attention in the teacher training course. The sociology component provides a more theoretical analysis of the concept of pluralism and attitude development, as well as an insight into various family structures and life-styles. Indeed, one of the stated objectives is 'to make students appreciate the diversity of society' (*Course handbook, 1993–94*, p. 20). However, in educational circles the view is put forward that the curriculum materials offered are quite selective and may portray a biased view of reality. For instance, chapters on religious festivals may only pay lipservice to them.

The only other area in the primary school curriculum where one can see some timid references to multiculturalism is in creative education. The art component expresses its general aim in these terms: 'The course aims at increasing the students' knowledge of the creative arts at primary level *relevant to the socio-economic background* of the primary school in Mauritius' (ibid., p. 38) [our emphasis]. One can deduce at least an intention of considering social background in terms of the cultural reality, although it is clear that the main intention is more to enhance their competencies in the creative arts themselves. However, when the content is analyzed, it does not reveal any clear multicultural dimension since it is expressed in rather broad terms. Emphasis is more on developing specific creative skills: 'The study of form, expression, manipulation and creativity through making different kinds of puppets in various media.'

In 'creative needlecraft', on the other hand, objectives are expressed much more clearly in terms of attitudes which are usually found in multicultural educational programmes. Among a list of eleven objectives, one in particular attracts the attention: 'Develop respect for oneself and others as individuals, and encourage the development of a caring attitude, a sense of values and a sense of responsibility and service towards others' (*Course handbook, 1993-94*, p. 42).

Once again, it is difficult to see from an examination of the content of this course how such an objective is going to be achieved, since the emphasis is more on the study of textiles, fabrics or the methodology of teaching this subject. It is possible that the content of the various disciplines is being expressed more in relation to the cognitive and identifiable aspects of the programme, but that attitudinal objectives are still being fulfilled but not evaluated.

Several other subjects form part of the teacher education programme, but are not actually taught in the primary school, such as 'audio-visual education', 'design and technology', 'educational studies' and 'music'. These courses are intended to equip students with knowledge, skills and attitudes to increase their competencies as professional teachers. It is in 'educational studies' and 'music' that multicultural elements are more apparent and are included formally in the description of the course. Indeed, the word 'multicultural' appears only once in the *Course handbook*, and that is in 'music': 'The course will have a multicultural approach' (p. 45). It aims at providing teachers with basic skills in music with a view to helping them to encourage children enrolled in their classes 'to make music through singing and other related activities'. Although the course is based mainly on a Western-oriented model, the multicultural element is introduced through the use of various instruments, for example 'the tabla', and through musical material derived from the various cultural traditions existing in Mauritius.

Within 'educational studies', the sociology of education course seems to lend itself most to multiculturalism, though a theoretical framework for the analysis of the concept is also provided by other components, such as the psychology of education in its analysis of the socio-affective, linguistic, moral and general personality development of the child. The philosophy of education and comparative education include topics such as 'Society and the school system', 'Social aspects of education' and 'Education, instruction and culture'. In the sociology of education, however, the issue of pluralism is tackled more directly through discussions on 'The social environment of the primary school child, the process of socialization and the role of the teacher in a plural society'. Students are first exposed to a theoretical framework on the concept of pluralism through research carried out in other societies, and an analysis of the issue in Mauritius, but are made to relate it to their profession as teachers. The course generally aims at developing in students an understanding of the socio-cultural context of the primary school child and the teaching/learning process in schools. They are finally encouraged through projects and group discussions to analyze the implications of multiculturalism on their role as teachers.

So far we have analyzed the multicultural elements of our teacher-training programme as evidenced in the *Course handbook* for students. We have seen that although multiculturalism is not a primary aim of the whole programme it does appear quite clearly in some components, such as 'Social studies', 'Educational studies' or 'Music', and in a more implicit way in areas like 'Creative education'. However, as a general rule, the content outlines are expressed in quite broad terms and it is possible that when they are translated into practice, multicultural elements might become more

151

evident. We have therefore considered it more imperative to go more deeply into the 'hidden curriculum' in order to get a more comprehensive picture of the issue. This is what we shall deal with in our next section.

ANALYSIS OF THE CURRICULUM: THE HIDDEN PERSPECTIVE

The other strategy used to analyze the curriculum consisted of structured interviews with individual staff members from all departments involved with the Primary Teachers Training Programme (General Purpose). To ensure standardization, all interviews were carried out by the same person and each lasted about an hour. The interviews were carried out over a two-week period and the purpose of the research was explained to all thirteen staff members who were chosen to participate. These people were selected because: (a) they were involved in the primary training programme; (b) they belonged to a particular ethnic group; and (c) they were available. As far as possible, an attempt was made to select staff members from the three main ethnic groups represented among the staff: Muslims (two persons); general population (five persons); and non-Muslims of Indian origin (six persons). In some cases, this choice was determined by the person's involvement in the training programme or in two cases — audio-visual education (Muslim) and music (general population) — because there was only one person involved.

The interviews explored three main dimensions: (a) the content of the courses offered; (b) the methodology used; and (c) the lecturer's own perception of multicultural education and their expectations from the different cultural groups among that cohort of primary certificate students. There was a mixture of closed and very open questions to allow the interviewees to speak freely on the selected topics. We will now analyze each of these three dimensions.

Course content

The questions asked on this issue dealt with: (a) the selection of content; (b) the selection criteria; (c) whether the same content was taught to all students irrespective of their ethnic origins; (d) whether lecturers felt that pluralism or a multicultural perspective was present in any form in their courses; (e) what type of assignments were given, who chose the topics, and whether they necessitated a knowledge of the various cultures existing in Mauritius.

The objective was to find out whether multicultural elements were incorporated in any part of the curriculum, even in an informal manner. The rationale underlying the first three questions was related to the theory that multiculturalism has essentially to do with the provision of equal opportunities to all students and adaptation of course materials to the perceived needs of individual students (Arora & Duncan, 1986; Banks & Banks, 1989). Question 4 aimed at making respondents reflect on the possible presence of multicultural components in their course through having to explain and apply the content of their subjects in their interaction with students. According to Banks & Banks, effective teaching includes among other characteristics the ability to incorporate the students' cultural background and experiences in order to enhance learning. Although multiculturalism as such may not figure formally in the content of the various syllabi, it could be possible that the lecturers concerned felt that it was necessary to relate their content to the cultural reality of the local context so as to make their teaching more effective and relevant. The last question was also based on the same rationale: students were given a choice in the type of course assignments required and intercultural components were thus indirectly woven into the programme.

Results

The content areas included in the programme have been devised by the staff after collegiate discussions in the departments concerned, except in those cases where only one specialist has been involved (audio-visual and music). All general purpose students follow the same course. The main criteria for selecting the content are: the entry level of the students; the content of the primary school curriculum; the needs of the students as perceived by the lecturers; the needs of the school and society; and the qualities of the teacher it is intended to train. Students rarely have a say in the selection of the content, though there is some flexibility in their choice of assignments, as we shall see later. It is almost universally felt that all students, irrespective of their cultural background, have to be trained to achieve competence in the various subjects offered by the programme. Their competence upon entry is rarely judged in terms of ethnic origin, but rather in terms of whether they have prior knowledge of the subject, and if they do, whether that level is satisfactory. In EVS Science, for example, many students may not possess a scientific background, having only studied science up to the third form of secondary schools. The perceived need in this case is for students to acquire basic concepts in science so that they will be able to grasp the EVS curriculum they will be required to teach.

No ethnic group among the Mauritians stands out from the others because of its lack of scientific training at entry point. However, one group of students is perceived to be relatively weak in many academic subjects: the Rodriguans. They need an intensive upgrading course before they can tackle the programme confidently and, in such courses as the EVS Social Studies, they may experience difficulties due to their unfamiliarity with the multicultural lifestyle of their Mauritian colleagues. They receive special help from volunteers during 'lunch-time tutorials', but there is no real official policy of incorporating their specific cultural experience in the programme. This group is expected to assimilate the content. It must be pointed out, however, that many lecturers feel that there is a need to give special attention to this group. Nevertheless, because of the large number of general purpose students involved (383) and the very tight schedule, they are unable to do so.

In many cases, a multicultural approach is being adopted in the actual teaching of the subjects. Intercultural components are automatically included in the explanations and tasks assigned in an attempt to make the content relevant to the teaching context. This is less true of areas that emphasize the acquisition of skills, such as physical education and design and technology, or in those with a more universal approach, as in pure science or mathematics. Sensitivity to cultural diversity is more apparent in languages, health and nutrition, creative education and audio-visual education.

Both the English and French departments aim mainly at developing specific skills pertaining to these languages, but when dealing with comprehension, the choice of texts for English reflects the intercultural richness of its heritage. The same applies to French when students are trained in 'exploitation des thèmes' for the development of oral skills during the methodology component. Texts on festivals or cultural traditions give rise to discussions on pluralism and even to gender, racism and ethnicity.

Health and nutrition, which forms part of the EVS Science component, inevitably draws on the cultures of different ethnic groups as far as eating habits are concerned. The department is especially sensitive to the intercultural issue and, while teaching about 'balanced meals', cannot ignore the fact that there are vegetarians and non-vegetarians, and that food taboos exist for some cultures. The cultural dimension is integrated informally into the content during discussions. For instance, in a lesson on various ways of preparing food, students were encouraged to share and discuss how each ethnic group cooked rice. The cognitive concern was to help students acquire knowledge about nutrition, but the affective aim was to develop a sense of respect for cultures other than one's own and to encourage the sharing of cultural experience. Student participation in this type of discussion is high and enthusiastic.

Likewise, the creative education component, while developing specific skills and aesthetic values, carefully weaves multicultural elements into its programme. A topic like 'stained glass', for example, naturally leads to its presence in Catholic churches which, in turn, broadens into a general discussion of places of worship, their architecture, design, use of colours and so on. A particular example of cultural sensitivity is the avoidance of hair to make paint brushes and avoiding images of the pig, in deference to certain beliefs in the Muslim faith. Attitudes of respect and tolerance towards other cultures are encouraged without the students feeling that the culture of others is being imposed on them.

Positive knowledge of cultural diversity is also revealed in the type of assignments that students are encouraged to undertake. In the more academic fields, they take the form of projects or essay writing, thus broadening their knowledge of cultural practices and life-styles of the various ethnic groups in Mauritius. Social studies and the sociology of education, for instance, encourage students to investigate festivals or socialization patterns in cultural groups other than their own. Creative needlecraft involves students in making greetings cards for different cultural occasions, like Divali, Eid or Christmas. Free composition in art may represent Indian, Muslim or Catholic weddings. An interesting example comes from the audio-visual education course. Each student is asked to work with one child, preferably from a cultural group other than their own. They are then required to experiment by teaching a specific skill to that child, to evaluate whether the chosen skill was adapted to the child's level of maturity and background, and relate the experience to his colleagues in the class. In the process, the student becomes intimately acquainted with at least one aspect of the cultural life of the context he or she has chosen.

We shall conclude this section with a brief reference to one component which does not figure in the training curriculum, but which also helps to develop a multicultural attitude among students, namely the tutorials or activities taking place twice a week. Students normally follow lectures by guest speakers on selected issues such as drug education, or they are divided into groups for tutorials. They normally select the group they want to join according to their own interests. One such tutorial group was run on 'values' for one term and was selected by two groups of eighty ethnically-mixed students. The tutorial entailed the discussion of religious as well as general values, and the strategies that can be used for teaching them. While the content was not primarily multicultural in itself, the discussions sharpened the students' cultural sensitivity (the dominant theme was 'Create a space for everyone') and the high level of participation was indicative of students' interest in this affective domain.

A dual strategy is being adopted on the curriculum: formal and informal. Some areas address themselves directly to multiculturalism and try to clarify the concept of pluralism by imparting knowledge about the cultures existing in Mauritius. However, an interdisciplinary approach is also evident in that such knowledge is intricately woven in most areas across the curriculum but in a less formal manner. The only group whose cultural experience is excluded from the curriculum is the Rodriguans.

METHODS TO DEVELOP INTERCULTURAL EDUCATION

Structured interviews were also used to investigate this dimension. While conscious of the fact that this may not be the best strategy to find out what methods are being used to develop the capacity for intercultural education, we were limited by time constraints and by the fact that students would be on teaching practice for one term. We were fortunate, however, in that the conclusions can be checked against the findings of an on-going evaluation of the Primary Teachers' Certificate Programme (Nankoo, Raghoonundun & Veerapen, 1994), which contains a detailed analysis of the methodology based on observation and questionnaires.

In our interviews, the respondents were asked to:
1. Describe the various teaching strategies they normally used.
2. Pinpoint the ones they thought were more appropriate to enhance intercultural education.
3. If group work was a technique, describe how the groups were formed.
4. State whether it was possible to consider individual learning rates.
5. State whether students were given the opportunity to be responsible for their own learning and develop their critical thinking; describe the methods used in this connection.

It must be pointed out at the outset that, since multicultural education was not a primary objective in many fields of study, the methods used had not been devised with this purpose in mind. Their principal aim was increasing teacher effectiveness and enhancing learning. However, as pointed out by Larke (1992), with the proliferation of diverse classrooms in the 1990s: '. . . considerations of race/ethnicity and equity are essential characteristics of effective teachers'. In other words, and particularly in Mauritius, an effective teacher nowadays cannot afford to ignore the multicultural perspective in education. It is for this reason that we consider this study on the methods used for teacher training at the MIE as still relevant, although these methods were not primarily designed with an intercultural objective. The aim was to find out whether students were offered a variety of methods which they could use according to the diverse contexts and needs they would face in the classroom. As Larke (1992) points out, such teachers are those 'possessing a wealth of instructional strategies for diverse classrooms, such as co-operative grouping, mastery learning or experiential learning'.

'Co-operative grouping', we felt, was an interesting dimension to investigate further, in that it seems particularly effective in developing cohesion among different cultural groups, and possibly could enable the tutor to provide individual attention when needed.

Another important approach to be imbedded in a programme geared towards multiculturalism, according to Burger (1994), is one that is learner-centred, one that 'values and encourages individual thinking, but discourages dominance, conformity and subservience'. He advocated, among other measures, the necessity for 'individualized learning' and that students should be made responsible for 'what they study, when they study it and how to study it'. In such programmes, the tutor's role is more that of a facilitator, a manager of the learning process, rather than the traditional 'guru', the only source or reservoir of knowledge. In this context, our last question attempted to find out if self-learning experiences were being provided to students and how they were being encouraged to think critically.

Results

Most lecturers felt that they were limited in their choice of methods by the very circumstances in which the training course was being carried out. Eight groups of between thirty and sixty students were being run concurrently during the week with limited staff. This did not leave much room for alternative action, however imaginative the lecturer and willing to innovate or experiment! An acute lack of resources in terms of equipment, transport and library facilities (the library could only accommodate thirty-eight students at a time!) puts further constraints on the lecturers' choice of methods.

However, our investigations reveal that, in spite of these constraints, students *are* being exposed to a variety of teaching strategies. These range from lectures, demonstrations, brainstorming, group work, practical work, project or field work, to discussions, peer-teaching, video and slide projections, questioning and case studies. In general, the more 'academic' subjects, such as languages, mathematics, EVS or educational studies, tended to rely more on lectures, discussions and brainstorming, while the other areas seemed to use demonstrations and activity-based learning methods, with a higher incidence of practical work.

The study by Nankoo, Raghoonundun and Veerapen (1994) provides a detailed quantitative analysis of the frequency with which each series of methods is being used in the various disciplines. Their results are based on systematic observation, as well as questionnaires, and are consistent with the responses obtained in our individual interviews. But their significance for our study is that they also reveal that, by the end of the course, students have been exposed to a wealth of instructional strategies which they can employ in the classroom. It must be added that, while being exposed to the actual methods during instruction, students receive a more theoretical basis for using the various teaching strategies and classroom management skills in the different methodology courses as well as the 'social psychology of teaching' within educational studies. Furthermore, when dealing with topics such as 'teacher expectations' or 'non-verbal communication', students are made to reflect upon their own expectations of their pupils, who come from various social and economic backgrounds, and thus become aware of the possibility that, even unconsciously, they might be prejudiced.

One method which all the lecturers interviewed seemed to favour was group work. This is confirmed by the study of Nankoo et al. (1994), which shows that in the sixty-six sessions observed, this method was being used on forty-one occasions. It is also true to say, however, that group work may have been used more to encourage student involvement and as a means to provide individual attention in the context of large groups, rather than out of a desire to develop cultural integration. Nevertheless, all respondents singled out group work as one of the most effective methods in multicultural settings.

The way in which students were allocated to particular groups were in most cases by the students' own choice, often determined by such factors as geographical or sex grouping, or interest in a particular subject. Only in the science courses did the lecturer insist that the group leader be someone with a scientific background, whenever possible. On no occasion was ethnicity determinant in grouping, with the exception of social studies, where the lecturer insisted that a group of students doing a project on, say, a Muslim festival should consist mainly of non-Muslims. Indeed, all the interviewees saw this method as conducive to multicultural understanding precisely because it provided students with the opportunity to work with colleagues of diverse backgrounds.

The group usually focuses on the assigned task with the desire to succeed. The team spirit thus engendered very often results in close friendship and a natural cohesion, respect and tolerance. It is interesting to note that co-operative grouping in creative needlecraft was seen as one instance where it was possible to develop mutual understanding between Mauritian and Rodriguan students through sharing each other's cultural experiences. It was also quite effective in building up communication skills — as in puppetry, where each group had to improvise dramatized sketches in front of the whole class.

The other two dimensions investigated by the final questions were self-learning and critical thinking skills, and the methods used to promote them. Our respondents once again stated that they felt limited by the large size of the groups and the time constraints, but saw discussion and brainstorming, together with the project method, practical and field work as the most appropriate for sharpening these same skills in the students. The use of these methods varies according to the nature of the disciplines taught. Practical work and projects are used more often in areas like creative education, design and technology, or physical education. They can be carried out either on an individual basis or in groups, and aim at making the students directly responsible for their own learning. In design and technology, for instance, each student has to choose a project — such as the making of an educational toy — and justify the making of that particular article through a survey of different toys, carry out an evaluation of its relevance, costs, feasibility and viability, select one idea from a series of possibilities, and then translate it from the abstract to the concrete by designing it and making it in a creative and original manner.

In creative education, each student is required to present a portfolio of all the work completed during the course. This work is presented to the class, discussed and evaluated. The primary objective is to enable students 'to develop respect for other people's work', and at the same time to view one's own work in a critical and responsible way. The work of the whole group is then mounted in an exhibition, the purpose being to achieve a sense of pride for one's work among the students. 'Individualized learning' is stressed by these approaches, so that all students are able to express themselves at their own pace in an imaginative and creative manner. The staff also sees this as one of the rare opportunities to give individual attention to the students, to develop a more meaningful relationship with them, while helping them to develop their own self-esteem.

An interesting example of 'practical work' was given to us during movement education. Students were asked to come up with as many ways as possible of travelling with a ball across a certain distance. The most original and imaginative suggestions were made, such as crawling backwards or pushing the ball with one's nose or elbow. Apart from all the fun and amusement involved, the purpose of the exercise, we were told, was to make students realize that there could be no 'winner', and each way of doing the exercise was valid, even if different. One of the central themes of multicultural education — respect for difference — was being transmitted here in a most enjoyable and effective manner.

Discussion and brainstorming were also seen as two strategies that encouraged critical thinking, either in small groups or with the whole class. The field of educational studies lends itself particularly to this kind of exercise. Students are encouraged to analyze issues in an objective manner and to assess the relevance of pedagogical theories based on their experience. In the sociology of education, where multicultural issues are dealt with more directly, the seminar approach seems to encourage more open discussions and a clearer willingness to share cultural experience. The philosophy of education 'is critical thinking', we were told, in that the major aim of the discipline is to make students realize that there is 'no one or absolute truth'. Any particular issue discussed during the philosophy of education is merely a pretext to develop the 'philosophical mind' and 'thinking skills'.

The development of logical and scientific modes of thinking is also the specific objective of the mathematics and science courses, achieved through discussion, experimentation and field work. It is evident that none of the methods employed so far is ever used in isolation, but rather in parallel according to need. For instance, a project leading to field work may start with a brainstorming session, followed by group discussion and personal research in the library, before any data is actually collected in the field. Individual self-learning habits, critical thinking, co-operative grouping and communication skills may all receive stimulation in the context of a single project.

Field work, it was felt, helps students to develop objectivity since the results are based on the observation of facts. It develops their critical thinking in that they are expected to make an analysis of the observed facts and synthesize them into a comprehensive picture of the phenomenon being studied. Individualized learning is enhanced, the students' involvement in their own learning is maximized, and the tutor acts more like a moderator or facilitator than the sole reservoir of knowledge. An interesting remark made to us by a science tutor was that the *process* of learning and the evidence of autonomous learning skills were considered student achievements as important as the actual findings of the study when it came to evaluating the project.

Conclusion

Our analysis of the methodology used in teacher training has revealed that, in general, teaching strategies were not designed specifically for the purpose of achieving multicultural education. This is possibly because the need was never perceived since there is already great cultural congruence in Mauritian society, as well as among the students. However, students were being exposed to a wide range of instructional strategies which could apply to a multicultural context.

Among these, co-operative grouping seemed to be most effective in achieving cultural cohesion. Such strategies encouraged student involvement, the development of critical thinking and self-learning techniques, and ranged from practical and project work to field work, discussion and brain-storming. Although these methods are used with varying frequency according to the subject being taught, they are used across the curriculum and are therefore being reinforced. Finally, intercultural education may achieve more when it is woven in an informal and natural way into the students' daily lives rather than when it is being imposed. To use Bourdieu's phrase (Bourdieu & Passeron, 1966), it is *une culture acquise sans effort ni intention, comme par osmose* [it is a culture acquired with neither effort nor intention, like a second skin] that stays with the individual for life.

IDENTIFICATION AND ANALYSIS OF SUCCESSFUL EXPERIENCES IN TEACHER TRAINING FOR INTERCULTURAL EDUCATION

It is obvious from our analysis of the curriculum and methodology that no teacher training programme exists in Mauritius specifically designed to develop intercultural education. Yet it is also apparent to any observer that students from various ethnic groups do not show any signs of racial or cultural conflict, but rather a spirit of tolerance, respect and understanding for different cultures. They seem to have assumed their own culture in a natural manner and accept in a similar way the cultural differences of their colleagues.

Evidence of this comes from a concert presented by the students on 'Music Day'. The show included a wide variety of songs, dances and sketches drawn from the various musical traditions existing in Mauritius. It was possible to see there a lady from the general population dressed in a sari and singing an oriental song quite naturally, and a Muslim student equally convincingly performing a *sega* in Creole.

It seems that the objectives of multicultural education are being achieved spontaneously. It seemed worthwhile, therefore, in this section to try to understand how such cultural cohesion has come to the fore in the training programme.

We must point out immediately that we cannot claim that the multicultu-ralism displayed by the students is the unique outcome of the training experience. To make such a claim would have required pre- and post-training verification, which was impossible as the present research started in the middle of the training course. Furthermore, all students are subjected to multicultural experiences in the outside society while attending the MIE. As pointed out by Gayan and Thancanamootoo at a paper presented to the International Conference on Multicultural Tertiary Education (South Africa, April 1994): 'Radio and television ensure daily the exposure to several languages, styles of fashion, the diverse musical traditions and ways of thinking characteristic of the different cultures existing here.'

Our students have also received a certain amount of multicultural training during their own schooling, since multicultural components have been integrated into both the primary and secondary curricula in order to 'Mauritianize' them. It is therefore quite difficult to isolate any training factor from all the others in order to prove that it is the one variable resulting in cultural congruence. However, it is quite possible to study those aspects of the training experience which *consolidate* the intercultural 'respect for difference' that seems to be a 'core value' of all Mauritians, to use Moore's (1984) phrase. Our investigation has therefore been directed to this end and has been based on a dual approach: participant observation and structured interviews with the same sample of thirteen lecturers involved in the Primary Teacher Training Course for general-purpose students.

Our first proposal is derived to some extent from our analysis of the curriculum and methodology of teacher training carried out at the MIE. We believe that multicultural education is effectively achieved because an interdisciplinary approach is adopted, rather than a mere course on cultural matters being attached to the programme. This is the view of McClelland and Varma (1989):

We believe that all initial teacher training courses, both PGCE and B.Ed., should be permeated with the principles underlying a genuine pluralist approach to education. All providers of in-service training should ensure that the courses they offer have this pluralist perspective.

The benefit of such an approach is that the integration of cultural components in the various subjects ensures that the learners do not feel a sense of cultural imposition and therefore are not inclined to offer resistance to them. They are all the more readily accepted when they are incidental to the main learning tasks. It is quite possible that the success of the multicultural programme is due to the fact that those participating in it are not aware that multiculturalism is a primary objective. Our experience seems to confirm Bourdieu's theory of learning *sans effort ni intention* [with neither effort nor intention] as the most effective in the cultural domain. Students seem to accept multicultural components perhaps because they are presented in an informal and natural manner, as and when the need is felt.

The same principle applies to the methods being used in multicultural education. Co-operative grouping was most effective in this context precisely because it placed students in a diverse cultural situation, but concentrated their efforts towards the achievement of the particular academic task in hand. The resulting cultural interaction and group dynamics were not perceived as the primary objectives and, since they were incidental to the learning task, their effect was strengthened. It is common knowledge that the impact of the hidden curriculum is more lasting than that of the formal curriculum, and that attitudes and values are 'caught rather than taught'. The informal approach, whereby cultural components are skillfully woven into the process of explaining a particular concept — as in creative education or science — seems more adapted to the transmission of desirable attitudes. They are more readily accepted because they are seen as *relevant* to the explanation and to the students' needs. If the strategy had been too obvious or artificial, especially on culturally sensitive issues, the contrary effect might have been produced and resistance provoked.

Our next major assumption is that teacher training for intercultural education is more effective when the teacher trainers themselves have internalized the positive attitudes towards cultural differences and themselves provide role models for the trainees. Multicultural education is perhaps essentially an *affective* enterprise as much as a cognitive one. In such a sensitive area the attitudes of the trainer are as important as his/her knowledge of diverse cultures. As pointed out by Burger (1994): 'No lecturer can teach this attitude [multiculturalism] to his students if he does not possess it himself.'

Our investigations therefore attempted to study the trainers' own attitudes towards their students, their perception and expectations of the different groups and their views about the issue of multicultural education in Mauritius. Our findings are essentially based on the interviewees' responses to our questions. The weakness of such an approach is that it is difficult to establish the sincerity or validity of the responses, which could reflect what the respondents consider to be a politically correct answer. The relevance of the responses to the different questions was therefore continuously verified in an effort to ensure validity. We also verified them against the responses on content and methodology to see whether there was some congruence between attitudes, perception, and their translation into concrete terms.

The respondents were asked:

1. Whether they felt that cultural issues should be discussed with students or ignored altogether.
2. Whether multicultural education involved any specific training in terms of knowledge, skills and attitudes for the students.
3. Whether the same teaching strategies should be used for the various ethnic groups among the students.
4. Which ethnic group of students did they feel performed better, and why.
5. Which group showed the least achievement and why.

Our objective in the first three questions was to check the respondents' sensitivity to the issue of multicultural education as a whole, and their awareness of what it implied for their own work as trainers. As Arora and Duncan (1986, p. 49) argue: 'Multicultural education is as much attitude as it is a pack of materials or a set of ideas. It is a whole curriculum which involves an attitude to life'.

In the second set of questions, our objective was to study the trainers' perceptions and expectations of the diverse groups they were teaching. A fundamental principle in multicultural education, in Brophy and Good's view (1986), is that teachers 'do not expect all students to make progress at the same pace, but expect all students to know the basic skills or to meet at least the minimum specified objectives' (quoted in Larke, 1992). They do not, in other words, expect students to differ in achievement because of their race or ethnic background. They should show the same concern for all students and should be 'able to interact positively with students whose ethnic backgrounds are different from their own' (ibid.).

The responses to the last question could give us an indication of the lecturers' perception of particular ethnic groups in terms of performance and thereby show whether their expectations were, in fact, determined by ethnicity.

Results

At a conceptual level, views were somewhat divided on the desirability of discussing cultural issues. At least four respondents preferred either to ignore the issue or to discuss it only when the need arises. One of them felt that he himself lacked the proper training to tackle such issues: he was apprehensive that such discussions might result in creating more conflict than understanding, and that students might feel obliged to project and defend their culture in the face of the others. It comes as no surprise that the reservations expressed above occurred in those areas of the training curriculum where cultural elements were less apparent: physical education; audio-visual education; design and technology; and mathematics.

The great majority of respondents, however, felt that discussion of multicultural issues was essential because it formed part of reality. In visual arts, for instance, the view expressed was that multicultural education should form part of the entire curriculum and students should be trained to be 'sensitive to difference', in order to eradicate prejudice. The creative needlecraft respondent saw such education as a necessity in order to develop tolerance and respect for others. Some felt that these issues were best tackled in disciplines other than their own, but that they should still have a place in the curriculum since future teachers need to develop an under-standing, an acknowledgment and an appreciation of cultural differences if they are to function effectively at the classroom level. One language department went even further and added that not only culture but racism and sexism should also be tackled during teacher training, since much contem-porary literature deals with these issues. When these findings were checked against content and methodology, those respondents who were convinced of the necessity to discuss such issues were generally involved with the same areas of the teacher-training curriculum where multicultural components were found. This congruence between the ideational and the behavioural confirms our assumptions that the beliefs and convictions of the trainer are determinant in achieving multicultural objectives.

Most respondents also felt that training in multicultural education involved essentially the development of desirable attitudes and, to some extent, this could be achieved by the acquisition of knowledge about the diverse cultural traditions of our country. Again, although most agreed with the necessity of such training, some respondents (mathematics, physical education, audiovisual and science) stated that it was best tackled in disciplines other than their own, since such issues were not particularly relevant to their principal objectives which were more geared to the acquisition of specific concepts or skills relating to their subject. However, these same respondents felt that the encouragement of group work could perhaps informally foster those skills required in achieving integration among cultural groups. It is interesting to note that one respondent, who was apprehensive but not averse to the idea of multicultural training, expressed the view that the trainer was the one whose training needed to be broadened before he/she could confidently try to integrate it into that discipline. Once this training had been received, he felt that there were distinct possibilities for such integration, for example students could choose to work on a model of a temple, church or mosque as a project, or on different styles of furniture drawn from different cultural traditions. The process of making such models would inevitably make students appreciate in very concrete terms the variety of architectural designs or styles, and thereby enhance respect and tolerance for cultural difference.

In all the other areas, the need to train students to develop positive attitudes toward cultural differences was quite strongly emphasized. Respondents saw this objective best achieved by providing students with knowledge of the different cultures and ways of life, either in a formal manner by including them in particular disciplines such as the sociology of education or social studies, or more directly by integrating such components across the whole curriculum. It was further emphasized that students needed to develop an *in-depth* rather than superficial understanding of the different cultures in order to be able to develop the versatility needed to teach in diverse contexts. It was unanimously felt that the most desirable attitudes in the Mauritian context were openness, tolerance, respect and care. One respondent further stressed that, in order for such training to be effective, the trainer needed to be an 'integrating factor' by internalizing such attitudes and acting as a role model for the students.

In terms of teaching strategies, the unanimous view was that students should be differentiated more by their academic level than their ethnic origins, since all students were expected to achieve the same objectives and were exposed to the same curriculum. It was felt that those students who were experiencing difficulties in learning should be given individual attention during tutorials wherever possible. Ability was not generally determined by the students' ethnic group.

This result was further confirmed by the responses to our second set of questions. Almost all those interviewed maintained that high performance was not determined by ethnic belonging, but rather by other factors, such as the secondary school attended, the entry level of students, students' aptitude or previous knowledge of the subject or, in some cases, their sex. Most respondents found it difficult to pinpoint one specific ethnic group as consisting of high achievers, with the one exception that will be discussed later. However, trainers' expectations and perceptions of students differed according to their department. In areas that did not require a prior knowledge of the subject, like music, audiovisual, design and technology or creative education, lecturers did not expect students to show different abilities since they all had to 'start from scratch'. Differentiation, if any, was perceived more in terms of special individual aptitudes, but not at all in terms of ethnic origin.

In other disciplines, it was the entry level of students that influenced the trainers' perceptions: the language department felt that all students had the same linguistic problems; mathematics and science were more interested in the mathematical or scientific background of students; EVS (social studies) found girls more involved and participating than boys. In only one case did the interviewee mention a specific group as being more proficient than others: the 'Rodriguan group' was acknowledged as the highest achiever in physical education. The reasons given for this performance were that blacks are better motivated for sport and are more physically fit than other groups. This remark is interesting in that, while there was no perception of differential ability on ethnic lines among Mauritians, the Rodriguans are seen as a distinct ethnic group, even though they belong to the general population category, which includes many Mauritian students as well.

This perception of the Rodriguans became more evident in the responses to our last question about which group was seen as the lowest achievers. Nine departments identified Rodriguans as a distinct group showing the lowest ability, for various reasons: lack of interest; low participation; no skill in open discussion; shyness; low academic level. Other justifications for this situation included their difficulty in adjusting to a different context, their lack of material facilities, their isolation and alienation from their Mauritian counterparts. One respondent even saw them as anti-Asian or hostile to mainland Mauritians. However, in design and technology, music and audiovisual education they were judged to be as equally proficient or committed as other students. As mentioned earlier, in physical education they were considered better than other students. Again, in physical education ethnicity was seen to determine ability, as Asian students were generally viewed as less proficient. However, in parts of the teacher-training course involving theory, Rodriguans were less able to grasp concepts than other groups, possibly because of educational or economic disadvantage. This distinction is further confirmed when we compare the two sets of respondents who viewed Rodriguans in terms of ability: in the more academic subjects, the Rodriguans were low achievers; in the more skill-oriented areas they were perceived as performing equally well or better than others.

Our findings seem to confirm our hypothesis that the attitudes and expectations of the trainers themselves are very often determinant in the success of multicultural education. The general cohesion and mutual tolerance among Mauritian students is reflected in the trainers' own positive attitudes towards the different cultural groups in Mauritius. It is possible that, as Mauritians, they share with their students a 'fundamental world view', though they 'may still differ in cultural manifestations, such as dress, gestures or vocabulary (Sohn, 1994). This 'fundamental world view' includes mutual respect for culturally different groups in Mauritius and is evident in the trainers' conviction about the need to incorporate such values in the teacher-training programme. Among Mauritian students and trainers there is a sense of 'shared identity' (Jackson, 1986), because, in spite of different cultural manifestations, they share a common cultural experience and it is quite easy for trainers to 'understand the nuances of context in students' behaviour' (Noordhoff & Kleinfeld, 1993). Since their expectations of Mauritian students are not generally influenced by ethnicity, but by other factors such as entry level, aptitude or secondary school attended, it becomes clear that they do not 'expect all students to know the basic skills or to meet at least the minimum specified objectives' (Larke, 1992) irrespective of their cultural background. It is consequently quite possible that the trainers' own attitudes and convictions are being transmitted in their daily interactions with students. They are evidently successful in achieving multicultural objectives in the case of Mauritian students, but definitely less so as far as Rodriguan students are concerned, precisely because their own perceptions towards this group are rather negative. The Rodriguan group may experience a sense of isolation or exclusion because these same perceptions may have been unconsciously transmitted to the Mauritian students.

Some respondents pointed out that, since they were trainers themselves, they did not know much about the Rodriguan students' background and culture, except what they could glean from the media on rare occasions, and consequently they found it difficult to integrate these students into the programme. Others stated that sheer lack of time and resources, and the large size of groups acted as deterrents to such integration. It is also evident that where lecturers' expectations or perceptions were positive, as in physical education or music, Rodriguan students seemed to find it less difficult to perform well. It would have been useful to investigate the students' own feelings, but time constraints did not permit us to do so.

CONCLUSION

Our study of attitudes and perceptions among teacher trainers has revealed some quite interesting facts about teacher training in a multicultural setting. The interdisciplinary approach, combined with the inclusion of specific cultural components in the social sciences, was found to be particularly adapted to this type of context. In terms of teaching strategies, informal and indirect strategies — where multiculturalism seemed almost incidental to the main academic tasks — seemed to promote the desirable attitudes and values.

But, most importantly, the curriculum and teaching strategies will only be effective if the trainers themselves have internalized positive attitudes about cultural differences and are willing to acquire the knowledge needed to embrace other people's cultures. In other words, the training of trainers is a prerequisite for the success of any multicultural teacher education programme. Finally, the promotion of multicultural values among teachers may be accelerated if the education sector is adequately supported at the societal level by the media and if there is a political will to encourage cultural understanding and tolerance.

REFERENCES

Arora, R; Duncan, C. 1986. *Multicultural education: towards good practice*. London; New York, Routledge & Kegan Paul.

Baker, P. 1976. *Towards a social history of Mauritian Creole*. York, United Kingdom., University of York. (Unpublished doctoral dissertation.)

Banks, J.A.; Banks, C.A. 1989. *Multicultural education: issues and perspectives*. Boston, Allyn & Bacon.

Barz, R.K. 1980. The cultural significance of Hindi in Mauritius. *South Asian studies* (London), Vol. 3, No. 1, p. 1-13.

Beaton, P. 1854. *Creoles and Coolies or five years in Mauritius*. London.

Bernardin de St. Pierre, J.H. 1773. *Voyage à L'Ile de France* [Voyage to the Ile de France]. Vol. 1. Paris, Découverte, 1983.

Brookfield, H.C. 1958. Pluralism and geography in Mauritius. *Geographical studies* (London), Vol. 5, No. 1, p. 3-19.

Brophy, J.; Good, T. 1986. Teacher behaviour and student achievement. *In:* Wittrock, M., ed. *Handbook of research on teaching*. New York, Macmillan.

Bourdieu, P.; Passeron, J. 1966. *Les Héritiers* [The Inheritors]. Paris, Editions de Minuit.

Burger, A. 1994. *Easing the transition from mono to multicultural education: the role academic staff development can play at the Vaal Triayle Technikon*. (Paper presented at the International Conference on Multicultural Tertiary Education, South Africa, April 1994.)

Course handbook. 1993-1994: Teacher's certificate--Primary. General purpose. Port Louis, Mauritius Institute of Education.

Furnival, J.S. 1988. *Colonial theory and practice*. Cambridge, Cambridge University Press.

Gayan, S,; Thancanamootoo, S. 1994. *Multiculturalism and education: the Mauritian perspective*. (Paper presented at the International Conference on Multicultural Tertiary Education, South Africa, April 1994.)

Haraksingh, K. 1988. Structure, process and Indian culture in Trinidad. *Immigrants & Minorities* (London), No. 17, p. 113-22.

Jackson, P. 1986. *The practice of teaching*. New York, Teachers College Press.

Jayawardena, C. 1966. Religious beliefs and social change. *Comparative studies in society and history* (Cambridge), Vol. 8, p. 211-40.

——.1980. Culture and ethnicity in Guyana and Fiji. *Man* (London), Vol. 15 (n.s.), p. 936-50.

Jumeer, M. 1984. Les affranchis et les Indiens libre au 18eme siècle (1721-1803.) [The freemen and free Indians in the eighteenth century]. Poitiers, France, University of Poitiers. (Unpublished doctoral dissertation.)

Jeffcoate, R. 1976. Curriculum planning in multiracial education. *Educational research* (NFER, Windsor, United Kingdom), Vol. 18, No. 3, June.

Kuczynski, R.R. 1949. *Demographic survey of the British colonial empire.* Vol. II, p. 707-805. London, Kelley.

Larke, P. 1992. Effective multicultural teachers: meeting the challenges of diverse classrooms. *Equity and excellence* (Westport, CT). Vol. 25, Nos. 2-4, p. 133-38.

McClelland, V.; Varma, N. 1989. *Advances in teacher education.* London, Routledge.

Moore, J. 1984. Exporting European core values: British and French influences on education in Mauritius. *European journal of education* (Abingdon, United Kingdom), Vol. 19, No. 1, p. 39-52.

Nankoo, J.; Raghoonundun, N.; Veerapen, T. 1994. *Evaluation of primary school certificate programme.* Port Louis, Mauritius Institute of Education.

Napal, D. 1962. *Les constitutions de l'Ile Maurice* [The constitutions of Mauritius]. Port Louis, Mauritius. (Archives Publication 6).

Noordhoff, K.; Kleinfeld, J. 1993. Preparing teachers for multicultural classrooms. *Teaching and teacher education* (Oxford), Vol. 9, No. 1.

Ramyead, L.P. 1985. *The establishment and cultivation of modern standard Hindi in Mauritius.* Moka, Mahatma Gandhi Press.

Simmons, A. 1976. Class or communalism? A study of the politics of Creoles in Mauritius. *In:* Rotberg, R.I.; Kitson, eds. *African diaspora.* Cambridge, Harvard University Press.

Smith, M.G. 1965. *The plural society in the British West Indies.* Berkeley, University of California Press.

Smolicz, J.J. 1988. Tradition, core values and inter-cultural development in societies. *Ethnic and racial studies* (London), Vol. 11, No. 4.

Sohn, J. 1994. *The need for a multicultural perspective in education.* (Paper presented at the International Conference on Multicultural Tertiary Education, South Africa, April 1994.)

Stein, P. 1982. *Connaissance et emploi des langues à l'Ile Maurice* [Knowledge and the use of language in Mauritius]. Hamburg, Burke.

Toussaint, A. 1974. *The role of trade in the peopling of Mauritius.* Paris, UNESCO. (Paper presented at the Meeting of Experts on Historical Contacts between East Africa and Madagascar on the One Hand, and South East Asia on the Other, 13 May 1972.)

CHAPTER IX

Teachers and multicultural education in Poland

Andrzej Janowski

INTRODUCTORY COMMENTS

The comment with which I will begin the present article is not very encouraging: that very little knowledge of multicultural education in Poland can be gained from the IBE questionnaire. The reasons are twofold: first, there is hardly any multicultural education in Poland; second, what exists is not discernible from mass questionnaires of the kind supplied.

I hope that what will follow will make it clear why I am expressing such views here.

I have decided to supplement the present article with an overview of Poland's national minorities and of the status of minority education because I believe the situation may otherwise be difficult to understand. A careful reader will be able to draw two conclusions:

– Nationality-wise, Poland is a highly homogenous country, with no more than three to four per cent of its population constituting minorities. Indeed, the percentage cannot be calculated precisely, for there is no obligation to disclose nationality in official documents. Hence, estimates must be used.

– A measure of the demand for teaching in a minority language is the size of this minority. All told, there are just over 200 minority language teachers throughout Poland. To put this in context, the whole Polish system of education employs approximately 600,000 teachers.

Given the numbers of minority language teachers, schools (170) and pupils (just under 12,000) it is obvious that not many new teachers are being trained to teach minority languages. Furthermore, the fact that there are five minorities and that they are dispersed all over the country makes it impractical for a single institution to train a large number of students to work in minority-oriented schools.

Elementary school teachers (who teach the first three or four primary school grades) are trained in two ways in Poland: they can take a five-year Master degree course in elementary education at universities or higher schools of education, or they can take shorter, more practice-oriented three-year Bachelor degree courses at universities, higher schools of education or at an independent (although provided with assistance) Teachers' College of Elementary Education. At present, elementary education courses, sometimes combined with pre-school education courses, are offered by twenty-one universities and higher schools of education. 14,000 students are currently enrolled, including 2,500 in their final year. There are seventeen Teachers' Colleges of Elementary Education, where there are a total of 1,000 students in the first year, 500 in the second year and a small number in the final third year (the majority of the colleges only opened in autumn 1992).

No colleges or universities in Poland train elementary school teachers to work with minority pupils. The obvious reason is the small extent of minority schooling. The question arises, therefore, as to the training received by prospective teachers of minority pupils.

First, these teachers may be graduates of language and literature studies. Although in the course of these studies they receive a certain educational background, it is more useful in teaching older rather than young children.

Second, they may be graduates of institutions that train teachers for Polish schools. It is assumed that they know their native, minority language from home, and will perfect it in a minority language teacher association or through training in the region where the language is spoken.

The demand for minority language instruction varies greatly from minority to minority.

PROFILES OF POLAND'S MINORITIES

Germans

Germans constitute Poland's largest minority. Before the political changes of 1989, Polish authorities recognized them officially not as Germans but as 'indigenous people', which implied they were of Polish origin and although Germanized, Polish 'in essence'. It was believed that efforts should be made to re-Polonize them instead of enabling them to use the rights of a national minority. The educational system in the regions inhabited by Germans did not even provide for the learning of German as a foreign language. In the wake of the political transformations of 1989, some people openly declared themselves German. Many of them could not speak German, because there had been no one to teach them, and their children had been denied the opportunity to go to a German-language school. In this situation the priority was to give them a chance to learn the basics of the German language and only afterwards think about instruction in this language. Thus, in the school year 1990-91, courses of German were offered to older primary school pupils, a three-year course at a German Language Teachers' College was opened in Opole, and the Department of German Studies was established at Opole's Higher School of Education. The demand for German language teachers was in part satisfied by teachers arriving from Germany.

I have included all these details in order to show the circumstances that have led to the sizeable and highly nationally-aware German community expecting more than just lessons in German. The German community is now waiting for schools with German as the language of instruction and once its basic needs are satisfied, it will probably seek to have German language kindergartens.

Belarusians

Although a large community, Belarusians seem to have problems with self-identification. They believe themselves threatened with Polonization, even though the authorities have taken no such action. In fact, Polonization takes place with abandonment of the traditional Belarusian rural environment and the move to large cities, where young Belarusians melt into the Polish community. Two factors seem to intensify the Belarusians' self-identification problem:

– Different language and peasant cultural models are combined with a different religion. Whereas most Poles are Catholic, Belarusians have very close ties with the Orthodox Church.
– The Belarusian language does not have a very strong position in the Republic of Belarus. In the 1980s, most of the Belarus population spoke Russian, while Belarusian had disappeared from schools. Now Belarusian is being revived, but its diversity slows down the process.

These two factors, as well as the absence of strong traditions of organization and the low financial standing of the community, result in Belarusians making poor use of the opportunities afforded by the current educational laws. No attempts, for instance, have been made to establish a chain of schools with Belarusian as the language of instruction. Hence there is little demand for elementary school teachers who can instruct in Belarusian. An observer has the impression that this community identifies more with the Orthodox religion than with Belarus.

Ukrainians

Ukrainians are today a minority, but once formed a compact community in Poland's south-eastern borderland. Soon after the Second World War, most Ukrainians were resettled in the USSR, partly in the Ukraine and partly in Siberia. Those who remained became the core of the Ukrainian partisan movement, which fought for independence against the Polish and Soviet armies. Unable to beat the partisans and inspired by the Soviet example, the Polish authorities deported the entire Ukrainian population from its historical settlements and dispersed it all over northern and western Poland. Efforts were made to place no more than a few Ukrainian families in any one village. For many years afterwards they were not allowed to return to their native regions. Given how scattered the community was, it took a great deal of self-determination to retain and transmit to children the sense of being Ukrainian. However, a relatively large number of Ukrainians succeeded in doing so. Ukrainians are a community with a strong national awareness, who love their homeland, traditions and customs. They are also a community capable of organizing. Their basic education-related problem is their geographical dispersion. Ukrainian schools and classes are of necessity very small, and the few larger ones must have boarding facilities. Furthermore, Ukrainians are divided by their religion, which is Greek Catholic for some and Orthodox for others.

Lithuanians

The small Lithuanian community lives close to the Lithuanian border. Lithuanians have high national awareness, are articulate in presenting their demands to the Polish authorities, and capable of working communally to defend their interests. There are no tendencies to Polonize. A factor that brings the Lithuanian community closer to Poland is that it is predominantly Catholic.

Slovaks

Slovaks live close to the Slovak border. Although the Slovak language is very similar to the dialect spoken by neighbouring Polish highlanders, there is no particular tendency to Polonize. Most Slovaks are Catholic.

EDUCATION OF NATIONAL MINORITIES IN POLAND: AN OVERVIEW

Formal and legal environment

The languages of Poland's national minorities are taught at all educational levels, including kindergarten, primary and secondary school and higher education.

Teaching of minority languages is organized by the school-running institutions at the request of parents in primary and of pupils in secondary schools.

The area of national minority education is regulated by the Educational System Act of 7 September 1991 and the ruling of the Minister of National Education of 24 March 1992 concerning the organization of teaching to support minority pupils' national, ethnic and linguistic identities.

In the school year 1993-94, minority languages were studied by 11,694 primary and secondary school pupils in 165 schools and by sixty-eight six-year-old Slovak, German and Ukrainian children in four pre-school facilities.

Minority language teaching institutions employ 257 teachers and include:

- Seventeen primary and secondary schools with mother tongue as the language of instruction, attended by approximately 900 and 500 pupils, respectively.
- 153 primary and secondary schools with mother tongue as an additional subject, with approximately 9,550 and 750 pupils, respectively.
- Eight inter-school mother tongue teaching centres with approximately 300 pupils.

Minority mother tongue instructed classes have fewer pupils than classes at Polish schools and can be organized for more than seven and fourteen pupils in primary and secondary schools, respectively.

Schools with instruction in minority languages teach the history and geography of native countries. Schools with additional minority language teaching may supplement history and geography courses with elements of the history and geography of native countries. The decision rests with the body of the schoolteachers.

Mother-tongue instruction applies to all subjects except Polish language, literature and history. Schools with mother-tongue instruction issue bilingual certificates. The number of hours of teaching in the mother tongue equals that in the Polish language. Secondary school pupils must take the mother tongue as a final examination subject.

Curriculum development and review, selection of textbook writers, syllabus design, staffing and in-service teacher training are areas where minority associations have participated, working together with the Ministry of National Education. They have also taken part in the preparation of regulatory national minority education-related documents and papers.

Legal regulations concerning the educational rights of minorities are not disputed. The Polish law in this respect complies with the Conference on Security and Co-operation in Europe (CSCE) document, the Convention on the Rights of the Child, and other international regulations.

Implementation of minority educational rights and the operation of minority language teaching institutions are supervised by heads of regional educational boards and their plenipotentiaries.

Minority languages are taught only at public schools and kindergartens. To date no-one has sought to establish non-public schools to this end.

German minority education

The number of Germans in Poland is estimated at 350,000–450,000. They live chiefly in the Silesian provinces of Katowice and Opole.

Before 1990 there was no teaching of German as a minority mother tongue in Poland. This was due to the ban on German language teaching in Silesia and non-recognition of the existence of the local German minority by the Polish authorities.

The year 1990 saw the beginning of teaching of German as a foreign language in Silesia, and in 1992 teaching of German as a mother tongue was initiated.

Initially, the wishes of many parents could not be fully met due to the shortage of qualified teachers of German and pupils lacking home-acquired German language basics. This problem has been partly solved in cooperation with German minority associations, which co-finance teacher training programmes, assist in establishing contacts between Polish and German schools, recruit teachers from Germany, and so on.

Significant benefits have also been obtained from the three-year in-service teacher training programme. German language teachers are trained at the Teacher Training Colleges of German in Raciborz and Opole and at the Department of German Studies of the Opole Higher School of Education. Language courses are also run for teachers in service.

In the school year 1993-94, courses of German as a mother tongue were available at forty-five primary schools and one kindergarten. Some 5,178 pupils were enrolled. Courses last three hours per week. The number of schools offering German-as-a-mother-tongue courses has increased to forty-five from twenty-eight the year before, with the number of students up 100 per cent. Further growth is planned in 1994-95.

The 1994-95 school year will also mark the commencement of the teaching of German as a mother tongue in the province of Czestochowa.

German schools use textbooks received from the Goethe Institute at Munich.

German language and literature can be studied at several universities.

Belarusian minority education

The Belarusian minority in Poland is estimated at 200,000–250,000. Belarusians live mostly in the north-eastern province of Bialystok. This minority comes second with respect to the number of pupils enrolled in mother tongue courses.

Belarusian as a mother tongue is studied by 3,596 pupils, including 2,904 in forty-one primary and 692 in two secondary schools in Hajnowka and Bielsk Podlaski. Courses last three hours per week.

Although there is a choice of the mother tongue teaching format, the Belarusian minority has no schools with Belarusian as the language of instruction. No parents have as yet declared their children's readiness to attend such schools. There are no private Belarusian schools, either. The interest in studying Belarusian is falling, due largely to the migration of the younger generation to cities.

There were seventy-nine teachers of Belarusian in 1993/94, a few more than the year before.

New Belarusian language and geography curricula have recently been designed and are being introduced in school year 1994-95. Several new Belarusian language textbooks have also been written.

Belarusian Master of Arts courses are available at Warsaw University.

Ukrainian minority education

Estimates put the Ukrainian minority in Poland at 200,000–250,000. The Ukrainian minority once lived in south-eastern Poland, but a special operation in 1947 resettled and dispersed them all over northern and western Poland.

The Ukrainian minority comes third in terms of numbers of pupils, after Germans and Belarusians. Recent years have witnessed a rise.

In 1993-94, Ukrainian language courses were available in eight of Poland's provinces, in one kindergarten (Przemysl, eighteen children), four primary and three secondary schools with Ukrainian as the language of instruction, and forty-eight primary and one secondary school with Ukrainian as an additional subject, as well as in one inter-school centre. All told, sixty primary and secondary schools have more than 1,600 Ukrainian pupils. The existing school network almost fully satisfies the educational needs of the Ukrainian minority.

The standard of teaching at schools with Ukrainian as the language of instruction is evaluated as very high.

There is, on the other hand, a certain lack of textbooks. Recently changed, the new Ukrainian language teaching curriculum requires new textbooks. These, however, have taken a long time to write. Some old Ukrainian textbooks are therefore being adapted, and the Ministry of National Education will finance the purchase of primers from the Ukraine.

The development of curricula of Ukrainian history and geography, under the patronage of the Ukrainian Teachers' Association, is now nearing completion. But new textbooks, readers and dictionaries still need to be published.

Ukrainian is taught by eighty-two teachers. Teachers may also be recruited from the Ukraine. Four major schools are currently being modernized and remodelled. There are plans to build or buy a facility to house the future Ukrainian secondary school in Przemysl.

Ukrainian language and literature Master of Arts courses are available at the universities of Warsaw, Cracow, Lublin, Poznan and Szczecin. Courses in Ukrainian are also offered by the Rzeszow and Slupsk Higher Schools of Education.

Lithuanian minority education

Poland's Lithuanian minority is 20,000-25,000 strong. Lithuanians live in north-eastern Poland, close to the Lithuanian border.

Lithuanian is studied by 795 pupils in seven primary schools and one secondary school with Lithuanian as the language of instruction, five primary schools with Lithuanian as a subject and one inter-school centre, all in the province of Suwalki.

In cooperation with the Association of Lithuanians in Poland, teachers of Lithuanian designed a new curriculum of Lithuanian as a mother tongue in primary schools. The curriculum has been in use since 1992.

The same group initiated the development of a Lithuanian history curriculum, later approved by the Minister of National Education. Lithuanian geography and language curricula are being finalized, and Poland's first Lithuanian history school textbook and a new Lithuanian language textbook for the final-year primary school pupils will soon come out.

Lithuanian is taught by thirty teachers, but only nine are graduates of Lithuanian language and literature studies, with others holding degrees in different subjects.

Lithuanian Master of Arts courses are available at the University of Poznan.

Schools for the Slovak minority

There are some 25,000 Slovaks in Poland. They live in southern Poland, close to the Slovak border.

In school year 1993-94, Slovak was studied by 483 children in thirteen schools and thirty-two children in two pre-school divisions in the Nowy Sacz province. There are two schools with Slovak as the language of instruction, attended by 142 pupils, as well as ten primary and one secondary school with Slovak studied as an additional subject by 312 and twenty-nine pupils, respectively.

In recent years the number of schools offering optional Slovak courses has decreased; however, the number of pupils in attendance has remained in a stable range of 470-490.

The group of twenty-one teachers is mostly made up of Polish citizens of Slovak nationality. They all have a good educational background and formal qualifications to teach their subject. Some of them graduated from the universities of Bratislava and Prague, and one has a Ph.D.

Slovak studies can be pursued at two Polish universities, in Cracow and Katowice.

Recent years have seen the introduction of a new Slovak language curriculum written by teachers from Slovak schools in Poland under the guidance of experts from the Slovak Republic. Work has also started on curricula of Slovak history and geography.

As far as textbooks are concerned, Slovak schools are at an advantage compared to other minority schools. Use is made of textbooks published in the Slovak Republic, especially in lower grades. Several useful textbooks of the Slovak language were also published in Poland between 1991 and 1993, and work is in progress on dictionaries, grammar books and workbooks.

Educational problems of the Romanies

Poland is home to some 25,000 Romanies. So far, no special educational facilities for Romany children have been opened and they are therefore educated in Polish schools. Their low rate of success at school, which stems in part from the lack of command of the Polish language, has compelled certain educational circles to look for solutions to reduce the educational

179

problems encountered by these children. By way of an experiment, a few Romany classes have been established to teach early school age Romany children.

The results of this experiment, together with a questionnaire which the Association of the Romanies in Poland has in mind, are likely to help develop a concept of education of the Romanies in our country.

Educational problems of other minorities

Poland has a community which is called 'Lemkos'. Some of the Lemkos consider themselves an ethnic group of the Ukrainian nation and others believe they are a separate nation. It is difficult to estimate how numerous Lemkos are. Like Ukrainians, they are dispersed over northern and western Poland. The teaching of Lemko as a mother tongue began two years ago in five locations.

Poland also has a very small Jewish community. With only 15,000 people, it is just a tiny part of Poland's pre-war large Jewish population. This community has recently instigated certain educational initiatives, including the opening of a kindergarten for Jewish children in Warsaw.

Poland is also home to an ethnic group, the Kaszubi. Inhabitants of northern Poland, Kaszubi do not define themselves as a nation. They use the Kaszubi language, which some linguists consider a remote dialect of Polish literary language and others regard as a remnant of an old and long-forgotten West-Slavonic language. At the request of the Kaszubi community, the Kaszubi language is taught in one primary and one secondary school.

POLISH STEREOTYPES OF NATIONAL MINORITIES

The decision as to where to present the questionnaire was influenced not only by my knowledge of the geographical distribution of each minority but also by awareness of Polish stereotypes and attitudes towards them. Some basic information on the latter is now in order.

Generally speaking, there is no single stereotype of the 'stranger' in Poland, but different attitudes towards different minorities.

Germans

Shaped over many centuries, the stereotype of a German contains some mutually contradictory elements. Many people still have vivid memories of Nazi atrocities during the Second World War. For forty-five years, these memories were used for propaganda purposes by the communist régime, which said or implied that a German threat was always present. On the other hand, large numbers of younger and better-educated Poles were meeting Germans like those who helped Poles on a mass scale in the 1980s with food aid. Poles have always been impressed with German industriousness, order and organizing skills, so much so that these qualities are commonly called 'German'. Poles are also impressed by German affluence. Nevertheless, I think that the average Pole was mentally unprepared for the emergence of a few hundred-thousand-strong German minority within a few months of the 1989 breakthrough. Many Poles suspected and, I believe, still suspect, that willingness to improve one's standard of living has been a more usual motive to declare oneself German than national awareness. The traditional sense of distance was historically intensified by many Germans being Protestants, but since most of the Silesia-based Germans are Catholic, this factor no longer comes into play.

Belarusians

A few dozen years ago, many Poles rejected the national aspirations of Belarusians, maintaining that the Belarusian language was a peasant, contaminated variety of the Polish language, that Belarusian culture boiled down to folklore and that higher culture was present only in Russians or Poles. Although such attitudes seem much weaker now, some traces have remained in the public mentality. The attitude towards Belarusians is influenced by their attachment to the Orthodox religion, which clashes with the stereotypical Polish perception of this as merely the Tsar's nineteenth century instrument with which to Russianize Poles.

Ukrainians

Some 100 years ago, Ukrainians were perceived as Belarusians were sixty years ago: as an obscure people situated somewhere between Poles and Russians. The developments of the twentieth century, and in particular Ukrainians' determination to fight for their native land, rendered this stereotype obsolete. Regrettably, its place was taken by another. In attempts to win independence, Ukrainians for centuries came into conflict with Russia or Poland or, at times, both. The Second World War saw frequent fighting between Poles and Ukrainians on the occupied territories, followed by mutual accusations of innumerable atrocities. Hence came about the stereotype of the Ukrainian as a murderer and criminal. Poles prefer to forget that the deportation of large numbers of Ukrainians from their homeland was a classic example of the application of the 'collective responsibility' principle. This stereotype of Ukrainians was also furthered by communist propaganda. It is a paradox of the collective mentality that non-communist Poles identified with the communist repression against Ukrainians without any particular qualms.

Lithuanians

Although Lithuanians provoke a less emotional response than Germans or Ukrainians, some Poles think they should regret having their own, independent state, instead of one united with Poland, as it was in the eighteenth century.

Slovaks

The minority which the average Pole is least aware of. If at all, emotions are only stirred by this people among a small population in the mountains of southern Poland.

This was an overview of the stereotypes attached to our country's largest minorities. Experts on minorities point out, however, that it is two presently small minorities, the Romanies and Jews, whose populations are estimated at 25,000 and 15,000, respectively, that evoke the strongest feelings. Anti-Romany resentment probably stems from lack of understanding and dislike of their lifestyle. The anti-Jewish feeling has most likely nothing to do with the actual behaviour of the few Holocaust survivors but is a throwback to old tensions and controversies, which sometimes find expression in the common consciousness in the form of searching for Jewish roots or mentality in people who nowadays neither declare themselves to be, nor feel like, members of the Jewish community.

DESCRIPTION OF SAMPLE SELECTION

In the light of what I have written about teacher training and the small scale of minority education, it becomes obvious that a teacher trainee questionnaire-study will in most cases reveal the attitudes of Poles who have neither contacts with nor awareness of national minorities. Still, in an attempt to obtain some data on attitudes to multicultural education, I decided to conduct the study in the following regions:

Opole

Capital city of the German minority region. A total of 140 questionnaires were distributed among elementary and pre-school education students in

their two final years at the Higher School of Education. Groups 1, 2 and 3**
were, respectively, Poles, Germans and Romanies.

Bialystok

Capital city of the Belarusian minority region and at the same time a city
with a higher education institution in close proximity to the Lithuanian
community. The study was conducted among elementary and pre-school
education students in their two final years at the local branch of Warsaw
University. Questionnaires were completed for Poles, Belarusians and
Romanies as groups 1, 2 and 3**, respectively, by thirty-three students, and
for Poles, Belarusians and Lithuanians by forty-three students.

Olsztyn

Capital city of a once extremely diverse, now nationally uniform region.
The seat of the Higher School of Education is in close proximity to the
Lithuanian community. The study covered twenty-nine students from the
faculty of arts and humanities and the selected study groups were Poles,
Belarusians and Lithuanians.

This exhausted the number of higher education establishments where the
questionnaire might reveal multicultural problems.

Additionally, I decided to collect some data from a region devoid of any
national minorities. My reckoning was that responses there would reflect
beliefs or stereotypes unaffected by actual contact with representatives of
the studied groups.

Thus, I distributed fifty questionnaires covering Poles, Romanies and
Jews among the senior-year elementary education students at Warsaw
University as well as thirty-eight questionnaires among pre-school and
elementary education students at Warsaw's Teacher Training College. The
first nineteen questionnaires covered Poles, Ukrainians and Germans and
the remaining nineteen asked about Poles, Belarusians and Germans.

Since my first impression of the completed questionnaires was of the
superficiality of the obtained information, I decided to supplement it in an
untypical way. Courtesy of the Association of Ukrainians in Poland, I was
able to obtain sixteen questionnaires from teachers working at schools with
Ukrainian as the language of instruction.

DESCRIPTION OF FINDINGS

To begin with, I would like to discuss the teacher trainee questionnaires, and only afterwards deal with the special and unique Ukrainian school teachers' questionnaire.

The bulk (97 %) of the questionnaires distributed among teacher trainees were completed by women. Teaching is largely a feminine career in Poland, with the rate of feminization in elementary education running close to 100 per cent. The average age of the respondents is twenty-two. Since in most cases their parents have no degrees, they are the first generation to have received higher education.

The questionnaires have shown some opinions, especially those concerning the work of the teacher, to be very similar, irrespective of the town of residence and actual contact with national minorities.

In particular, the same responses were given to question 1, as to what is important and what unimportant in education. Vital importance was usually attributed to the following objectives:
– to have confidence in oneself;
– to show understanding for others;
– to develop morals;
– to express oneself easily;
– to develop the imagination;
– to be able to read, write and count;
– to have self-respect.
The following objectives were judged 'not very important':
– to be an active citizen;
– to show respect for authority.
'Does not concern school' was the usual choice towards 'That boys should act like boys, and girls like girls'.

Similarly, there was considerable agreement as to the 'First three main functions of a teacher' (question 6), with the usual choices being:
– to transmit knowledge;
– to help pupils develop their skills;
– to help pupils learn about themselves.
A relatively frequent choice was also 'to help pupils integrate into their societies'.

All of the studied groups gave similar reasons for choosing a teaching career, including:
– because I like to be amongst children;
– because it is a fascinating occupation;
– because education leads to greater success in life.

'Because I like to explain things and communicate my knowledge' was also frequently chosen.

Approximately half the respondents declared their willingness to teach after they have obtained teacher's certificates. Twenty per cent intend to continue with other training or studies and another twenty per cent do not know what to do.

Let us now discuss in greater detail the 140 questionnaires distributed in the town of Opole.

The studied communities included Poles, Germans and Romanies. Almost all respondents expressed interest in working exclusively with Polish children, with only a few saying they could speak German, and three and one, respectively, willing to work with German and Romany children. Strikingly enough, these answers were given in the capital city of a province with a thirty per cent German population. Of course, this is the result of the developments I have described above. When the teacher trainees made the decision to study elementary education a few years ago, the German issue was only just emerging. At that time the management of the Higher School of Education was presumably not interested in it, either. Opole has recently become home to some interesting ideas concerning the German issue, which I will present later on, but they have not really influenced the respondents' course of studies as yet.

An analysis of answers to question 2, 'Do you think it is easy or difficult for this group to achieve the following objectives' reveals an interesting propensity for stereotypes. As we know, there are as yet no schools with German as the language of instruction; nor are there any Romany schools. German children who only a few years ago would not admit to being German most definitely speak Polish at school, and hardly any Romany children can be found at schools at all. It is therefore hard to tell who the respondents have in mind when saying that some objectives are difficult or easy to achieve. One gets the impression that the answers are the result of a stereotypical perception of both Germans and Romanies rather than a judgment based on social or educational facts. All of the answers form a very distinct pattern: that it is generally difficult for Poles to achieve various educational objectives, but easy for Germans and very difficult for Romanies. Moreover, it is particularly easy for Germans to achieve the objectives which Poles ascribe to them, such as:
- to have confidence in themselves;
- to be orderly and punctual;
- to be active citizens;
- to form part of their community;
- to show respect for authority.

The same objectives are difficult to achieve for Poles, and very difficult to achieve for Romanies. As for analysis of why educational objectives are difficult to achieve (question 3), the most frequently mentioned causes include 'the parents' socio-economic level' and 'the number of pupils per class' with respect to Polish children; 'parents' expectations of the school' and 'the teachers' level of training and/or qualifications' with respect to German children; and 'the parents' socio-economic level' and 'the pupils' mother tongue which is not the language of teaching' with respect to Romany children.

The most frequently chosen remedies include 'to set up supplementary courses for pupils experiencing difficulties' and 'to reduce the number of pupils per class'. Ideas such as 'to group pupils in various classes according to their abilities and interests' and the proposal 'to organize separate schools and classes according to the pupils' mother tongue' are resented. Incidentally, the respondents' dislike of the latter demonstrates their disapproval of the current state policy on minority education.

The analysis of social distance (question 4) reveals the lack of a significant difference in respondents' perceived social distance from Poles and Germans. In most cases the symbol of Poles touches that of the respondent, and the symbol of Germans is within the radius of 2.5 cm. The symbol of Romanies is mostly placed within the radius of 5 cm. As is shown by answers to question 7k, the distance is related to levels of knowledge and contacts. Most of the respondents said 'I have had friends or acquaintances from this group' with respect to Germans and 'no contact' or, less often, 'other types of contact' (with 'beggars' sometimes added) with respect to Romanies.

The questionnaires distributed in the town of Bialystok fall into two sub-groups, with the first, of thirty-three examples, covering Poles, Belarusians and Romanies and the other, of forty-three examples, covering Poles, Belarusians and Lithuanians. Since both groups had similar compositions, I will discuss the results jointly.

On the whole, the answers do not point to any significant differences between Poles, Belarusians and Lithuanians in terms of the potential for achieving educational objectives. In other words, the same level of difficulty is involved for all three nationalities, with only two exceptions: respondents think that, compared to Poles, it is particularly difficult for Belarusians 'to form a part of their community' and 'to be active citizens'. However, things are totally different with respect to Romanies. Romanies, respondents say, find it very difficult 'to develop morals', 'to be orderly and punctual', 'to adopt clean habits', 'to be active citizens' and 'to be able to read, write and count'.

What makes it very difficult for Poles to achieve educational objectives is 'lack of teaching means and materials', 'the number of pupils per class' and 'the teachers' level of training and/or qualifications'. Belarusians and Romanies, in turn, are especially impeded by 'the pupils' mother tongue which is not the language of teaching' and 'the gulf between life at school and life in the family'. The difficulties of Lithuanians resemble those faced by Poles.

The remedies to improve the quality of education most frequently selected include 'to set up supplementary courses for pupils experiencing difficulties', 'to reduce the number of pupils per class' and 'to adapt teaching materials to the needs of various cultural groups'.

As regards social distance, Poles are placed not further than 2.5 cm from the respondent's symbol. The distance from Belarusians and Lithuanians is a little greater, but still holds within the range of 2.5 cm to 5 cm. The attitude to Romanies is much more unfavourable, with the distance usually marked at 5 to 10 cm. Indeed, many respondents mention numerous Belarusian friends, but have almost no contact with Romanies.

Two persons within the sample stated their nationality as Polish-Lithuanian, three as Belarusian and two as Polish-Belarusian. Seven respondents said they could speak Belarusian, five would like to work with Belarusians and one with Romany children.

Twenty-nine questionnaires were filled in by teacher trainees at the Faculty of Arts and Humanities, Higher School of Education, Olsztyn. The studied communities included Poles, Belarusians and Lithuanians. The results are almost identical with those of the parallel group in Bialystok. The distance from Lithuanians is slightly greater than from Belarusians, but the difference is insignificant. The vast majority of the respondents do not know what they will be doing once they have obtained their teacher's certificates. They do not seem to have strong motivation to become teachers. One person indicated a command of Lithuanian and another said he was Ukrainian but did not declare willingness to work with Ukrainian pupils.

The fifty questionnaires distributed among elementary education students at Warsaw University investigated attitudes towards Poles, Romanies and Jews. Predictably, a vast majority of respondents had never had anything to do with these or any other minorities, which did not, however, prevent them from expressing categorical viewpoints, especially with regard to difficulties in achieving educational objectives. Jews are perceived by the Warsaw respondents as Germans are by those from Opole. The Warsaw respondents believe that it is always easier for Jews to achieve educational objectives than for Poles, let alone Romanies. I think that such responses do not originate from analyses of educational opportunities of the existing Jewish community but reflect the old stereotype of cunning Jews who always manage to achieve their objectives. Possibly, some admiration both for Jews and Germans also comes into play. At any rate, at 2.5 to 5 cm, the social distance from Jews is not very significant, whereas Romanies are placed 5 to 10 cm from the respondents.

Questionnaires were also distributed among pre-school and elementary education students at Warsaw's Teacher Training College. Nineteen questionnaires covered Poles, Ukrainians and Germans and another nineteen asked about Poles, Belarusians and Germans. The two groups of respondents were composed of individuals who on the whole had never had any contacts with any national minority and whose attitude towards Germans could have been shaped by contacts with Germans from West Germany. Germans were noticeably elevated by the respondents, the common opinion being that they had an easy educational life, whereas Poles and Ukrainians had to cope with difficulties. Yet the distance from Ukrainians and Belarusians was smaller than from Germans, as if the sense of community with those whose lives are more difficult was emphasized.

Some of the Warsaw and Bialystok questionnaires were administered by individuals known and liked by respondents. These individuals asked the respondents to write down any questionnaire-related comments that came to their minds if they so wished. The comments were anonymous and written on extra pages. Out of a dozen or so comments, some are worth quoting.

Let us start with the most categorical statement. A twenty-year old female student from Warsaw wrote that she had only 'very superficial' contact with Germans and had not 'met any Belarusians at all'. Then she went on to say: 'I am nationalistic. I think that everyone has his or her place and should not go where they are not wanted, unless to travel. But I would never have let people like Germans, Russians, Romanians, Bulgarians, Jews, Romanies [the latter two underlined] into my country. It is a mistake that they are here'.

Two more negative statements:
'The Ukrainian and German communities have a rather negative attitude to Poles. I have nothing against either, but am concerned about their expansion on Polish land.'

'I do not know much about the two communities—Germans and Ukrainians. My major concern is that if the schools of these minorities had the same rights as Polish schools, ours could be ousted.'

And a couple of statements on a different note:
'I think that this minority [Belarusians] has opportunities to develop its culture in the Bialystok region. Belarusians sometimes suffer at the hands of

Poles, but these are sporadic occurrences which testify to the low culture and awareness of these Poles.'

'I have had Belarusian and German friends. These friendships have lasted for eight years now and they do not differ in any special way from my other friendships.'

Finally here is a uniquely mature statement by a twenty-four-year old from Bialystok:

'The Belarusian problem does exist. It is about the lack of social awareness. We realize that another culture exists next to ours but we lack specific knowledge about it. Poles themselves face the problem of finding their place in the contemporary world and this must be the reason why they are not widely interested in other communities.'

POLES AND MINORITIES IN THE EYES OF UKRAINIAN TEACHERS

Of the sixteen questionnaires filled in by teachers from schools with Ukrainian as the language of instruction, four were completed by men and twelve by women. Seven of the respondents were aged below thirty, another seven were aged between thirty and fifty and two were much older.

With respect to educational objectives, Ukrainian teachers attach particular importance to the following:
– to be aware of their responsibilities;
– to show understanding for others;
– to be familiar with their own culture;
– to form part of their community;
– to weigh up their options;
– to be able to read, write and count.

They do not attach much importance to the objective 'to show respect for authority'. In their opinion the three main functions of a teacher are:
– to transmit knowledge;
– to help pupils develop their skills;
– to help pupils to be familiar with their own culture.

They became teachers for the following reasons:
– because it is a fascinating occupation;
– because they like to be amongst children;
– because they like to explain things and communicate their knowledge.

The questionnaires filled in by the Ukrainian teachers dealt with three nationalities: Poles, Ukrainians and Germans. Again, the answers displayed the familiar judgement that it is easier for Germans to achieve educational objectives, especially those stereotypically regarded as German: punctuality, order, civic activity, studiousness and clean habits. Clean habits, for example, are considered easy to adopt for Germans, more difficult for Ukrainians and most difficult for Poles. However, certain objectives in the area of psychological development are much easier to achieve for Ukrainians than for Germans and Poles, including 'to show understanding for others' and 'to develop morals'. It must be an expression of some unfamiliar Ukrainian stereotype of Poles that the latter are believed find it easiest 'to have a sense of pride' and 'to have self-respect', much more so than Germans, not to mention Ukrainians, for whom, teachers say, it is very difficult to develop these kinds of attitudes.

There are two major obstacles to pupils achieving the educational objectives set by the Ukrainian teachers—'lack of teaching materials and means' and 'the gulf between life at school and life in the family'. The teachers approve of most of the proposals mentioned in point 5 except for 'to mix pupils from different cultures in order to encourage exchanges and mutual learning'.

As far as social distance is concerned, it is less for Poles (approximately 2.5 cm) than Germans (approximately 5 cm).

When distributing the questionnaires, members of the Association of Ukrainians in Poland encouraged respondents to make extra comments. Some are definitely worth presenting.

'The Ukrainian teacher is proud to contribute to the development of his country.'

'A Ukrainian teacher does not always feel good. . . . The distance from the Ukraine makes it difficult to transport materials necessary for cultural development and learning. I mean books, national costumes, musical instruments, objects of worship, etc. Regardless of such difficulties, a lot is being done, and this is very gratifying.'

'Regrettably, the negative stereotype of the Ukrainian is still present in Polish consciousness, which breeds intolerance or, worse, leads to victimization.'

'The teacher feels underestimated, is evaluated as inferior to teachers of other subjects. Feels lonely.'

One respondent points out that the unfavourable stereotype of the Ukrainian is perpetuated by the media: 'If the choice is between a respectable Ukrainian and a Polish drunk and layabout, the Pole is chosen. Everybody except Ukrainians have the right to love their homeland and be proud of their origins.'

One of the younger generation of teachers commented very interestingly on transformations in the Ukrainian community itself: 'Our fathers' generation deliberately avoided contacts with Poles, isolated itself from the society it happened to live in, to preserve its national identity. That generation cannot easily adapt to the present circumstances and is mistrustful of any signs of opening up towards the Polish community. Sadly, I feel inclined to include also the older generation of Ukrainian teachers in this group. They often do not acknowledge that it is within the Polish environment that we must nurture our culture and language. To succeed, we must enter this environment, get to know it well and let them get to know us—we must inform, make suggestions . . . I am concerned that teachers at Polish primary and secondary schools with minority pupils are not formally kept up-to-date on the situation of these minorities. It seems to me that teachers—both of Ukrainian and Polish origin—should feel co-responsible for their pupils because it is they who will decide the future.'

The last sentences of this comment can be understood as an expression of the need to introduce multicultural education into teacher training.

CONCLUDING REMARKS

I began this article by signalling that there was no multicultural education in Poland. I hope it is now clear why I think so. Mention should be made, however, of steps taken in two institutions that will help change this negative opinion in the future.

An ethnic prejudice prevention programme for primary schools has been developed by psychologists Wieslaw Lukaszewski and Barbara Weigl of Opole's Higher School of Education. The programme is being tested.

A conference on 'Multicultural education: needs, expectations and stereotypes' was organized by the Bialystok branch of Warsaw University. The conference was attended by experts from abroad. I was told by the organizers that the idea of the conference was to open new roads and research subjects, so that the Bialystok institution would become a specialized centre for multicultural studies.

REFERENCES

Ministry of National Education. *[Education of national minorities: Report of the Ministry of National Education.]* Warsaw, 1993. (In Polish.)

Wierzycka, L.; Holuszko M. [National minorities: some comments and observations.] Spoleczenstwo otwarte., 1993. (In Polish.)

[Ukrainian minority in Poland: Report of the Polish members of the Experts' Commission for National Minorities at the Polish and Ukrainian Presidents' Consultancy Committee]. 1994. (In Polish.)

CHAPTER X

Teacher training for multicultural education in Senegal

Mourtala Mboup

Senegal is a multi-ethnic country. The Wolofs are the largest ethnic group (43 per cent of the population); they are followed by the Pulaars (23 per cent) and the Sereers (14.8 per cent). Wolof is the most widely spoken language of the country; almost 71 per cent of the Senegalese use it as their first or second language.

At first sight, it is tempting to say that there are no problems of an intercultural nature in Senegal. In fact, this was the attitude most people revealed when interviewed by the author about multicultural education. Relatively speaking, Senegal has been spared open conflicts of the purely inter-ethnic type, and true social peace has reigned for a long time in the country, especially in the large towns. The urban zones have experienced a merging, facilitated by the common use of the Wolof language and common faith in the principles of Islam. This is true to the point that it is impossible to distinguish between Wolof and other children on school playgrounds in urban zones. All the children speak Wolof in the breaks and sometimes even during classes. This standardization is seen as a sign of social cohesion.

POSITIVE EXPERIENCES IN TRAINING FOR MULTICULTURAL EDUCATION

Introducing national languages in pre-school education

It was only in 1977, seventeen years after political independence, that the Senegalese authorities created the National School for Pre-school Teachers

(ENEP). In 1978, official instructions emphasized the need 'to establish the mother tongue in pre-school classes'.

The ENEP had two ways of recruiting for training two types of pre-school teachers. First, holders of the DEFEM (Diploma awarded at the end of middle school studies, at the end of the first secondary cycle) were recruited through an entrance examination and trained for four years. Secondly, holders of the Baccalaureate who passed the ENEP entrance examination received one year's training.

Apart from the specific aspects of the psychology of the Senegalese child which the ENEP syllabus stresses, the introduction of national languages was the most important point with regard to the multicultural dimension of this training. In addition to the post of lecturer in linguistics, there were posts of lecturers in national languages. The latter had the responsibility of training student teachers to conduct all educational activities in the national languages.

If we speak of this ENEP experiment as a positive one in relation to the question of multicultural education, it is only because of the nobility and pertinence of the principle upon which it is based. In reality, this experiment was far from efficient and satisfactory. As early as 1982 an assessment seminar identified a certain number of difficulties and inadequacies linked to the training given at the ENEP:

1. In particular, the insufficiency and inadequacy of theoretical and practical training;
2. The absence of linguistic training in certain instructors, due to the fact that at the beginning the ENEP did not give classes in all the national languages. The instructors who had opted for certain national languages did not know how to write them;
3. The lack of liaison between the linguistic content at ENEP and the requirements at the level of practical application. For example, instructors met problems of terminology, dialect variations, borrowing, etc.
4. The lack of adequate training for the instructors themselves and/or the special nature of their status.

In fact, the linguistics classes were often given by French teachers who were not specialists in the subject. Similarly, the national languages were usually taught by part-time lecturers whose other activities scarcely left them with any time to fully take part in the life of the establishment (meetings to assess the weaknesses of the training, interdisciplinary coordination of syllabuses, etc.). But these inadequacies were not enough to justify questioning the pertinence of introducing national languages in pre-school classes, especially as since 1984 all educational activities in all sections of pre-school classes have been conducted in the national languages (Joola, Pulaar, Wolof, Manding).

Introducing national languages in elementary education

In 1971 the introduction of national languages was made a mandatory and essential part of the education system. A certain number of decrees and official declarations followed, stressing the urgency of the task.

The contents of official declarations showed a growing awareness of the problem. One official text stated: 'We think that as long as we, the Senegalese, continue to teach our children a foreign language, whichever it may be, without teaching them first of all their mother tongue, our people will remain alienated' (1972). But it was not until 1978 that these intentions began to appear in a concrete way in the form of experimentation in primary schools.

This experimentation consisted in the opening of ten television classes starting in 1978 and three non-television classes starting in 1979. Later, in 1981/82, six other classes were opened, including three in Joola, two in Pulaar and one in Sereer. As far as the training of the teachers for these classes was concerned, we should point out that those in the first stage (1978/79) only received two weeks' training which was provided by the CLAD (Applied Linguistics Centre of Dakar), the IFAN (Fundamental Institute of Black Africa) and the DA (Office of Literacy) with the collaboration of individual research scholars. For two weeks, television teachers followed periodic training sessions for exchange of information. As for teachers during the second stage (1981/82), they received three months' training organized by the CLAD. The training programme was based essentially on initiation into the writing of national languages in the first stage, with the addition of general linguistics, applied linguistics and some elements of grammar in the second stage.

From the point of view of the internal functioning of these experiments, there was a marked difference between the television and non-television classes. In the first, teachers were provided with broadcasts approximately every two weeks by the Centre for Educational Television Production of Senegal (TSS) situated in Dakar. Each cassette had with it an instructional sheet including the objective of the broadcast and advice on how to exploit it. The teacher of such experimental classes was asked not to watch the film before showing it to the pupils. The reason for this was that the teacher should be subjected to the conditions of a broadcast by national television in case television teaching were to be applied generally.

In the second stage, almost everything was left to the initiative of the teacher. This created a number of problems related to the lack of textbooks and a precise syllabus. One teacher of this type of class, when questioned, stated that he had made his own teaching material and translated the French syllabus into Sereer. He admitted that he had serious problems with the terminology, especially when teaching arithmetic and grammar, the two subjects that had not been the subject of any appropriate research on terminology by specialists in the field with the aim of translating certain scientific concepts.

The teachers of television classes, in spite of the teaching instructions they received, also had to face certain problems. Some of them considered that certain broadcasts did not satisfy the objective mentioned on the corresponding instruction sheets. In both types of classes, and during the first stage as well as the second, the teachers were inadequately trained.

Apart from these problems of an educational nature, there was also the problem of reticence on the part of the parents to send their children to these experimental classes. Some of them quite simply withdrew their children from the classes. This reaction was due not so much to disapproval by the parents as to their fear that their children would make slower progress than the others. Since school is considered here as a means to get ahead in society, it is easy to understand their fear of seeing their offspring lose the chance of becoming 'somebody'. All these problems compromised the work of the experimental classes. The non-television classes of the first stage were purely and simply converted into traditional classes. As for the six classes opened in 1981, four of them have been closed: two in Oussouye, one in Matam, one in Dakar.

If we decided, in spite of these results, to class the introduction of national languages and the training of teachers for this purpose under the heading of positive experiments, it is because they illustrated two facts of vital importance for the future of the school in Senegal. On the one hand, pupils in the experimental classes obtained results comparable to those of pupils in the other classes, according to the teachers. In the opinion of the teachers, the results were not due to the use of television broadcasts, but to the use in school of the language that the children use in their home environment. It is clear that the children understand certain subjects, such as addition, far more easily when they are taught in their own language.

On the other hand, this experiment showed clearly that even if it is true that national languages are highly suitable for use in teaching, it is also true that to guarantee success it is essential to have a good linguistic policy, together with an appropriate syllabus. In fact, the difficulties experienced by teachers in the creating of educational material and the adoption of the appropriate terminology are, respectively, the result of the lack of suitable training and lack of specialized literature at the national level.

However, this appears to be a task that the Senegalese authorities are tackling at present. A Ministry for Literacy and the Promotion of National Languages has just been created. The director of the ministry is a former research scholar in education who used to train education inspectors. When we met the Minister, his team had just begun its work and was therefore unable to provide us with any documentation.

The role of teachers in mass literacy policies

The CNREF (National Commission for the Reform of Education and Training) was commissioned following the EGEF (States General of Education and Training) to reflect on the issue of national languages, and made a number of proposals based on an assessment of the situation in Senegal. Its Commission No. 2, responsible for studying the introduction and widespread use of national languages, considered that in order to put an end to the practice of conducting isolated experiments in literacy and the teaching of national languages, as has been the case in Senegal since independence, there must be a global and coherent linguistic policy. In fact, until that point the government had only introduced a so-called 'functional' literacy policy, aimed at workers in certain national enterprises.

Commission No. 2 stressed the need to adopt a clear policy of systematic promotion of national languages and identifying the measures that would facilitate such a policy. Among the measures suggested for the promotion of national languages was the proposal for a mass literacy programme. This programme would help restore to national languages their value and place, their role as an instrument of communication and management in all sectors of national life.

Among the points supposed to lead to the desired objectives was stressed in particular the training of the training personnel themselves, whose role will be described later in the description of the adopted strategy. Teachers, of course, were a main target in view of the nature of their profession and their presence throughout the national territory. The Office of Literacy (DA) was put in charge of operations.

The first training session for teachers in national languages took place in 1984. In all, 180 teachers from ten administrative regions of the country (18 per region) were trained for two weeks in transcription and reading. They were allotted six national languages. The global strategy that was adopted foresaw the creation of education cells in primary schools to train the first teachers. Thus, each of these 180 monitors was given the task of training

100 of his colleagues in his region in one year, which would make it possible, nationally, to train 180,000 teachers.

Primary school inspectors, who were initiated in national languages during their initial training, were made responsible for the conduct of the project, with one inspector per department. A second, post-literacy phase was planned; unfortunately it was not undertaken because of a lack of funds.

Later, in 1991, another project involving 1,000 mass literacy classes was undertaken by trained teachers. We do not know if any assessment was made of this operation. But it appears obvious that it was an experiment in teacher training which would certainly increase the ability of teachers to work towards intercultural objectives.

TEACHER TRAINING SYLLABUSES AND INTERCULTURAL EDUCATION

Officially, the new teacher training colleges in Senegal are comprehensive centres which train teachers for the primary and pre-school sectors. They are expected to give student teachers skills and attitudes based on knowledge of the Senegalese child, and Senegalese school and society. They also aim to initiate education research and modern techniques of leadership through close collaboration with the national structures of applied research. The type of teacher required must be ready to assume the role of a development agent capable of playing a full role in the promotion of community life. This also means that apart from his/her professional obligations, the teacher should be a person of culture, sociability and action who plays a full role in the process of social change, in the sense of improving the standard of living in the area where he/she has been assigned.

Three expressions fully describe the desired profile of future teachers: know, know how and know how to be. Since it is obvious that all these objectives could not be achieved in one year, the creation of in-service training is planned. This should make it possible for teachers to complete and perfect the basic training received at the teacher training colleges while they are working in schools.

The various subjects taught in the syllabus cover: educational activities; general teaching skills; psychology; professional ethics and law; national languages; practical training and initiation in technology; initiation in research and leadership. If we examine everything of a cultural nature in the objectives, contents and activities for each subject, it will be possible to show the multicultural dimension of this training, insofar as it exists.

Objectives and contents of different subjects

General teaching skills. The official syllabus states clearly that at the end of training, the student teacher should be capable of understanding how educational action only makes sense in relation to a set of values accepted by a given community at a given moment of its history. In addition to other, more technical skills, he/she should be capable of showing the relationship between professional techniques and the values that inspire them.

In addition to the classical headings concerning class management (order, assessment, testing techniques, etc.) the following three themes figure in the contents: the morals and social aims of education; the purposes and objectives of pre-school education; and the main movements in pre-school classes.

Educational activities. Among the objectives of this subject, and in addition to the objectives of mastering the contents, it is important that the teacher know Senegalese society well enough to adapt his activities to the specific environment to which he has been assigned. It also requires the teacher to be modest, well-balanced and moderate. The content of educational activities includes themes such as study of the environment, music and craftwork as well as practical training.

Psychology. The overall objective of this training is knowledge of the child aged 2 to 13 years. Also important are the main themes of modern child psychology which stress behavioural studies and the development of the child on the mental, social, emotional and psychomotor levels. In addition to these classical themes, the syllabus stresses a certain number of points, in particular at the level of educational activities. For example, the official text states the need to base experiments and hypotheses on experience on the ground in specific environments. It is, in fact, a practical rather than theoretical psychology which takes into account the specificity of the Senegalese child. With this in mind, observations of children in and out of the school situation, as well as interviews with them and specific case studies, are planned.

Initiation into education research and leadership. Parallel to his technical documentation skills and background studies, the student teacher must acquire the ability to manage one or more groups within his class, the school or the school-environment cell. Practical work in workshops and application exercises on the ground are planned, with the particular aim of initiating the future teacher into participating in the school.

Linguistics and national languages. The objectives of this subject can be summed up in the following sentence from the syllabus: 'Student teachers are capable of transcribing, reading and writing at least two national languages.' In order to do this, emphasis will be placed on comparative study of the French alphabet and the alphabets of national languages, the study of vowels, consonants, the noun and its use, and initiation to literature: the study of stories, legends and proverbs.

There is one detail in the syllabus that makes us think that even if the general outline drawn by the official texts appears to be in favour of multicultural education, it will not be effectively applied. This is the fact that there is no evaluation of the performances of student teachers in national languages in the final examinations. Moreover, during our interviews we understood that the student teacher's choice of national language is not necessarily taken into consideration when he is assigned to a particular area. This explains how somebody who has been trained in Joolaa and Sereer can find himself working in Louga where almost nobody speaks these languages.

Other activities. The official syllabus recommends that teacher training colleges conduct other activities which call for outside collaborators. These activities could be organized in the form of seminars, conferences or debates, and could cover such themes as hygiene and health, population studies and the study of family life, environmental studies, etc. Collaborators could be people working in specialist institutions; for example, the Division for the Supervision of School Health could send one of its employees to a school to talk about hygiene and health.

SUITABILITY OF TRAINING METHODS FOR MULTICULTURAL EDUCATION

The new method

In the official teacher training syllabus, the general method adopted is one which stresses the vocational aspect of this training. This can be seen in the brevity of the so-called initial training (it is supposed to be continuous thereafter). The objective is not, therefore, to provide academic training, but rather to dispense vocational skills. This is why the organization of educational activities is such that the activities, according to official instructions, are in keeping with the progress from theoretical studies to practical studies, with feedback at the end of the practical side and a systematic exchange of ideas.

By trying to stress the practical side of vocational training, the objective is to link all actions and behaviour to the principles that justify them. In reality, the weekly timetable is shared in the following way: 43 per cent for theoretical studies and 57 per cent for practical studies. In addition, the classes of general education and the teaching of activities must always be followed by a session of application which may take the form of a mini-class or a trial class, followed by critical analysis from the instructor. Workshop sessions are also included, still following attempts to place emphasis on the practical side, which makes it possible to acquire the knowledge and know-how necessary for initiative, research, leadership, practical training and technology.

By giving priority to the practical side and to on-the-ground experiments in which the student has to face local facts of life, the student teacher is given a real opportunity to build up his ability to deal with a multicultural environment.

Background studies

When the method of exchange between theory and practice is correctly applied to a subject such as 'background studies' it can lead to the development of aptitudes for intercultural education.

In any case, this was highly feasible in the old regional training colleges (ENRs) where it was compulsory to spend a session in a selected background, followed up by a written dissertation. The most important objective of these sessions was to enable the student teacher, through direct contact, to discover the reality of what would probably be his future field of action, from a geographical, historical and sociological point of view. The principles of the session stipulated that the general context to be studied should be in the region where the ENR was situated. They also stated that the themes should be worked out and supported by pluridisciplinary teams consisting of teachers of the subjects of background studies and sociology, and public employees of the services working in rural areas. Finally, the activities undertaken should include agricultural work and every training session should be sanctioned by a report written by the student teacher.

Much importance was given to the theme 'from theory to practice' which underlies the background studies session. The session was held in three stages, one in each of the first three years of training. During each of these, student teachers spent three weeks in a rural area and one week writing their reports on the sessions and meeting their instructors to discuss their work. During the first stage, the student teachers were supposed to show general but precise knowledge of the area they were studying. At the end they were expected to write a monograph on the area in question.

The second stage was devoted to detailed study and criticism of an important aspect of social and cultural life, concerning either the social and economic development of the area or concerning its ecological or climatic specificity. Finally, in the third stage, in addition to an in-depth study and refinement of the first conclusions, a study of the resources, activities, values or handicaps thus identified was of utmost importance.

Whereas in the old structure of training this course was spread over four years, today it is a matter of counting on the efficiency of continuous training, for which there is still no formal structure.

CONCLUSION

Senegal is, then, by its very nature and population, a multicultural society. The six officially recognized national languages correspond to the existence of at least six communities which are culturally different. However, it is also true that certain factors, for example the very large majority of the population belonging to the Muslim religion, as well as the existence of a local language for communication, Wolof, considerably reduce problems of inter-ethnic conflict.

But although serious social problems are rare, education problems of a cultural nature are evident in the education system, especially at the primary level. First of all, the language of instruction is always French. Also, a large number of teachers do not speak a national language other than Wolof, which causes serious problems in the early classes in rural areas where there is a minority of Wolofs. It has, in fact, been proved that in order to convey certain difficult notions, the teachers are obliged to speak the language of the children, especially in the first years of primary school.

Today, renewed interest in national languages and their introduction into the education system are recognized by everyone as a necessity. Language associations run by intellectuals have been created and are grouped together within the National Union of Language Associations (UNAL).

A ministry with responsibility for the promotion of languages and literacy has also been created. The Minister himself told us that UNAL is today his closest partner. Institutes of research and training such as the National Institute of Study and Action in Educational Development (INEADE), the Office of Literacy (DA), the Fundamental Institute of Black Africa (IFAN), the Applied Linguistics Centre (CLAD) in Dakar, the Higher Teacher Training College (ENS) and the National School for Teachers and Social

Workers (ENEAS) are all involved in the promotion of national languages. These provide material for the national bibliography which nurtures pertinent and original ideas.

Since 1977, some experiments have been conducted at the primary teaching level with the aim of rehabilitating national languages. This is the case with the introduction and generalized use of national languages in pre-school classes, and the creation of pilot classes where experiments can be conducted at the primary school level. Even if they were not always well conducted, at least they have the merit of being pertinent and audacious in theory.

The training of teachers, in theory at least, also pays attention to local cultural values. But the main problem is still the same: work must be done to ensure that the theories are in fact applied and given the maximum chance of success. Unfortunately, since schools are almost totally financed by the State – which is today on the verge of bankruptcy – most of the best initiatives are held up due to lack of funds. It is increasingly clear that extra-budgetary, non-governmental sources of financing are required in order to face the challenge. On the other hand, thirty years of international technical co-operation with mixed results means that any attempt to bring aid from abroad must be considered with great caution.

We think that if an adequate multicultural approach is to be established within the Senegalese education system, it will be necessary to seek institutional support in order to strengthen the national capacity for research and management. The existing research, training and administrative institutions ask for nothing better. Since the economic crisis has led the State to opt for shortened training for teachers, supposing that it will be continuous, it is therefore be advisable to help the country develop its training structures in this field. Social partners such as UNAL should also be closely associated in any project concerning multicultural education.

Within the framework of the present UNESCO:IBE project, UNAL would appear to be the best partner. Let us remember that this project is not concerned with a form of technical assistance which implies direct on-the-ground action; instead it supports local participants in the search for new methodologies. These people should be capable of using their local knowledge to enhance the cultural heritage of the country by, for example, translating the scientific concepts which it is essential to master today.

Therefore, each cultural community should itemize those elements relevant to its heritage which should be enhanced and passed on to future generations through the education system. This work, which can only be conducted by pluridisciplinary teams, will, of course, rely on the study of stories and legends, oral literature in all its forms and information given by elders. This requires people working on the ground who are devoted to their work and capable of understanding society from the inside.

The language associations within UNAL, whose main objective is the defence of the values of their respective communities, are without a doubt the people who could provide the liaison in such an enterprise. By making them into special collaborators, we will give each of the communities the opportunity to have their say. The work of UNESCO's International Bureau of Education (IBE) would consist in guiding the people in charge along lines of thought that have already been marked out, and toward appropriate research themes. At the centre of comparative education, the IBE is in a position to help them take advantage of the positive experiences of other countries. Thus, for example, relevant methods and approaches in the field of ethno-mathematics could be suggested. All of this, naturally, would be in agreement with the relevant government institutions, such as the Ministry in charge of the promotion of languages and literacy. The product of this task of compilation would be the subject of a working document and at a later stage would be made available to research centres for use in the writing of schoolbooks and teachers' manuals for public schools.

Senegal is fortunate to have an institution such as UNAL. It would be interesting for the IBE to suggest creating this type of association in other countries concerned by the project where there are no equivalents at present. It would give each community more responsibility for its own destiny. This would indeed be a form of democratization and a safe guarantee of the establishment of an authentic education system

REFERENCES

Châu, T.N.; Caillods, F. Financement et politique éducative: le cas du Sénégal [The financing of educational policy: the case of Senegal]. Paris, IIEP, 1976.
Conférence d'états africains sur le développement de l'éducation en Afrique, 1961. *Final report*. Paris, UNESCO, 1961.
Corina, B.A.; Jolly, Stevart F. *L'ajustement à visage humain* [Humane adjustment]. Paris, Economica, 1987.
Durufle, G. L'ajustement structurel en Afrique (Sénégal, Côte d'Ivoire, Madagascar) [Structural adjustment in Africa (Senegal, Côte d'Ivoire, Madagascar)]. Paris, Ed. Karthala, 1988.
INEADE. *Rapport et évaluation des CDF* [Report and evaluation of the CDF]. June 1989.
Kasse, M. *Sénégal: crise économique et ajustement structurel* [Senegal: economic crisis and structural adjustment]. Paris, Ed. Nouvelle du Sud, 1990.
Ndoye, M. L'ajustement et le secteur de l'éducation [Adjustment and the education sector]. *In: Les conséquences sociales de l'ajustement structurel au Sénégal.* [The social consequences of structural adjustment in Senegal]. February, 1992. (Cahier de l'IDEP.)

Niang, M. *Population et éducation: le cas du Sénégal* [Population and education: the case of Senegal]. Paris, CILSS (Institut du Sahel), 1985.

Senegal. Ministère de l'éducation nationale. *L'école nouvelle* [The new school]. Dakar, 1986.

—. *Etude du secteur de l'éducation et de la formation* [Study of the education sector and training]. Dakar, 1986.

—. *Financement public des dépenses courantes d'éducation de 1983-84 à 1987-88* [Public financing of current expenditure on education from 1983/84 to 1987/88]. Dakar, 1989.

—. *Education pour tous: politiques et stratégies pour les années 1990. Le cas du Sénégal* [Education for all: policies and strategies for the 1990s. The case of Senegal]. Dakar, 1990. (National report presented at the International Conference on Education, Geneva, 1990.)

Sylla, A. *L'école future pour qui?* [The future school for whom?]. Dakar, Enda, 1987.

CHAPTER XI

The training of Tunisian school-teachers and intercultural education

Coordinated by Mohamed Miled

INTRODUCTION

Mohamed Miled

This paper is a contribution by the National Institute of Educational Sciences to an International Bureau of Education (IBE) project aimed at the promotion of multicultural and intercultural education in the training of teachers for primary schools. In the case of Tunisia, analysis of the multicultural element is of little relevance because Tunisia is ethnically homogeneous and enjoys linguistic and religious unity, even if the present national culture has its origins in a number of different cultures. The regional differences that were linked to the conflicts between certain tribes at the time of French colonization have, with time, been considerably smoothed out.

Thus, this study will deliberately restrict itself to the definition and analysis of intercultural options in Tunisia's education system today and, in particular, to the part played by intercultural education in the training of primary school-teachers.

Tunisia is immediately obvious as a suitable case for the application of such an approach because of its favourable geographic situation (between Europe and Africa, with a central position in the Arab world and the Mediterranean region) and because of its history, rich in cultural intermixing.

The different values based on the knowledge, understanding and respect of others, for what they are and for the ways in which they are different, can only lead to the harmonious blending of individuals within society if they are treated with the necessary seriousness at school. The introduction of these values in the teaching syllabus is of great interest for the training of student-teachers, making them more aware of their own roots in their own societies, but also developing in them the intellectual qualities they need if they are to understand the cultures of others in a calm, impartial way.

Nevertheless, the presentation of foreign cultures with the aim of achieving better understanding risks two problems, depending on the educational context. The first is the danger that the civilization of the other will be reduced to a set of stereotypes and caricatures that will, paradoxically, lead to misunderstanding, distrust and even rejection. The second danger, on the contrary, is that of reaching, often unintentionally, an over-estimation of the value of other civilizations, which may cause the depreciation, and even the rejection, of one's own culture.

Intercultural education, which must guard against both these dangers capable of bringing discredit upon it, is, at the level of education thinking and practice, in fact based on the demonstration of possible interaction (two-way movement) between the culture of the learner and that of others. It is the teacher's responsibility to avoid having this diversity reduced to a simple statement or juxtaposition of other people's experiences; 'What matters,' according to L. Porcher, 'is the building of relationships, meeting places and connections between the various cultures.'[1] By objectively and impartially studying the relationship between cultural models, the learner will develop the ability to make comparisons, to judge the other in a sensitive, relativist way and to recognize the other in what is different about him.

Thanks to these skills, among others, the pupils will be capable of moderation in the positions they adopt; they will show tolerance and understanding towards people who are different from themselves.

These three notions are one of the basic principles of the Tunisian education system which, according to the law of 29 July, 1991 seeks to strengthen Tunisian national identity, to develop the pupils' civic sense and feeling of belonging to national, Maghreb, Arab and Islamic civilization and to confirm their openness towards modernity and human civilization.

This openness must 'prepare young people for a way of life in which there is no room for discrimination or segregation based on sex, social background, race or religion.'[2]

This manner of thinking, shown in the text of the law, is applied in the conception of learning material for each discipline and the development of teaching methods and tools. Openness towards the world, through language learning for example, can be seen in the teaching of at least one foreign language, in this case French, which is an instrument for the promotion of intercultural education through the intellectual functions that it requires of the learner. According to the law of July 1991, the learning of a foreign language allows pupils to 'have direct access to the products of universal thinking, techniques, scientific theories and human values, and prepares them to follow evolution and contribute to it in a manner that will bring about the enrichment of national culture and its interaction with universal human culture.'[3]

These values aimed at developing tolerance and acceptance of others and their differences are presented in the objectives and in the learning material used in teacher training in Tunisia. Teachers are trained today at higher institutes of teacher training (ISFM) where students study for two years after passing their baccalaureate, following thirteen years of primary and secondary education. Their training includes specific academic subjects related to the various disciplines and activities linked to educational theory and practice.

When approaching Arabic literature and its peculiarities, the student-teacher is made aware of its interactive links with other foreign literary models. In the syllabuses of the ISFM, Islamic thought, traditionally presented from the same angle, is based on the idea that Islam did not originate independently of the cultural facts that preceded it.

The French syllabuses, based on the principle that access to another language is closely linked to the clear understanding of another culture, help the student-teacher to have an instrument that provides an opening onto the outside world and a less subjective means of appreciating his own culture.

The philosophy syllabus, based on the principle of diversity in the study of different themes and on the importance of critical thinking, helps the student-teacher to avoid egocentric or ethnocentric approaches.

In history and geography, the majority of the syllabus is devoted to foreign countries which gives the student-teachers an opening onto other countries and develops their skills of comparison and relativism.

Acting as a support for the acquisition of the knowledge and attitudes peculiar to each discipline, the training of the student-teacher and the content matter of education sciences favour the principle of the autonomy of the learner and that of interactions in class.

These monographic analyses, conceived according to the same methodological framework, show that the intercultural dimension is an important element of these training syllabuses and the stated objectives. At the same time, they help the reader to refer to similar themes and approaches within the various disciplines. Nevertheless, this study deliberately did not take into consideration the reality of the class situation, the different conditions under which these syllabuses are applied and the degrees to which intercultural objectives are achieved.

TEACHER TRAINING FOR INTERCULTURAL EDUCATION

Ahmed Chabchoub

At the cultural level, Tunisia has been fortunate in two ways: fortunate to be a culturally and linguistically homogeneous country and—no less important —fortunate to be situated in a multicultural geographic environment. The closeness of Italy, France and Spain, but also the Middle East,[4] places Tunisia in a situation in which it is obliged to practise values of openness and tolerance, i.e. to develop in its children intercultural attitudes and inter-community dialogue.

This preoccupation, in fact, matches the philosophy of the international organizations on the subject of intercultural education. We read in the recommendation of the forty-third session of the International Conference on Education that 'intercultural and multicultural education . . . is designed to promote respect for cultural diversity and mutual understanding and enrichment.[5]

The Ministry of Education and Science is conscious of the fact that it is teachers who are the key to improving education systems. In October 1989, parallel to the general education reforms, the ministry began the task of restructuring teacher-training institutes. This reform introduced four principle innovations; these innovations, in our opinion, favour a greater openness towards other people and therefore form a part of intercultural education.

1. *Longer schooling.* Since October 1989, schoolteachers have received two years of higher education.[6] Longer schooling, as it takes place in an institute of higher education, can only further the development of a sense of objectivsm and rationality; this is reinforced by the importance granted to the arts in the official syllabuses.

2. *Arts.* Disciplines such as philosophy, psychology, history, geography, educational sciences, etc., occupy a third of the timetable in the first year and slightly over a third in the second year. In addition, the content of the syllabus is quite modern in education sciences (see details later). The legislators hope that these measures will encourage qualities of reflection, openness towards others and relativism in the student-teacher.

3. *Foreign languages.* French is taught in teacher-training institutes five hours per week in the first year and five hours per week in the second year (i.e. one-sixth of the total hours on the timetable). This has two purposes: to strengthen the linguistic skills of the student-teachers (most of whom will have to teach French in primary schools)[7] and also, at the same time, to allow them to learn about the literature and culture of a foreign country. The second objective is strengthened by a programme of correspondence with French and Belgian student-teachers and sessions at foreign institutes.[8]

4. *The education sciences syllabus.* Spread over two years, the education sciences syllabus includes the following subjects:
   (i)   introduction to the educational sciences;
   (ii)   general child psychology;
   (iii) general education skills;
   (iv)   teaching theory and method.

Aware of the fact that educational training is the key to teacher training, the legislators created an avant-garde curriculum which will inevitably promote intercultural education while teaching about other subjects. It can be summed up as follows:

1. The introduction of new education theories: Rousseau, Rogers, group dynamics, constructivism, cognitivism, etc.
2. A prominent place is accorded to comparative education and the history of education systems throughout the world (one-fourth of the first-year timetable).
3. An analysis of the complex relationship between education and modernity (one chapter during the second year).
4. The place accorded to teaching theory and method in the second year. Through its philosophical and epistemological presuppositions, teaching theory and method leads the individual to complete autonomy through the importance granted to the learner's personal accumulation of knowledge.[9] The theory and method system is, in fact, the only education system which pays particular attention to the ideas of the students and takes them into consideration in the teaching/learning situation.[10] Literature on education and intercultural studies stresses the fact that pupils must be allowed to express their thoughts if they are to be gradually encouraged to overcome their prejudices and accept and understand other people.

An IBE document states: 'Experience proves the importance of taking into account the ideas of the pupils and their obstacles to learning in order to achieve positive teaching. The analysis of the ideas of the pupils is a powerful tool to be used towards this objective. It can be very useful to develop solidarity and peace between the various communities because this allows the analysis of beliefs related to racism and xenophobia'.[11] Thus, it is essential for teachers to develop the ability to analyze the ideas of the pupils and the obstacles to their learning process.

This relatively modern syllabus material is to some extent strengthened by the recommendations of the official syllabuses. The lecturer in the educational sciences working in teacher-training institutes is recommended to: encourage dialogue between students and teachers and avoid authoritative lecturing; give the student-teachers project work and allow them to guide group work; encourage personal research.

This methodology should favour the modernization of syllabuses and, therefore, promote the emergence of self-confident, autonomous individuals capable of listening to others and conducting a dialogue with them.

In addition to all this, in October 1994 an integrated syllabus was introduced: population studies. The integration of the concepts and methods of population studies affects three subjects taught in teacher-training institutes: educational sciences, social science and biology. Here we shall only examine the integration of population studies in the syllabus for the educational sciences, and in particular the integration of the methodology used in population studies. By stressing active group methods, the need to make the learner autonomous and the objective of rationalizing behaviour, the methodology of population studies ties in with the general aims of teacher training in the institutes, i.e. the desire to train a teacher who is both dynamic and capable of training rational citizens open to others and ready to collaborate, not only with their own co-citizens but also with their neighbours and foreign counterparts.

Conclusions

The promotion of intercultural/multicultural education in a centralized education system like that of Tunisia must inevitably pass through the reform of the teacher-training system. Under the effect of multiplication, any well-conducted educational innovation can be expected to reach the majority of children in less than ten years. Yet there is an important point to be considered: in order to have teachers who are well-prepared for intercultural education (or for any other form of innovation) it is not enough to simply work out curricula and recommendations. It is essential that those responsible for the training (in this case the lecturers in the institutes) be sufficiently well-trained themselves to manage the innovation, so that it can be successfully introduced into the education system.[12]

It is this uphill struggle that the Ministry of Education and Science is undertaking at present. It asks: what training should be given to instructors in teacher-training institutes to create the flexible attitudes needed for the promotion of innovations such as 'intercultural education'?

INTERCULTURAL EDUCATION AS PART OF EXTRACURRICULAR TRAINING IN HIGHER INSTITUTES OF TEACHER TRAINING

Abdelmagid Greb

High-school graduates who enter a higher institute of teacher training (ISFM) soon realize that the training they receive in these institutes is not only characterized by a diversity of disciplines. The fact is that in the ISFM the students will also acquire a certain number of qualities that will serve them in the exercise of their duties as a teacher, putting all the advantages and chances of success on their side – 'We do not teach what we know, we teach what we are'. Students learn to live in a community, with all the demands and virtues that that implies. Emphasis is also placed on extra-curricular activities, especially social and cultural activities intended to back up their training and give them the kind of preparation that is required for a profession which is becoming more and more demanding regarding the general culture of the teacher.

From cultural to intercultural

UNESCO defines culture as 'the whole complex of distinctive spiritual, material, intellectual and emotional features that characterize a society or social group. It includes the modes of life, traditions and beliefs, the arts and letters, while incorporating in its value system the fundamental rights of human beings.'[13] Since cultural models are principally passed on through education, this definition gives an idea of the enormity of the task of school institutions which set out not only to promote the acquisition of culture, but also to act as agents for cultural development. In the ISFM, the act of training is, in fact, based on the principle that the school should not only pass on to the coming generations certain values and knowledge, but it must also train responsible citizens. It must be able to modify individual and group mentalities in order to bring about those social changes that will lead to progress, justice and peace. The realization of these objectives implies that the act of training must take various forms, it must develop at several levels and no longer be confined to traditional lessons, however rich they may be. It must let informality play an important role, thus allowing the

211

individual to appear as he or she really is and not as they ought to be, and to achieve an identity structure strong enough to overcome regional and national narrow-mindedness and open up to the world, to be themselves, but to be without fear, without restraint, without shame, without boasting, to dare to be what they are deep within themselves–but it does not mean to despise others or to want to change, judge or criticize them at any price. If we like to be recognized for what we are, we must, consequently, recognize others for what they are. Gandhi said on this subject: 'The golden rule of good behaviour is mutual tolerance because we will never all think in the same way, we will only ever see a part of the truth and from different angles'. In fact, we have more and more proof that the 'self' is built only through 'otherness', that it develops and blossoms only in relation to others, with all that that implies in being open to difference, being committed and going beyond oneself. By promoting family life and social and cultural activities, we teach the student-teacher to recognize the advantages of communication, to share knowledge, beliefs, ideas and the deepest thoughts, feelings and emotions. Communication implies, therefore, sharing, exchanging, openness, transparency and mutual understanding, even communion. It makes it possible to learn how not to take refuge in silence, solitude, things left unsaid, and how to get rid of prejudice which is often a source of unhappiness for oneself and for others.

The actions of the ISFM to promote intercultural training are, then, based on two desires: to make it possible for student-teachers to get to know how their own culture is in every way unique and different, and to confer on them a set of values and intellectual and moral qualities which will allow them to have easy access to other cultures which see the world differently– to go towards the other, to accept them as they are and to engage with them in a dialogue based on curiosity and generosity. If the dialogue is to be fruitful, it is essential that it be conceived in a spirit of partnership. Each of the two partners should formulate his desires, questions and poles of interest in order to make them converge into themes and projects of common interest. A true dialogue implies, therefore, a strong partnership so that it does not become a dialogue between the deaf or a monologue in disguise, so that each partner does not hesitate to take the best of what the other has to offer. It is, of course, obvious that a society which is confident about its own culture can face outside influences and take advantage of them, whereas a society that is on the defensive, closed in on itself, is more firmly attached to sterile tradition.

There is no lack of examples to illustrate this: Arab civilization at the height of its greatness (from the ninth to the fourteenth century A.D.) benefited enormously from the knowledge of the Greeks, Persians and

Chinese, and the process of modernization in Japan in the last century was the result of a careful combination of new techniques and indigenous skills. The French anthropologist Claude Lévi-Strauss observed that all cultures include a mixture of exchange and borrowing. One of the factors which appears to play a role in the success of development is if the culture is open to other ideas, and if it is willing and able to assimilate the ideas of other cultures. Intercultural training that hopes to achieve results requires the individual to know his own culture in all its diversity so that he can open his arms to other cultures and either take advantage of what they have to offer or reject it. It is in the numerous aspects of their own culture that individuals can find the instruments that will help them to assimilate other cultures.

Dialogue between cultures is not a new idea. The only notion that has emerged recently is that of a dialogue that is mutually accepted in an atmosphere of peace and respect for identities, a dialogue that does not block the potential creativity of local culture, that does not reduce society's ability to resist the penetration of undesirable influences and foreign cultural models and that does not lead to mechanisms of rejection or channels of self-denigration. Today, rather than seek to dominate, different cultures can be enriched by their differences and can inject each other with new life.

An essential dimension of training

It is hardly necessary to repeat that every culture sees the world differently and that these different perceptions which are almost always based on objective facts and situations, such as the phenomena of the environment, give rise to different interpretations in different cultural contexts. But the identical results that different peoples have obtained by applying varied techniques to practical problems in fields such as housing, agriculture and medicine, also prove that even if the type of solution chosen is inspired by the natural or cultural environment, the solution itself is always inferred by those laws that command the destiny of our species.

The common nature of this destiny is becoming more clearly defined and more obvious in the era of the global village (a term invented by the Canadian Marshall McLuhan) due to the rapid development of telecommunications which is shrinking the planet. If the school opens to the environment, in the future it will open to the whole earth in order to give people a global vision of problems and contribute efficiently to the arrival of a world order which will integrate economic, social and cultural dimensions and where basic human aspirations to progress, peace and justice will find their rightful place.

UNESCO's charter says it clearly when it states that 'peace based exclusively upon the political and economic arrangements of governments would not be a peace which could secure the unanimous, lasting and sincere support of the peoples of the world.'[14]

The phenomenon of the universalization of human relationships must, therefore, be accompanied by a rise in the level of awareness and an increase in the types of exchange and communication between different cultures, a task that is both arduous and exalting for the educational body: arduous because of the violence of all kinds that is tearing us apart today— in particular the violence caused by extreme nationalism; and exalting in the sense that it aims at an acceptance of the values of tolerance, human solidarity and respect for others, and the consideration that human rights are the common heritage of the human race.

A few positive experiments at the ISFM

The experiments undertaken in the field of extracurricular intercultural training were inspired by the considerations described above, but in particular by two principles that it is useful to recall:

1. For student-teachers, intercultural education must start with knowledge of their own culture so that it does not lead to mechanisms of self-defence and the rejection of other cultures, or to the phenomenon of self-denigration.
2. Recognition of others is a task requiring long training taking different forms in order to know others and accept their differences.

Since the other person may be one's immediate neighbour, it is important that training in the ISFM be mixed at an age when both the physical and psychological differences between the sexes, and even within the same sex, are the most striking. Offering young people in search of their own identity the possibility to share a lasting common experience is to bring them to accept others in the ways in which they are identical and different.

The students are partially mixed in the boarding sections, meals and indoor activities. Their communal life benefits from the informal nature of these activities which give true opportunities for communication and exchange and lead the students to think again about their concepts of the lives of others, to ask questions about themselves and to redefine their ideas. The management of diversity, necessary because it is a source of enrichment (did Victor Segalen not write 'Variety is decreasing and that is a great danger to the world'?), led us to increase the number of meetings between institutes. We organized, in particular, two sessions of holiday camps bringing together, at the same time, student-teachers from six institutes in the south of the country into an institute in the north and those from six institutes in the north into an institute in the south. Man's management of his environment has been throughout history one of the main forms of cultural expression and the natural reflection of the concept of utilizing the space allotted to inhabitants, to their way of life and social organization; through these meetings we intended, apart from the advantages of putting young people in touch with one another, to give each student-teacher the opportunity to discover other aspects of his own culture by becoming familiar with different ways of life and management of the environment. It must be said that by the end of these meetings, an enormous amount of misunderstanding had been uncovered and erased and a great number of prejudices overcome, even though Tunisia is a small country with great cultural homogeneity.

In order to emphasize this open attitude towards others and to rehabilitate the idea that man must be aware that he belongs to the unique, yet diverse, human race, we promoted exchanges with teacher-training establishments abroad, and in France in particular, through the system of twinning, for which the agreements specifically stressed the objectives of intercultural education.

To allow Tunisian and foreign student-teachers and their instructors to have, even for a few days, a common experience can only be of mutual advantage and enriching to all, on the one hand because cultures are increasingly intermingling, thanks to the various means of communication, and because on the other hand, in spite of differing external features, human beings have the same joys, same anxieties and the same basic questions.

INTERCULTURAL EDUCATION
IN HISTORY AND CIVIC EDUCATION SYLLABUSES
AT HIGHER INSTITUTES OF TEACHER TRAINING

Amara Ben Romdhane
Taoufik Ayadi

Intercultural education is one of the basic options of the Tunisian education system which has been undergoing in-depth reform in recent years. And although the intercultural dimension is a major preoccupation of all branches of education and is part of the modules of the higher institutes of teacher training, it is the syllabuses for history and geography which are the most explicit, insofar as they develop precise content material, in-depth texts and educational tools related to intercultural education.

In the following table, we shall select from the syllabuses the themes which illustrate intercultural choices (left-hand column); they are then linked to the learning objectives and appropriate recommendations (right-hand column).

This analysis of syllabuses shows that intercultural education is solidly rooted in the very foundations of Muslim Arab civilization and it is not a recent phenomenon, nor is it something that has been imposed.

Thus the student-teacher learns that the emergence of new values arises from a heritage which is common to all civilizations. Moreover, while it has benefited from outside influences, Tunisia, at the crossroad of civilizations, has made considerable contributions to other Mediterranean countries.

Civic education

If we refer to the laws on the Tunisian education system, we observe that civic education as an autonomous branch in schools was conceived for the following three purposes:

1. To make student-teachers more aware of themselves by teaching them those values that are required to help them integrate in a constantly changing social environment.

2. To develop in student-teachers an awareness of belonging to their own nation and community through respect for the laws and regulations of their different institutions, while maintaining a rational approach to these institutions. This objective also makes it possible for them to become familiar with the cultural, political and social values of their country, thus strengthening their attachment to the country, its culture and history.

3. To develop in student-teachers an understanding of others and an international understanding, so that relations between national and international institutions and organizations working for peace and equal relations between peoples may be strengthened.

Similarly, the education system links these three objectives to the promotion of a kind of education that guarantees human dignity, rights and liberties, in order to shape citizens who are proud of their country, who are ready to work for human rights and respect for others, and for peace and friendship between peoples.

In Table 2, we select from this syllabus the themes related to intercultural education and we show how they correspond to specific educational objectives.

TABLE 1. History.

Contents	Objectives and recommendations
– Prehistory – Ancient civilizations – The Maghreb countries in the Carthage era and the era of the Numidian kingdoms.	Teachers are expected to include: – The influence of different civilizations on the Western Mediterranean region; – The role of Carthage in the introduction of Eastern civilization to the Western Mediterranean; – The fact that Tunisia today is the product of contributions by different civilizations;
– The Christian West and its relations with the Muslim/Arab world.	– To encourage awareness of the diversity of environments and civilizations; – To teach the common nature of political power in the West, this power being based on the Church until the end of the Medieval era.
– The French Revolution – The Renaissance in Europe	– To stress the emergence of new ideological values which, as they spread across vast regions of the world, had an obvious influence on Mediterranean countries, including Tunisia; – To make it possible for the learner to become more aware of his rights and duties and to play a responsible role in society.
Contents Objectives and recommendations	The contemporary Arab renaissance. – To help the student-teacher to understand the Muslim Arab world in its diversity and in its unity and to show that the decadence was to a large extent linked to the withdrawal of that world, together with the lack of any rational process, and that the height of Muslim-Arab civilization was essentially due to the openness of the Arabs towards others (diversity of cultures, tolerance, borrowing from other cultures and constant reference to reason). – to show what Arabs have contributed to world civilization. (They served as intermediaries between Eastern culture and Western culture, and made great contributions to the enrichment of human civilization).
– Tunisia, the crossroad of civilizations; – Its links with the West and the consequences of those links.	To show that in the nineteenth century there was a reformist movement in Tunisia which favoured change in political, social and education structures and in particular: – the creation of the military school of Bardo (1840) which introduced modern education and the use of foreign languages (French and Italian); – the abolition of slavery (1846); – the establishment of the first trial of a modern constitution, formalized by the fundamental pact (1857) and the constitution (1861).

217

Teacher training and multiculturalism

TABLE 2. Themes related to intercultural education.

Learning content	Objectives and recommendations
The State	Illustrate the diversity in the conception of the State by thinkers of different cultures: Plato, Ibn Khaldoun, Hobbes, Rousseau, Hegel, etc.
The Fundamental Pact (1857) and the Constitution of 1861, the first constitution experienced in the Muslim Arab world.	Show that this constitutional experience, the result of contact between Tunisian thinkers and modern political culture, engendered respect for the individual and his rights, equality before the law for all, regardless of religion and origin, freedom of religion, etc.
– General principles of the Tunisian constitution of 1959; – Rights and duties in the Tunisian constitution.	Lead the student-teacher to an understanding of the principles on which this constitution was based: – attachment to human values common to all peoples, – solidarity between peoples fighting for liberty and equality, – respect for individual integrity and freedom of conscience and religion.
Learning content – World political regimes.	Objectives and recommendations Show the different types of government in human societies and explain the reasons for their differences and changes throughout history. This objective will lead the student-teacher to grasp the importance of understanding and recognizing others, starting with the diversity of political regimes.
– The multi-party system and the law on political parties in Tunisia.	Stress political plurality in the organization of social and political life, with respect for the interest of all. However, political trends and parties must not be based on any form of intolerance, exclusion or discrimination.
Learning content The National Pact (A charter signed on 7/11/88 by all political parties and the main governmental organizations in Tunisia).	Objectives and recommendations To consolidate the values of tolerance and ban all forms of extremism; To aim at a culture inspired by the Arab Islamic heritage, in particular in rational elements so that Islam can further adapt to modern requirements; To open up to the product of human thought and take advantage of it in order to develop awareness of the whole of the human race.

218

Human rights in: – Ancient civilizations – Islam – The French Revolution – The Fundamental Pact – The Universal Declaration of Human Rights and the various texts on the subject – The Tunisian Constitution	Make student-teachers aware of the diversity of ways of approaching this theme in order to show that human rights are a heritage common to all civilizations and an essential part of development today.
Personal status code	Show that this text is partly based on a text that originated in the Arab Muslim heritage and, on the other hand, on charters and universal declarations which guarantee human rights, as well as the rights of women in the West.
Contents Culture and society	Objectives and recommendations Stress the role played by educated people in the analysis of the present, in prospects for the future and in the building of mechanisms to bring different cultures together.
Information	Stress the importance of the role of information in awareness of other cultures and take care to vary the sources of information and remain objective enough to make impartial judgments.

INTERCULTURAL EDUCATION IN THE GEOGRAPHICAL STUDIES OF PRIMARY SCHOOL-TEACHERS

Chedly Baccar

In most French-speaking countries, school geography has often been the subject of criticism, sometimes bitter, by pupils and their parents as much as by the teachers themselves. Many hold against it its forbidding character with tedious lists of names and figures and its unclear utility for the academic, vocational and social lives of young people.

Others, who consider that geography 'is useful above all for making war,'[15] accuse those responsible for geography teaching of trying to hide from the eyes of the world the fact that geography is a powerful tool for those in power because it allows them to control the people of their own land better and to be better prepared for war against any outside adversary.

However, in the past few years there has been a certain rehabilitation of geography teaching, originating in the changes that have taken place on a worldwide scale. The vast amount of pictures and information that we

219

receive every day through the media in general and television in particular is in itself a justification for geography teaching, if only 'to put some order into the disorder of our personal image of the world.'[16]

On the other hand, the emergence of various threats to the environment and different forms of pollution in the world mean that geography has become the natural ally of ecology in the active struggle to inform young people. The universal dimension of problems of the environment and development, and the intensification of international exchanges at economic, social and cultural levels, have made of geography a special instrument for teaching the need to strengthen international solidarity.

By the middle of the 1960s, UNESCO had already worked out a project to this end entitled: 'Major project related to the mutual appreciation of cultural values of the East and West'. Its objective was to make 'geography contribute to teaching young people the useful notion of solidarity that should exist between all men and which UNESCO calls international understanding.'[17]

Today it is appropriate to ask what impact these new guidelines for geography teaching have had on national teaching and training syllabuses, especially on the subject of teaching international understanding and comprehension. It is this question that we shall try to answer by analysing the contents of syllabuses for training primary school teachers in Tunisia.

HOW SHOULD TEACHING AND TRAINING PROGRAMMES BE ANALYZED?

Any analysis of contents supposes the establishment of scales or, at least, the adoption of several basic principles related to the objective of the analysis. Since the objective is to discover the intercultural dimension of geography training of primary school-teachers, first of all we sought to find out how geography could contribute in a specific way towards bringing cultures closer together and developing a spirit of tolerance and respect for other cultures, independent of the country where it is taught.

Like all socialization disciplines, geography aims to integrate the young person into the country to which he belongs and into the world community. But in teaching syllabuses the balance between the objective of 'creating roots' and that of 'opening' varies considerably from one country to another, and even from one educational level to another within the same country; in geography, looking outwards towards other societies may be limited to the study of a few countries, just as it may include all the countries of the world!

We have decided, then, to consider the degree to which geography syllabuses look outwards to other societies and world problems (development, pollution, migration, etc.) as the first indication of the degree of commitment of these syllabuses to respect for other cultures and international understanding. The objectives of 'opening onto the world' are a qualitative indicator which makes it possible to find out if the desired objective is only of a cognitive nature (knowledge of other societies) or if it is also of a moral nature (teaching of positive values and attitudes with regard to these societies). Is it simply a question of giving information about other countries and the major problems of today's world? Or does it also develop in the learner, and in an explicit way, positive attitudes towards other societies in order to strengthen his spirit of tolerance, respect and solidarity in relation to all people on earth? The analysis of syllabus content, on the one hand, and the wording of the objectives, on the other, will make it possible to answer this double question.

Which syllabuses should we analyze?

At the beginning of this study on the intercultural dimension of the training of primary school teachers, it was intended that the analysis of content would not extend beyond the syllabuses employed in the ISFM. But because of their functional nature and their relationship to primary school syllabuses, teacher-training syllabuses include only a very relative openness towards the outside world, in geography as in other disciplines. Therefore, it was decided to consider the training received by teachers in secondary schools as an integral part of their general training and to include in the corpus of documents to be analyzed the teaching syllabuses of the four years of secondary school. The geography syllabus in the ISFM does in fact repeat certain parts of the contents of secondary school syllabuses, as we shall see later.

'OPENNESS TOWARDS THE WORLD'

Starting from the principle that the contribution of geography training to intercultural education depends on the degree to which this training is outward-looking towards the world and other societies, we sought to determine, first at the level of content and then at the level of the objectives of teacher training in geography:
1. The importance of this openness towards the world, all the knowledge that it covers and the areas which receive more attention;
2. The purposes of this openness at the cognitive and moral levels.

'Openness' in syllabus content.

Table 3 shows the distribution of the main themes and content of geography syllabuses integrated into teacher training, by year of study and type of teaching.

TABLE 3: The main themes and content of geography syllabuses.

Themes	Secondary teaching		I.S.F.M year %		% of total timetable	Year % timetable
General geography	General geography (physical)	1st	22.0	1st	50.5	45.5
	General geography (human)	2nd	22.0			
Regional geography	Geography of Tunisia and the Arab world	3rd	26.0	2nd	50.0	32.5
	Geography of the world today	4th	30.0			
Total			100.0		100.0	100.0

The table shows that the ISFM syllabuses repeat certain elements of the secondary syllabus, in particular the sections on general physical and human geography through which students learn to look outwards to the world, together with the geography of Tunisia and the Arab world; the objective of this is to give the student-teacher a greater feeling of belonging to his Tunisian and Arab environment.

It is also evident that 'openness to the world and other societies' is greater in secondary teaching (74% of the timetable) than in the ISFM (50%) because of the study of 'Geography in the contemporary world'. But globally the theme of 'openness to the world' constitutes around two-thirds of the timetable if we take into account all geography teaching given to student-teachers from the time they are in secondary school.

Specific content on 'openness to the world'

In geography, the study of other societies and major economic and social problems on the world scale is usually approached in complementary ways:

through general geography on the one hand, and regional geography on the other. The first, more global, makes it possible to understand the common destiny of all the people of the earth, through the diversity of natural, human and economic environments. The second is based on the study of certain countries taken as particular models of relationships between social groups and their natural environments.

General geography and 'openness to the world'

General physical and human geography takes up a little under half of the timetable allotted to the geography training of student-teachers (see Table 3). It is this subject which covers most of the theme of 'openness to the world' for student-teachers.

The following are among the themes studied in general geography which serve the intercultural dimension at the cognitive level:

In physical geography: The theme 'Major world climatic zones' gives the student-teacher a global view of the diversity of the world's bio-geographical environments. 'Natural threats and the degradation of the environment' includes the study of the ecosystem, its components, its balance, and its natural disasters—volcanic eruptions, earthquakes, floods, the extension and erosion of deserts—from the point of view of their zones of influence, their repercussions on the environment and possible means of dealing with these problems.

In human and economic geography: This is demographic geography which covers geographic distribution, demographic growth and its repercussions in developing countries, national politics with regard to population, migration in the world today. Also, world agriculture: diversity of the rural world, agricultural products and international exchanges, the world's food problem. Finally, world industry which covers energy sources and raw materials, world industrial structures, distribution of industry throughout the world; and world commerce which covers growth of international exchanges, structure of international commerce, degradation of exchange terms to the detriment of certain countries.

Regional geography and 'openness to the world'

As we stated above, the study of countries other than Tunisia figures less at the level of the ISFM (see Table 3), but on the other hand it figures in part of the syllabus of the third year and in the whole of that of the fourth year of the secondary school, the year of the baccalaureate. This syllabus, which is an integral part of the training of student-teachers, is devoted to 'Geography in the contemporary world,' approached from the angle of the unequal economic and social development in the world, and includes the study of the following themes:

1. Unequal development: the evidence, developed countries, developing countries, relations between the former and latter, aid for development.
2. The study of countries with different levels of economic and social development:
   (i) countries which are industrially very advanced: the European Union, the United States, Japan;
   (ii) newly industrialized countries: Taiwan, Singapore, the Republic of Korea;
   (iii) industrially developing countries: Brazil, Egypt.

At the end of this review of the geographical themes taught to student-teachers, themes which make an appreciable contribution to their knowledge and understanding of the contemporary world, we must ask the question concerning the purpose of it all: is it simply the acquisition of knowledge, or is it also the development of positive attitudes and behaviour with regard to others?

The objectives of 'openness to the world'

At the cognitive level, it is said that the objectives of the teaching of geography are to convey to the pupil knowledge on:
– General geography;
– The geography of Tunisia and the Maghreb Union;
– The geography of developing countries;
– The geography of industrialized countries;
– The problems of the modern world.

On the moral side, the official syllabuses state that at the end of his training in geography, the learner should be: 'proud to belong to Arab and Muslim Tunisia and the human race'; 'aware of the seriousness of questions related to population, economy and development'; 'aware of the problems of the environment and ready to play a role in solving them'.

Although geography syllabuses do not specifically speak of values such as tolerance, understanding and international solidarity, etc., they stress the fact that Tunisians are part of the international community, which implies that they accept these values. In the same way, awareness of the seriousness of problems of development and the environment and a willingness to play a role in solving them supposes a commitment in favour of international understanding and solidarity.

CONCLUSIONS

The analysis of geography syllabuses for primary school-teachers shows how much emphasis is placed in their training on looking outwards to the modern world. This openness, relatively greater in secondary school studies than in studies at the ISFM, first of all aims to help teachers to have a better understanding of the world in which they live, with its natural and human diversity, its economic and social differences, and the major problems and challenges that it poses to the whole of mankind. A second objective is to develop in student-teachers the attitudes and values which will strengthen their attachment to the international community.

However, the achievement of these objectives still depends on the degree of commitment of the instructors, their educational competence and the teaching methods and means put at their disposal.

NOTES

1. L. Porcher, Pédagogie interculturelle et stéréotypes. [Intercultural education and stereo-types] In: *Le Français aujourd'hui*, No. 70, June 1985.
2. Article 3 of the law of 29 July 1991 on the Tunisian education system.
3. Article 5 of the above-mentioned law.
4. C. Fitouri liked to say that Tunisia had its heart in the East and its soul in the West (cf. C. Fotouri, *Bilingualisme, biculturalisme et éducation*, Lausanne, Switzerland, Delachaux & Niestlé, 1983).
5. International Conference on Education, 43rd session, Geneva, September 1992, *Final report*, p. 19, Paris, UNESCO, 1993.
6. Before this date, teacher training ended with the Baccalauréat.
7. French is taught in Tunisian primary schools as a foreign language from the third year onwards at a rate of ten hours per week (i.e. one-third of the hours on the timetable).
8. See, in this study, the paper by A. Greb on extracurricular activities in the ISFM.
9. We should add here the recommendation to lecturers to give their students bilingual bibliographies. This can only promote openness towards foreign educational literature and experiences.
10. We also find this aspect in the theory and method of teaching science, for example. Cf. De Vecchi: *Les représentations des enfants et les modalités de leur prise en compte en cours de biologie* [Children's representations and the modalities of their consideration in biology courses]. Doctoral thesis, Université Paris 7, 1984.
11. International Bureau of Education (IBE) project on intercultural education, Geneva, 1994.
12. Most teacher trainers lecturing in institutes have come from secondary education. Apart from their personal qualities, none of them has received any specific training to be a teacher trainer.
13. International Conference on Education, 43rd session, Geneva, September 1992, *Final report*, op. cit., p. 18.
14. Constitution of UNESCO, Preamble.
15. Yves Lacoste, *La géographie, ça sert d'abord à faire la guerre* [Geography, its first purpose is to make war], Paris, Maspéro, 1976, 187 p.

Teacher training and multiculturalism

16. Pierre George, *Les hommes sur la terre, la géographie en mouvement* [Man on earth, changing geography] quoted in Pierre Giolitto, *Enseigner la géographie à l'école* [Teaching geography at school], Paris, Hachette, 1992, p. 10.
17. UNESCO–IPAM, *L'enseignement de la géographie* [Geography teaching], Paris, 1966, p. 15.

BIBLIOGRAPHY

Chabchoub, A. [*The basis of educational action.*] Tunis, 1988.
—. [*From teaching to learning.*] 1994. (In Arabic.)
Fitouri, C. *Bilinguisme, biculturalisme et éducation.* Lausanne, Delachaux et Niestlé, 1983.